Research for Social Workers

Research for Social Workers

An introduction to methods
2nd Edition

Margaret Alston and Wendy Bowles

Routledge
Taylor & Francis Group

LONDON AND NEW YORK

First published by Allen & Unwin, 1998

This edition first published in 2003
by Routledge
11 New Fetter Lane, London EC4P 4EE

Simultaneously published in the USA and Canada
by Routledge
29 West 35th Street, New York, NY 10001

and in Australia and New Zealand
by Allen & Unwin Pty Ltd
83 Alexander Street, Crows Nest, NSW 2065, Australia

Routledge is an imprint of the Taylor & Francis Group

British Library Cataloguing in Publication Data
A catalogue record for this book is available from the British Library

Library of Congress Cataloguing in Publication Data
A catalogue record has been requested

ISBN 0-415-30722-8 (hbk)
ISBN 0-415-30723-6 (pbk)

Typeset by DOCUPRO, Canberra
Printed by South Wind Productions, Singapore

10 9 8 7 6 5 4 3 2 1

CONTENTS

ACKNOWLEDGEMENTS

We would especially like to thank our editors Elizabeth Weiss and Catherine Taylor for their assistance and support in bringing out the second edition of this book. Jenny Coopes's cartoons flavour the chapters with just the right spice. Thank you to our friends Eddie Oczkowski and Veronica Paul who helped us over the rough spots with many useful suggestions. Thank you to our partners, as ever, for their ongoing support. We dedicate this work to Louise.

INTRODUCTION

We are delighted to bring you the second edition of *Research for Social Workers*. Since the first edition was published, social work research has developed and this edition reflects many of these changes. There is a new chapter on *Best Practice* and the chapters on statistics and action research have been completely re-written. All the other chapters have been updated with most incorporating new material.

Our initial aims remain the same:

- To make research methods accessible to students and social work practitioners with plain English explanations of research concepts and principles.
- To enable social work students and practitioners to undertake their own research by providing a step-by-step guide.
- To encourage the social work community to become critical consumers of research.
- To foster the new social work research culture which is emerging world wide.

As social work practice has become increasingly sophisticated, the place of research in social work has become more critical. Today, research is relevant to just about every area of social work practice: from the initial stages of an intervention, determining the needs of an individual, group or community; through to testing new ideas and deciding which course of action to take; and finally, to evaluating practice and justifying social work's existence. Springing from the research traditions of sociology and psychology, social work is now developing its own research orientation and knowledge base, providing fertile ground for social work theory and practice to flourish. However, many social workers still do not recognise the potential of research, nor its value for them as practitioners.

This book introduces research concepts and skills for social workers. It is for social work students as well as social work graduates who wish to brush up their research skills. Readers will gain not only an understanding of the principles and approaches which are most relevant to social work practice, but also a step-by-step approach to undertaking research in their work. *Research for Social Workers* deals with research issues from a social work perspective, using social work examples and incorporating social work based methods. It has been written as a guide for beginners in appropriately non-technical language, but it will allow readers to move into a research program with confidence and ability. As teachers, researchers and social workers ourselves, we, the authors, are committed to enabling social workers to include research as an essential part of their professional tool kits. This means becoming critical consumers of research, as well as confidently being able to incorporate research as part of everyday practice.

Today, social work research reflects the many differences in approach, politics and theory that exist in social work practice. Hence it is important that social workers understand the variety of research approaches available, and are aware of the different theories and epistemologies on which they are based, so that their personal approaches to research are more informed and explicit. Thus, the book begins with a brief exploration of what constitutes the range of social work research and how theories influence all aspects of research—from choosing the general topic area and the overall approach, to defining the problem and selecting methodologies.

Because this is an introductory text for beginning researchers, the various approaches are presented as ideal types to highlight the differences and the debates which surround them. However, we do not view the research process as consisting of mutually exclusive, dichotomous approaches (for example: inductive/deductive or qualitative/quantitative). In our own research we tend to use multimethod approaches and the examples chosen in the book reflect this. Nonetheless, for an introductory text, we feel it is important to set out the different approaches separately, so that beginning researchers can clarify the differences and identify the different orientations in existing research, as they develop their own conceptual approach to research practice.

In chapter 1 we sketch an outline of different approaches to social research, concluding with a discussion of the politics and ethics of research. In these times when many social work programs are under threat, it is particularly important to be aware of the various ideological and political agendas of the different stakeholders in the research process, and the policy and practice implications of the research we undertake. In chapters 2 and 3 we cover the issues involved in choosing your topic area and defining the problem. Steps in the research process are summarised in chapter 4, and sampling procedures are covered in chapter 5. Research methods which are most relevant to social workers—surveys, interviews, needs analyses, evaluation, action research, methods of establishing best practice and other methods—are discussed in chapters 6 to 11. Chapters 12 and 13 present different ways of analysing data and producing results, with reference to the various computer software packages available. Chapter 14 introduces statistical concepts and techniques. The book concludes with a discussion of how to ensure that research leads to action, and some of the most effective ways of influencing policy and practice (chapter 15). Finally the Appendix provides a detailed guide to writing your research proposal, including how to produce a budget.

As the aims outlined in the beginning of this Introduction are achieved, so will social work's voice strengthen, and with this, social work's ability to achieve its mission of advancing the cause of disadvantaged groups, overcoming oppression and working to improve well being for all people.

1 SOCIAL WORK RESEARCH

This chapter introduces you to social research. First, some reassurance. Research is *not* all about numbers. If you are one of those social workers or students who have had unhappy experiences with mathematics, do not despair! Social research is more about critical awareness, careful thinking and the ability to view situations from new perspectives than about numbers. In the twenty-first century, there are a whole range of approaches to research—some involving more mathematics than others. With the advent of computer software packages, it is more important to understand the thinking or logic behind the mathematics, and the theoretical perspectives behind the thinking, than to be able to calculate the numbers themselves.

In this chapter we examine some of the different forms of research and the power of the underlying beliefs which shape them. Quantitative, qualitative, emancipatory, feminist and postmodern influences on research methods are discussed. Each of these offers a range of possibilities for creative and exciting research for social workers. All these approaches can be used by social work researchers and are important for you to understand. As you will see, they are not necessarily mutually exclusive. Indeed, much research today involves a mixture of methods—that is, researchers use a 'multimethod' approach, selecting aspects of different approaches that best suit their purposes. As this is a text for beginning researchers, we present the approaches separately so that you can see how they have evolved, and so that we can introduce some of the debates that surround them.

In this chapter we also consider some of the important political and ethical issues that surround research, before moving on in later chapters to the 'how to' of different research approaches. First of all we discuss what social research is and why, as social workers, we should study it.

WHY STUDY RESEARCH?

Whether they realise it or not, most social workers are constantly doing research or research-like activities. Consider the following:

- A social worker wonders which counselling methods used by different workers in her team are most helpful to the young offenders they see on a regular basis.
- A community worker, in a new job at a council, has a brief to find out what the local community thinks of a planned development to build an industrial complex in some bushland containing a disused quarry.
- A worker in a church-based agency holds a regular group for homeless youth and suspects that many group members are facing similar issues and problems in their lives.
- A social welfare worker wants to know what effects the new respite care service is having for families who are under stress.
- A worker in the disability field, who has been asked to establish a new service for young adults, wonders what life is like from the perspective of the young people and what kind of services, if any, they would like his agency to provide.

All these situations require research skills if social workers are to address the questions and issues they face. The bottom line is: if you are to make informed decisions or carefully thought through actions/interventions, you need research skills.

More specifically, consider the following reasons for studying research.

Becoming an informed research consumer

Social workers are often confronted with government or interdepartmental reports in which research and statistics are quoted. If this is a familiar situation for you, you are probably uncomfortably aware that you may have taken such reports at face value, and, because of a lack of research understanding, you may not have the ability to critique such reports. You should heed Royse's (1991, p. 5) suggestion that:

> as an informed consumer, you ought to be able to know if too few subjects were interviewed, if the methodology was flawed, or if the

author generalised well beyond his or her findings. Research studies can be biased or flawed for a lot of different reasons, and you might not be able to detect these reasons without a basic understanding of research methodology.

All social research has a political imperative. Some reports may take liberties in the way research is presented in order to achieve or to bolster a certain perspective. Some departments, keen to downsize, for example, may disregard or under-report the success of certain programs. Some statistics may be used inappropriately or out of context to enhance an unsupported position. Likewise, some research reports might enhance positive findings in order to ensure continued funding. It is naive to think otherwise in an economic climate where large cuts have been made to welfare spending.

Consider also that when outside consultants are used by an agency or department to assess the organisation's functions, you should be in a position to critically analyse their work and examine whether or not they have given you a fair appraisal. It is imperative that you become an informed practitioner capable of dissecting the information on which decisions are being made about policies which affect your department or your programs.

Finding out about your practice

A second and equally important reason why you should have competent research skills is to allow you to justify your practice interventions in an informed way. It is not enough to rely on your intuition—intuition is susceptible to bias and may reflect your own values rather than client benefits. In these days of increasing accountability to funding bodies and to the people for whom the services are established, workers must be able to find out what the people they are working with want and need, how their interventions are affecting people's lives, and how their programs and approaches can be improved. More and more around the world social workers are being expected to work in an evidence-based culture; that is, to know if what they are doing is working or not.

There are a number of ways practice effectiveness may be assessed. For instance, as a practitioner, you may be called on to examine the effect of certain interventions on a group of clients. You might also be called on to justify your agency's effectiveness by providing an evaluation of the use of its services and the effects of the services on the client group.

Again, you might be called on to show you are meeting the needs of a particular target group (needs analysis). Often practitioners keen to continue a new program are expected to evaluate the program in order that its effectiveness can be demonstrated—that it is meeting its objectives, that it is developing as intended and producing desired outcomes (program evaluation). The future development of the program may depend on well-constructed evaluation research. As well, maintaining and indeed increasing your funding level may depend on your analysis of research conducted to justify a service (cost–benefit analysis).

It is also vital that you have the confidence and competence to act as a contributing partner in research projects. There are often occasions when your agency or department will conduct or contribute to a research project. Having an understanding of research methods will allow you to ensure that a social work perspective is part of the project.

Participating in the policy process

We also need to develop our research tradition so that we are better able to assess government social policies and to formulate such policies. It is our role as a profession to take a lead in the formulation of policy that affects the most vulnerable members of our community and to attack or support government policies. In the past social workers have not been known for applying pressure effectively—at any level of government—to change or modify policies. As an example, there has been little noise from the helping professions condemning the cuts in government welfare services and this is not aided by the lack of data supporting retention of services.

With improved research skills, you will be on firmer ground in joining in the policy process—in commenting on current policies or evaluations of policy and in developing a case for new or different policies.

Undertaking postgraduate education

Studying research at undergraduate level will facilitate your entry into Masters and doctorate programs. This reason should not be discounted, as it is our experience that students may be reluctant to pursue postgraduate study because of their lack of knowledge about research and their fear of attempting a major research project. Yet we need such students to build a strong theoretical and research base in order to upgrade the standing of our discipline. Of course you must also be aware that studying research at undergraduate level is a requirement of professional social work associations around the world and so is a basic requirement for those of you wishing to attain a social work degree.

Developing social work knowledge and theory

A very important reason for studying research is to aid in the development of social work knowledge and theory. Having studied, or being now involved in studying social work, you would be aware that the development of social work theories rests on the shoulders of practitioners who are able to test and evaluate their usefulness. We need these developments to come from social workers themselves and not from other disciplinary areas. For all these reasons, and more, you will benefit from the study of research methods.

Practising in an ethically responsible manner

Social work codes of ethics around the world support ethical research practice. For example, the ethical codes of the British, American and Australian social work associations all contain detailed sections on how to undertake ethical research. We discuss this in more detail later in the chapter.

WHAT IS SOCIAL RESEARCH?

From the discussion above, it can be seen that many different types of research are used in the welfare field. Which approaches you choose depend on the purpose of the research, your background and beliefs, the agenda of the organisation funding the research and, increasingly, the perspectives of the people and/or programs being researched.

Examples of the variety of social research used in the welfare field

- Needs analysis
- Action research
- Outcome evaluation
- Cost–benefit analysis
- Secondary analysis
- Content analysis
- Client satisfaction surveys
- Qualitative in-depth interviewing

Nearly all forms of research involve the search for patterns or themes—ways of simplifying a mass of information into meaningful stories or relationships. Good research helps us to make links, gain insight into apparent contradictions, explore new territory and raise difficult questions. In the process of searching for patterns or themes, all types of research involve some form of measurement. In chapters 2 and 3 we will explore the different types of measurement used in the process of translating broad research issues into researchable questions.

In the welfare field nearly all types of research are undertaken in order to make a decision or to take some action. If we go to the trouble and expense of undertaking a research project, it would be most disappointing if the finished report sat on a shelf gathering dust. It is often said that research is a means of putting off tough or expensive decisions. Instead of being the end of the process, your report should be the first step in changing a policy, deciding on an intervention strategy or setting up a new service.

Taking these considerations into account then, the definition of research (below) describes the way the term 'social research' is understood throughout this book. The research literature contains as many definitions of research as there are forms; this definition captures the broad elements that are generally agreed upon as being shared by most research that is undertaken in the social welfare field.

Definition of social research

Social research is the systematic observation and/or collection of information to find or impose a pattern, to make a decision or take some action.

It is difficult to define what is unique about research in social work. However, McDermott (1996) makes a very good beginning when she suggests that social work research:

- Would be research that arises from a particular theorisation of the acting subject within his/her social, political and economic context
- Would be research that privileges the research process as an intervention leading to the possibility of constructive change
- Would be research that enables the participation of the researched—the poor, the vulnerable, the oppressed and those who interact with them (p. 6)

In any definition of social work research we must ensure that we incorporate the tenets of the Social Work Code of Ethics that guide all aspects of our practice. The power of research as a tool for social change is fundamental to our understanding of the place of research in social work. Just as the goals of social work involve not just understanding the world, but actively intervening to change things in some way, so, too, does social work research involve action, decisions and change.

TYPES OF RESEARCH

The way that researchers find or impose patterns from or on the mass of information available, in order to make decisions or take action, depends very much on the beliefs and theories from which they operate. Before we decide what type of research to do, it is important to understand the assumptions and perspectives which underlie the major approaches to research, so that we are not 'blinkered' by our methodology or unaware of its limitations.

The different research approaches used today are best understood in the context of their history and how they developed in relation to each other. We will discuss five of the major research approaches, in order to demonstrate the variety that exists:

- Quantitative research
- Qualitative research
- Emancipatory approach
- Feminist research
- Postmodern research

These research approaches are summarised as ideal 'types' rather than actual descriptions of research as it happens in the 'real world'. The descriptions highlight the major differences between the approaches to allow you to distinguish between the different types and to think about which research methods would be most appropriate in different situations. In fact, many researchers use a variety of methods, the multimethod approach, and the different approaches themselves can have considerable overlap (Taylor 1993, Kumar 1999). We begin with what was until recently the dominant and orthodox form of research.

Quantitative research

Quantitative research is the oldest form of social research. It grew out of the natural science paradigm of the eighteenth and nineteenth centuries and the intellectual tradition known as 'positivism' (Mark 1996). This type of research is based on the idea that there is an objective 'reality' which can be accurately measured, and which operates according to natural laws which can be 'discovered' by rigorous, objective research (Marlow 1998). Just as a natural scientist in the nineteenth century might examine a rock and test its properties, so it is assumed that a social scientist can 'objectively' study a group or social system (Sarantakos 1998, Babbie 2001).

It is also assumed that the effect of the researcher's own presence is minimal or non-existent, so that 'pure' reality can be studied. That is, it is assumed that whatever the researcher is told, or observes, would actually be happening whether they were present to observe it or not (Mark 1996). Similarly, it is assumed that any other researcher who studies the same social phenomenon using 'accurate' research instruments would come up with the same findings (Gibbs 1991).

Originally, the people who were being studied using this approach were not included in the decision-making processes about the research (they were 'objects' for study rather than 'subjects' involved in the process). Indeed, often the only concessions made to them being people rather than the inanimate objects researched in the physical sciences were precautions taken to protect privacy, anonymity and safety.

Traditionally, researchers in the quantitative positivist tradition begin with ideas or theories about the world, which they go out and test empirically. Thus they carefully design the structure of their research and the concepts they are researching before they go out into the field. Going from the general to the specific, or beginning with the theory and testing ideas empirically, is known as the 'deductive' approach to research (Marlow 1998, Cournoyer & Klein 2000, de Vaus 2002). We will discuss how these ideas or theories are turned into researchable questions in chapter 3.

At the most extreme end of the quantitative spectrum of research methods lies experimental design. This type of research has recently experienced a revival in some areas of social work research, particularly in the United States and some parts of the United Kingdom (Trinder 2000). Experimental designs involve strict conditions including random assignment of subjects (people) to experimental groups (the group being given the intervention) and control groups (the group that does not have the intervention). The researcher manipulates the independent or treatment variable systematically to determine what effects treatment (intervention) has on the experimental group. Because people are randomly placed in the control and experimental groups, it is assumed that all the other factors (variables) which could influence or interfere in the effect of the treatment variable are balanced out between the two groups. Thus, any change measured in the experimental group can be assumed to be due to the treatment variable. Proponents of experimental design in social work argue that this is the only 'true' way of rigorously testing the effectiveness of interventions.

While experimental designs, also known as RCTs or 'randomized control trials' (Trinder 200), may be possible in some social work situations where a single intervention is being offered, such as correctional or prison settings, it is not always possible or desirable to randomly allocate people to experimental or control groups, because those in the control group will not receive the intervention—an ethical dilemma. In addition, critics of this approach argue that social reality cannot be reduced to simplistic manipulations of one variable at a time—life is much more complex than this. Rather than being 'objective', this approach is based on a world view that assumes humans act in ordered, rational ways. Critics of positivism and its offshoots maintain that these assumptions are not universal truths, but a particular theoretical perspective (feminist critics argue that this reflects a largely white, male, middle-class view of the world).

Due to these and other considerations, a whole range of quantitative measures has been developed which 'compromise' one or more of the conditions of classic experimental research design. For example, there are quasi-experimental single-case designs in which practitioners can evaluate the effects of their interventions with a single person, and non-experimental surveys and group designs where inclusion in the sample is not based on random allocation.

Quantitative researchers typically use techniques such as surveys, questionnaires and structured observations. Using statistics, they analyse the information they have collected to see if their ideas about patterns or relationships are supported by 'the facts' as revealed in their research. Because they are interested in 'truth' and discovering natural 'laws' of society, quantitative researchers place great importance on whether the people they study are representative of a whole population, and whether their results can be applied to this larger group. Various sampling and statistical techniques are used in attempts to ensure that conclusions can be 'generalised' (applied) to all the people in the population and not just to those who were included in the particular study.

Examples of quantitative research

- The census
- Large opinion polls
- Some forms of evaluation, e.g. outcome evaluations, cost–benefit analyses
- Research which aims to establish whether there is a relationship between two or more variables, e.g. Is there a relationship between income and religion?

Although quantitative research has provided many useful insights into the social world, some of its most basic assumptions attract stringent criticism. These have led to alternative research approaches. A general term for a variety of research methodologies that has arisen from critiques of quantitative approaches is 'qualitative research'.

Qualitative research

Instead of beginning with theories of patterns or relationships and testing them in the 'real world', qualitative researchers prefer to start the other way around and begin with their experiences or specific observations. They begin their research with no preconceived ideas, and allow the patterns or themes to emerge from their experiences. From careful observations, immersion in the world of the 'researched', in-depth interviews, and a range of other techniques, qualitative researchers build their theories from the patterns they observe in their data (sometimes called 'grounded theory'; see, for example, Strauss 1990). Thus, their approach is inductive: moving from specific observations or interactions to general ideas and theories. This is in direct contrast to deductive quantitative researchers who begin with general theories and move to specific situations. Whereas quantitative researchers aim to 'discover' universal social 'laws', and test theories which explain causal relationships, qualitative researchers are more interested in understanding how others experience life, in interpreting meaning and social phenomena, and in exploring new concepts and developing new theories.

In contrast to quantitative researchers who emphasise the importance of 'objectivity', and of research being 'value free', many qualitative researchers reject the whole notion of objectivity and argue that research can never be value free. Rather than assuming that there is an 'objective reality' which exists independently of people and can be measured, qualitative researchers believe that 'reality' depends on how people experience and interpret life. From this point of view, reality is 'socially constructed' and so cannot be separated from experience or measured from the outside. Instead, the challenge is to understand reality from the 'inside', from other people's perspectives.

A crucial part of such understanding is the way the researcher interacts with the researched, and how the two parties affect each other during the research process. This is another major difference between qualitative and quantitative research. Quantitative researchers believe that the researcher should remain separate from those being researched and that the researcher has minimal or no effect on what is being researched. Qualitative researchers maintain that this is impossible—instead, the researcher should acknowledge their own values, biases and position in relation to the researched. They advocate a research process which is a two-way interaction between the researcher and the researched in which the parties are on a more equal level, sometimes 'co-evolving' the research structure as they go. Thus, a qualitative researcher might conduct very flexible, open interviews so that the conversation can cover topics, perspectives and meanings that are important to the people being researched. Qualitative researchers reject structured surveys and interviews, arguing that these structures reflect the values, assumptions and 'social constructions' of the researcher rather than the perspective of the people being researched. According to qualitative researchers, quantitative methods distort reality because they only measure those aspects of it that are 'quantifiable'. Much of social life, qualitative researchers maintain, can only be understood in the context in which it is experienced and can never be captured in artificially structured questionnaires, which impose a particular view of reality upon the people being researched.

Similarly, qualitative researchers, unlike quantitative researchers, do not emphasise statistical procedures nor the importance of representativeness. Instead, they generalise their results using theory, logic, and further exploration and discussion of themes with the people with whom they are researching. Statistics can be used for limited purposes in qualitative research, such as summarising or describing what many people felt. Most purist researchers in this tradition, however, would not see any point in 'imposing' advanced statistical procedures on the information they have collected.

Examples of qualitative research

- A researcher spends several months 'hanging around' with a gang of 'street kids' to investigate their lifestyle and the issues that are important to them (participant observation)
- In-depth interviews are conducted with rural women and workers from relevant agencies to explore attitudes to domestic violence in the country
- Observations of council meetings and interviews with local councillors are conducted to examine how they perceive 'grass roots democracy'
- Meetings with groups of elderly residents in an inner-city suburb are held to understand their concerns and priorities and to find out what they would like from the local neighbourhood centre

---

Unlike quantitative research, which has its roots in positivism and theoretical disciplines closely related to it (for example, you might come across terms such as 'logical positivism' and 'postpositivism'), there are many different theories underpinning qualitative research which emphasise different aspects of it and which arise from different critiques of positivism. Some of the theories on which various types of qualitative research methods are based include: ethnography, symbolic interactionism and hermeneutics. Many textbooks on qualitative research methods contain descriptions of these different theories, which you will need to understand in more detail if you are going to attempt some of the qualitative techniques (for example, Berg 1995).

Qualitative research has had its share of controversy. One of the major criticisms of these methodologies is that they ignore the larger social structures and forces that influence existence by concentrating only on the microcosm of human experience. In this way, accusations of being 'apolitical' have been levelled at some qualitative researchers. Ethical questions have also been raised about some forms of qualitative research such as 'participant observation', where the researcher joins a group or community 'in disguise' and then publishes the results of their observations without the knowledge or consent of the people themselves. Still others have questioned the uses to which both quantitative and qualitative research has been put.

From our discussion so far, it might seem that qualitative and quantitative research are incompatible opposites, and indeed, up until the 1960s this was how the two schools were viewed (Pyke & Agnew 1991, Rothery 1993a, Taylor 1993). However, purist qualitative or quantitative researchers are rare. More commonly, researchers combine aspects of qualitative and quantitative methodologies to accomplish their purposes. Instead of viewing qualitative and quantitative approaches (or inductive and deductive thinking) as diametrically opposed, many theorists see them as different phases of a cyclical process of developing knowledge (Cournoyer & Klein 2000, Babbie 2001, de Vaus 2002). For example, de Vaus (2002) describes research as a cycle of theory building and theory testing which incorporates inductive and deductive approaches. Thus, researchers may begin with an idea which they explore in a qualitative fashion before testing more developed hypotheses using quantitative methods. Similarly, Cournoyer and Klein (2000) argue that the two approaches are two sides of the same process of science—just as necessary for each other as are the other parts of the cycle to do with logic and theorising versus information gathering.

Many researchers use both qualitative and quantitative questions to explore different aspects of the same issue in a questionnaire. Indeed, Part 4 of Sherman and Reid's (1994) book *Qualitative Research in Social Work* is devoted to five papers by different authors discussing how qualitative and quantitative methods can be integrated. Once you have understood the differences in qualitative and quantitative approaches, it is best to see them as both being useful and necessary skills for good researchers to have in their repertoire.

The third type of research which we discuss in this chapter, which has largely arisen as a result of critiques of purist forms of qualitative and quantitative research, is emancipatory or critical research, sometimes also called 'anti-discriminatory research' (Humphries & Truman 1994) or 'anti-oppressive' research. Some emancipatory researchers combine qualitative and quantitative approaches to achieve their goals, others may use more qualitative or more quantitative methods, depending on their purpose. What distinguishes emancipatory research is not its methodology, but its goals. Feminist research has become such a large and influential form of emancipatory research that it is now acknowledged as a form of research in its own right. We begin our review of these types of research with a brief introduction to emancipatory research followed by a closer look at feminist research.

Emancipatory research

During the twentieth century it became increasingly clear that research, and the knowledge it brings, is not essentially 'good' in itself; nor does it necessarily contribute to the universal betterment, as was originally believed in the eighteenth and nineteenth centuries. The use of the atomic bomb in the Second World War is seen by many as the end of the age of innocence for research. Even before this time, however, anthropologists had been disillusioned by the way the results of their research had been used for political and military ends in Africa during the First World War.

At the same time as it was being realised that research is used for various political ends, many social scientists were coming to see that research has largely been an instrument of the powerful, used against the powerless. Traditionally researchers have studied 'downwards': there are far more studies of indigenous people's culture than the colonists', of the working class than the aristocracy, of patients' behaviour than doctors', of consumer behaviour than corporations'. There have also been several published accounts of the difficulties of studying 'upwards', for example, studying white-collar crime or the culture of sociologists (Bell 1978, Punch 1982).

As these realisations were being made, challenges were being mounted from within the ranks of 'the researched' as to the value of research for them, and their right to be part of decision making about how research would be done. With the rise of consumer rights movements and of liberation movements worldwide, people who had traditionally been seen as passive 'objects' of research began demanding that research should have some benefits for them as well as for the researcher and those who sponsored the research. Indigenous peoples now insist on having control of research that is carried out in traditional communities, and on being part of the decision making about the aims, methods, results and recommendations of that research. Third World countries negotiate agreements, including the possibility that indigenous researchers will be trained as part of major international research projects on their soil, in return for allowing the research to proceed.

At the same time, people from groups who have previously been excluded from conducting research but are more usually the researched—women, people from races and cultures other than white Anglo-European/American, people with disabilities—are now entering the professions, including the research area. They are exposing discriminatory assumptions in much of what has been previously accepted as 'objective' research knowledge and methodology. They are also demanding that researchers be accountable to the people they research, not just to the people who pay for the research.

For example, researchers with disabilities have questioned the multi-million-dollar Human Genome Initiative, which aims to map in detail human genes and thus creates the possibility of being able to banish many 'medical frailties'. Morris (1992) has argued that such research:

> encourages an unthinking acceptance that the elimination of certain types of people and experiences is straightforwardly a good thing.

At the moment disabled people are being excluded from this debate which is being carried on within the medical and scientific communities (p. 17).

As with qualitative research, the theoretical traditions of emancipatory research come from a variety of areas including Marxism, feminism, critical and conflict sociology, as well as educative consciousness-raising theories such as those of Paulo Freire (1970). However, in contrast to both quantitative and qualitative approaches, emancipatory researchers argue that the point of research is not merely to study the world, but also to change it (Masters 1995, Grundy 1990). For too long, such researchers argue, research has been in the hands of the powerful, where it has been furthering the interests of the power elite at the expense of the powerless. The job of the emancipatory researcher is to uncover the myths, beliefs and social constructions that contribute to the continuation of the status quo, in order to reveal how power relations are really operating to control the powerless. In the process, emancipatory researchers aim to liberate, enlighten or empower those people who are subjugated.

Emancipatory researchers take for granted that research is never value free. What is important is whose side you are on. Emancipatory researchers deliberately 'take sides' with the people who are oppressed or struggling against their oppression. Thus, they are overtly political. It has been said that a mark of good research in this tradition is that it makes powerful people angry (see, for example, Baldry & Vinson 1991).

Emancipatory researchers sit somewhere between the purist quantitative and qualitative positions in terms of their views of 'reality' and 'objectivity'. They view society as being full of contradictions and tensions between dominant and oppressed groups, between those who impose their reality on others and those who are the 'other'. In this view, people are shaped by external forces operating in the interests of the powerful (similar to the assumptions of universal objective laws of quantitative researchers), but may also be aware of their oppression and attempt to resist the dominant group's version of 'reality' (similar to the beliefs about the importance of subjectivity of qualitative researchers).

With its growing body of literature, and contributions to many debates about the nature of research and knowledge, feminist research has become an important area of emancipatory research in its own right (see, for example, Nielsen 1990).

Feminist research

Like other forms of emancipatory research, feminist research is characterised by its goals rather than its methods. During the last twenty years this form of research has made an immense impact on society in general and on the position and role of women (Reinharz 1992, Sarantakos 1998). As an approach to research, it is in a stage of lively evolution.

In their quest to study 'the condition of women in sexist society' (Stanley & Wise 1990, p. 12), feminist researchers applied academic and research techniques to expose the sexism inherent in male-dominated social sciences and research (sometimes referred to as 'malestream research'). For example, feminist researchers highlighted the 'gender-blindness' of official statistics which made it impossible to determine the status and condition of women separately from the male 'head of the house' (see, for example, Roberts 1981, Oakley 1985). Thus feminist researchers showed how traditional ways of measuring the world have ignored or silenced women's viewpoints and position because the researchers literally cannot 'see' them.

'Feminist research' has been defined as a focus *on* women, in research carried out *by* women who were feminist, *for* other women (Stanley & Wise 1990, p. 21). From the beginning, feminist research was committed to changing women's lives.

During the earlier phases of feminist research, quantitative methods were seen as being 'male', while qualitative ones were 'female'. Since then, a plurality of approaches has developed: feminist researchers now use a variety of methods, including quantitative research, and have introduced some innovative techniques of their own in their task to study and improve women's lives. These include consciousness-raising groups, textual analysis and collaborative strategies such as keeping group diaries and discussing the meaning of results or presenting results back to respondents for interpretation with the researcher. Many writers emphasise that the ongoing debate within this plurality of multiple approaches is itself an important part of feminist research. They maintain that it is crucial that different approaches be respected and no single approach gain dominance as *the* form of feminist research.

In line with this thinking, Reinharz (1992) defines feminist methodology as the sum of feminist research methods. In her definition, feminist research is research which is done by researchers who claim to be feminist, or which is published in explicitly feminist journals and books, or which receives awards from organisations that give awards for feminist research.

Like emancipatory researchers, feminist researchers come from a variety of theoretical backgrounds, including socialist feminism, radical feminism, liberal feminism and Marxist feminism. Recently, many feminist researchers have been influenced by the work of poststructuralists and postmodernists. This chapter concludes with a brief discussion of postmodernism, particularly as it applies to feminist research.

Ten themes of feminist research methodology identified by Reinharz (1992)

- Feminism is a perspective, not a research method
- Feminists use a multiplicity of research methods
- Feminist research involves an ongoing criticism of non-feminist scholarship
- Feminist research is guided by feminist theory
- Feminist research may be transdisciplinary
- Feminist research aims to create social change
- Feminist research strives to represent human diversity
- Feminist research frequently includes the researcher as a person
- Feminist research frequently attempts to develop special relations with the people studied (in interactive research)
- Feminist research frequently defines a special relation with the reader

---

Stanley and Wise (1990, p. 38) propose a set of four basic assumptions about the world, based on the work of Margrit Eichler, with which they expect all feminist researchers would agree. These four points echo many of the themes discussed in relation to emancipatory research in the previous section.

Four assumptions of feminist research

- All knowledge is socially constructed
- The dominant ideology is that of the ruling group
- There is no such thing as value-free science and so far the social sciences have served and reflected men's interests
- The perspectives of men and women differ because people's perspectives vary systematically with their position in society

---

Feminist researchers often criticise the 'artificial dichotomies' which exist in mainstream research, for example the deductive/inductive split or the theory/method divide. They argue that instead of being separate or opposites, such concepts are inextricably linked to each other. For example, Stanley and Wise (1990) have said of the traditional inductive/deductive split:

> Researchers cannot have 'empty heads' in the way that inductivism proposes; nor is it possible that theory is untainted by material experiences in the heads of theoreticians in the way that deductionism proposes (p. 22).

Like many qualitative researchers, a feminist researcher often makes sure that the researcher includes herself as an essential part of the research process, and is explicit about her beliefs and background, how she became involved in the topic and about her relationship with the people with whom she is researching. Feminist researchers, in their quest for empowerment of women and understanding women's perspectives, may also develop close relationships with the people they involve in their research.

Examples of feminist research

- A researcher holds conversations with rural women over several months to discuss and write up their experiences of farming and attitudes towards these experiences
- A women's support group collects statistics and evidence about how domestic violence is dealt with in their region compared to other types of violence, in order to raise community awareness and to lobby for a women's refuge
- A social welfare worker involves her colleagues in a study of their daily work practices to analyse the similarities between social work and traditional 'women's work'
- Beginning with her own experience, a researcher explores the meaning of mastectomy in Western culture through an analysis of works of fiction, poetry and women's magazines

---

As is the case with quantitative and qualitative forms of research, feminist research has its critics. The voices of women from marginalised groups have not been heard in much of feminist research, despite its commitment to diversity. For example, lesbians, indigenous women, women from other cultures and women with disabilities have criticised much of feminist research for being dominated by white middle-class perspectives which exclude them, just as they are excluded by mainstream society (Meekosha 1990, 2000, Gunew & Yeatman 1993).

Terming much of the broad range of feminist research methodologies discussed above as 'standpoint/critical' feminist research, feminist social work researchers who support postmodern approaches, such as Fawcett and Featherstone (2000) and Trinder (2000), have launched some major criticisms of what has now become known as traditional feminist research. Trinder (2000), for example, analyses a piece of feminist research on violence to show how women's voices are presented as unproblematic and unified, and how a 'true' version of what constitutes violence, based on a feminist approach, is developed. This view, she considers, may exclude other equally valid perceptions and gloss over differences in the individual women's original accounts. Our review of the major approaches to social work research concludes with a brief brush with postmodernist research to illustrate just how wide the spectrum of research available to social workers has become.

Postmodern research

Most social work research discussed so far, both quantitative and qualitative, comes from a modernist perspective which ultimately falls back on a belief in a knowable, 'real' world, the truth of which can be discovered through rational processes (for example, Howe 1994). The postmodern world in which social work and social research now finds itself, however, challenges all this.

Instead of certainties and 'realities' which can be scientifically explored, postmodernism asserts that 'truth' or knowledge is created through language and meanings and is different for different people, depending on their experiences. Thus, instead of a single, knowable reality, postmodernist researchers speak of a plurality of voices, each with its own locally constructed reality. No single reality is more valid than another—indeed, diversity and difference should be celebrated (Sands & Nuccio 1992, Rossiter 2000). Instead of focusing on structural disadvantage or the study of fixed notions of 'men' and 'women', for example, postmodernist researchers turn their analysis to language itself (often termed 'discourse'), and 'to examining what voices women (and men) are using within the context of unequal gender and other social relations' (Trinder 2000, p. 51).

With its emphasis on language as the site for the complexities of how power is mediated through discourse and relationships, and its insistence that there is no single reality, postmodernism poses some fundamental challenges to social work which will keep theorists and researchers busy for some time (not least in trying to untangle the inaccessible language postmodernists use!).

Proponents of a postmodern feminist approach to social work research argue that postmodern research re-theorises the individual as an effect of the social, thus overcoming the problem of artificially distinguishing between the person and their environment (Rossiter 2000). Rossiter argues that this opens the way for a new view of social work's traditional claim to work with the 'person in environment' which offers an opportunity to 'unify social work as a democratic project' (Rossiter 2000, p. 29). Similarly, postmodernism could offer the prospect of a more complex understanding of how power operates between social workers and their clients.

Even proponents of postmodernism do not advocate an uncritical acceptance of its approaches within social work (for example, Latting 1995, Fawcett & Featherstone 2000, Rossiter 2000). Critics, on the other hand, argue that postmodernism threatens the very existence of social work because, with no fundamental reality or 'truth', how can one know if one is working towards social justice or injustice? What happens to the notion of ethical practice if there is no longer a standard against which to measure this? In her critique of postmodernism, Gray (1995) warns of the dangers of relativism and subjectivism undermining the notion of ethical practice in social work. Similarly Peile and McCouat (1997) and Wood (1997) discuss the problems of relativism while at the same time acknowledging the opportunities postmodernism offers social work to become more reflective and inclusive.

Conclusion and summary

In this brief review of some of the major approaches to research, we have attempted to show how important it is to understand the underlying assumptions, beliefs and goals of each approach and how these shape the way research is done. We have also argued that while some approaches are incompatible (for example, experimental design and postmodern analysis) many other approaches are not mutually exclusive. Some types of quantitative and qualitative research can be integrated to produce richer results than will be achieved by simply using one methodology or another. Research in the real world is messy and often cannot be limited to a particular 'ideal type'. Instead, researchers tend to use techniques and methods from a variety of approaches, depending on their purpose, as shown in the discussion on emancipatory and feminist research.

The important point to take with you from this discussion is that it is imperative that you are explicit about the theoretical and value framework from which you conduct your research. Similarly, an important aspect of being an informed consumer of research is that you can identify what theory or approach underlies the research you are reading. We conclude this chapter with a summary of the political and ethical issues which arise whenever a person becomes involved in research.

THE POLITICS OF RESEARCH

We now know that research is not a value-free endeavour which inevitably produces knowledge for the good of all people. Instead we must accept that research is a political activity with ethical and political consequences. Two fundamental and related political questions must be addressed before any research is begun. These are:

- Who is the research for? (Whose interests does it serve?)
- What is the purpose of the research? (How will the results be used?)

While we cannot always be sure how our research will be used in the long term, it is important to be as clear as possible from the beginning about the purposes of the research and whose interests it will serve.

Key players in the research process

One way to address these questions is to be clear about the key players who must be taken into account in the planning of your research.

Key players in the research process

- The researcher or researchers
- The people who are researched
- Sponsors who pay for the research
- People who will benefit from the research
- People who are targeted to be convinced by the research (e.g. policy makers)

From the discussion in this chapter it should be clear that the research process is rarely straightforward, but is rather the outcome of negotiations or bargains between each of these groups of people, who may have conflicting interests. Sometimes these categories will overlap: for example, if an organisation run by people with disabilities hires a researcher to investigate the housing needs and preferences of its members, then at least three of the above categories will be the same. The fact that people share categories does not necessarily make the negotiations any more simple, however! Still, when planning a piece of research, it can prevent many problems later if we can distinguish between who belongs in each category and what our own attitudes are in relation to this.

Who owns the research?

Another important question which again needs to be sorted out before research is begun is: who owns the research? In the early days of social research, it was assumed that the knowledge generated by research was somehow universally owned. Nowadays, research knowledge is more often treated as a kind of private property, which is owned by the people who sponsor (pay for) the research. If the people who commission the research do not approve of the results, they may refuse to publish it and the researcher may have no legal redress about this. To prevent as many difficulties as possible in this area, it is important to have a clear contract with the sponsor of the research, to specify who owns, and who is responsible for, the research data and outcomes.

Aspects to include in a research contract

- Who owns the data?
- Who owns the research instrument?
- Who owns the findings?
- Who owns the report?
- Who is responsible for the recommendations?
- Intellectual property rights

THE ETHICS OF RESEARCH

Just as research is never value free, ethics is a vital part of every research project. These days it is generally accepted that social research must meet five ethical criteria in order to be considered ethically acceptable. As we have discussed, these principles have been accepted not only because most researchers wish to conduct ethical research, but also because of the demands for a 'fair go' from the people being researched.

Five ethical criteria for research

- Autonomy/self-determination (includes informed consent and confidentiality)
- Non-maleficence (not doing harm)
- Beneficence (doing good)
- Justice (are the purposes just?)
- Positive contribution to knowledge

Adapted from Beauchamp (1982)

The principle of autonomy involves issues such as respect for people and their right to decide whether or not they will be involved in research. When asking people to be involved in your research, it is important that you can demonstrate that they have given their *informed* consent to participate. This means that they understand the nature of the research and its purpose, the risks for them, and what will be asked of them.

Other ethical aspects of the principle of autonomy include the right to *privacy*, including the right to withdraw from the process at any stage and to refuse to answer certain questions if they wish, the right to *anonymity* and the right to *confidentiality*. Confidentiality means that the information given to the researcher will not be divulged to others, except in reporting research results as agreed, and also that the information will not be used for any purpose other than the research.

Researchers are also required not to harm their subjects in any way and, conversely, to do some good, or to be of benefit, to the people who are being researched. Often in proposals to ethics committees you will be asked to document the risks your research might pose to the participants, and what measures you will take to minimise these.

Principles of justice or fairness are also ethical issues which, as we have seen, can be viewed differently depending on your perspective. Research is often a complex issue involving ethical dilemmas in which you may have to choose between undesirable alternatives.

Three questions which might help you to decide on the ethical value of your research project are:

- Would the participants be willing to do further research of this kind?
- Would I be happy for my own family to participate?
- What are the benefits for the people being researched?

The final principle—making a positive contribution to knowledge—involves issues of professional standards. You must ensure that your purpose is worthwhile, that your data are gathered carefully and that you have chosen appropriate methods of research design, data collection and analysis. Results must be reported honestly, and this should include any problems, errors or distortions of which you are aware. You cannot publish data that you did not collect, and you must not falsify data.

In relation to other researchers, it is imperative that you give credit and refer to others who contributed to your work. Plagiarism, or using other people's work without acknowledgement, is a serious offence in research and scholarship generally.

Social work codes of ethics

Many national social work codes of ethics are explicit in including research within their practice standards. For example, the National Association of Social Workers' Code of Ethics in the United States devotes Section 5.02, 'Evaluation and Research', to 16 ethical responsibilities that social workers have in relation to research and evaluation (NASW 1999).

Similarly, the Australian Social Work Code of Ethics (AASW 2000) includes a section (4.5.2 'Research', AASW 2000, p. 20) containing 14 clauses which applies the ethical principles discussed in this chapter to social work research. In addition, references to research appear throughout the general parts of the AASW Code. For example, social workers are to 'set and enforce explicit professional boundaries (with research participants) to minimize risk of conflict, harm, exploitation' (4.1.4 (g)).

Sexual conduct is forbidden with research participants (4.1.4 (h)) and anonymity is expected to be preserved (4.2.6 (g)). In addition to these clauses, which also relate to other people with whom social workers relate, the Code of Ethics states that social workers must promote the general ethical principles and standards of the Code when conducting research.

The new British Code of Ethics for social work adopted in April 2002 goes even further in its stipulations about how social workers should do research. In addition to the requirements listed in the other two codes, this code emphasises the anti-oppressive or empowerment focus of social work and reminds social workers to work together with disempowered groups, individuals and communities in devising and achieving research agendas (BASW 2002).

Having research included in social work codes of ethics in this way means that social workers who ignore or violate ethical principles when undertaking research face serious penalties imposed by their profession, which may affect their whole career.

The role of ethics committees

Most universities and major welfare and research institutions, such as large hospitals, government departments and research councils, have ethics committees which review research proposals before they are allowed to go ahead. Some organisations and professions also have research codes of ethics. When planning your research, you must find out the requirements for your particular situation. Usually you will have to document the ethical implications of your research for the committee before it can be approved. Often the questions on the form address the ethical principles outlined above. Filling out an ethics form will also help you to be clearer about the nature of your research.

Ethics committees play an important role in protecting the public from unethical research. They are part of ensuring that we are accountable for our actions. Universities and research institutions impose severe penalties if the procedures agreed to are not followed.

SUMMARY

In this chapter we have defined social research and introduced some of the major types of research. Principles of quantitative, qualitative, emancipatory and postmodern research are described in order to demonstrate the variety of research approaches that are possible, and the way that different approaches are shaped by their underlying beliefs about the world. We have noted the different theories on which the approaches are based, the different types of methods and techniques used, and how each form of research views the role of the researcher differently. All of these approaches are used by social workers doing research. Although for simplicity we have presented 'ideal types', in reality, social work researchers may use a mixture of some of these approaches depending on their purposes. It is important that you understand a variety of approaches if you are to have the flexibility to research different social work issues in the most appropriate way. It is also important that you are able to identify the underlying approaches of your own and others' research. Finally, we have discussed some of the political and ethical implications that researchers must consider before they begin their research.

QUESTIONS

1 What are the differences between quantitative, qualitative and emancipatory research?
2 What challenges does postmodern reseach pose?
3 What are the main tenets of feminist research?
4 With which forms of research do you feel most comfortable?
5 Why are politics and ethics so important in planning your research?
6 List some key ethical issues to consider in any research proposal.

EXERCISES

Find an example of one quantitative, one qualitative and one piece of feminist research. (Use your local library. Try journals or books of collections of research.) Answer these questions about each of the papers:
1 For whom was the research conducted?
2 What was the purpose of the research?
3 Are you told how the results were used? What actions or decisions were taken as a result?
4 Identify the people in the following categories:
   - The researcher/s
   - The participants or people being researched
   - Those who benefited from the research
   - Those who sponsored the research
   - Those who were targeted to be convinced by the research
5 Can you identify any conflicts of interest between these groups?
6 What were the theories underlying the research?
7 How was the information gathered?
8 How were the patterns or themes determined (how were the data analysed)?
9 What conclusions were drawn?

10 How is the role of the researcher discussed in the paper?
11 What role did the people who were researched play in the process of the research?
12 What risks existed for the people who were researched? For the researcher?
13 Were there benefits for those who were researched? What were they?
14 Do you think the participants would be willing to undertake further research with this researcher?
15 Would you have been happy to participate in this research?

FURTHER READING

Babbie, E. 2001, *The Practice of Social Research*, 9th edn, Wadsworth, California. Part 1, chapters 1 and 2, contains a good discussion of the foundations of social scientific inquiry and the different theories and paradigms which underlie research as well as an introduction to ethical issues.

Cournoyer, D. E. & Klein, W. C. 2000, *Research Methods for Social Work*, Allyn & Bacon, Boston. Chapter 1 provides an excellent discussion of the different ways of scientific knowing including a discussion of critical thinking and sociocultural influences. Chapter 2 comprehensively covers ethics including a section on sources of ethical conflict.

Fawcett, B., Featherstone, B., Fook, J. & Rossiter, A. (eds) 2000, *Practice and Research in Social Work: Postmodern Feminist Perspectives*. The first three papers in this collection set out the principles and debates around postmodern feminist research in social work; the following chapters provide some excellent examples of this type of research in a variety of fields of practice.

Fortune, A. E. & Reid, W. J. 1999, *Research in Social Work* 3rd edn, Columbia University Press, New York. Chapters 1 and 3 provide a good overview of the differences between qualitative and quantitative research and between political and ethical considerations.

Grinnell, R. M. Jr 1993, *Social Work Research and Evaluation*, 4th edn, Peacock Publishers, Itasca, Ill. Chapters 3 (Rothery 1993b) and 4 (Taylor 1993) discuss deductive (termed positivist) and inductive/qualitative (termed naturalistic) research; chapter 5 (Schinke & Gilchrest 1993) discusses ethics.

Humphries, B. & Truman, C. 1994, *Re-thinking Social Research*, Avebury, Great Britain. This book is a series of papers from the emancipatory research approach (termed anti-discriminatory research in the book). Chapter 1 provides an interesting critique of traditional research ethics and chapter 9 is about anti-discriminatory social work research, although all papers have relevance to social workers.

Nielsen, J. M. (ed.) 1990, *Feminist Research Methods: Exemplary Readings in the Social Sciences*, Westview Press, Boulder. Discussion of feminist methods.

Reinharz, S. 1992, *Feminist Methods in Social Research*, Oxford University Press, New York. Discussion of feminist methods.

Royse, D. 1999, *Research Methods in Social Work,* 3rd edn, Nelson Hall, Chicago. Chapter 4 contains a comprehensive review of quantitative research methods.

Sarantakos, S. 1998, *Social Research*, 2 edn, Macmillan, Sydney. Chapters 1 and 2 cover the differences between qualitative and quantitative research paradigms, as well as ethics.

Sherman, E. & Reid, W. J. 1994, *Qualitative Research in Social Work*, Columbia University Press, New York. Part 4 contains five papers (authors: W. D. Harrison, I. P. Davis, S.R. Bernstein & I. Epstein, B. Loneck, R. W. Toseland) which discuss integrating qualitative and quantitative methods in social work research.

Wodarski, J. S. 1997, *Research Methods for Clinical Social Workers: Empirical Practice*, Springer Publishing Co., New York. This book contains many examples and tools for undertaking quantitative research in social work. Chapter 6 offers a comprehensive description of experimental designs applied to social work.

Yegidis, B. L., Weinbach, W. W. & Morrison-Rodriguez, B. 1999, *Research Methods for Social Workers*, 3rd edn, Allyn & Bacon, Boston. Part 1 covers an overview of the differences between quantitative and qualitative research, and a detailed chapter on ethics.

2 CHOOSING YOUR TOPIC AREA

In the next two chapters we will explore choosing your research topic, and then examine how to transform the issue, problem or area in which you are interested into researchable questions. We will look at how both quantitative and qualitative researchers go about this process.

Sometimes this first step—choosing your research topic or problem and developing research questions—is also the step which brings the project to a halt before it has even started. Some beginning researchers become so overwhelmed by all the possibilities and the enormity of the task, that they never get on to the research itself. Rothery (1993b) has called this 'decidophobia'.

One of the main elements of 'decidophobia' is wanting to do too much at once. You cannot possibly solve all the problems, or even answer all the questions you have, in one research project! The first lesson in defining your research problem, then, is accepting that you will only ever be able to research a little part of the issue in which you are interested. This is often a disappointment to the beginning researcher. Be warned, and warn those with whom you are researching: you will always have to narrow down your research topic and address only *some* of the issues that interest you. Defining the research topic is a crucial step in this process. It can be a big help in overcoming 'decidophobia', and enabling you to get on with your research.

The first step in defining the issue or problem to be researched is to determine the general area. Yegidis et al. (1999) make the point that this first step is crucial, and should be framed as a problem statement rather than as a question. As we saw in chapter 1, often a research area presents itself during the course of your work, or from personal experience. Alternatively, you might answer an advertisement for funding for a research topic, or be approached by someone from your organisation about a project. However the research topic presents itself, before you leap into planning the project or even narrowing down the topic area, it is important that you are aware of your own values and preferred theoretical perspectives, and how these will influence the whole way you conceptualise the project.

THEORY, VALUES AND YOUR RESEARCH TOPIC—THE IMPORTANCE OF A CONCEPTUAL FRAMEWORK

Inevitably, the theories from which you operate, your beliefs about the world and the values you hold, whether you are conscious of them or not, will influence the research topic you choose, and the way you go about researching it. For example, if you are asked to evaluate a residential facility for people with disabilities, the way you approach this will depend on how you see the problem. If you hold a largely functionalist view of the world, you may assume that staff and residents are working together to achieve the program's goals, so you may only interview staff, or perhaps staff and residents together, as part of your evaluation. If, however, you are coming from a more conflict–critical tradition, you may assume that the staff and residents will have different, even opposing views, so you will design a project that seeks those views separately. Perhaps you may choose only to interview staff, or only to interview residents—if you operate from certain perspectives it may not occur to you to interview the other. In addition, a feminist researcher would want to ensure that the results for men and women, whether staff or residents, could be analysed separately.

Similarly, a person immersed in symbolic interactionism might be most interested in how the facility is experienced by the residents themselves, and spend considerable time understanding their perspective about how the institution is run. This researcher may analyse the interactions between staff and residents in terms of how meanings are developed and shared. Another researcher from a critical perspective, on the other hand, may be more interested in uncovering the power differentials between staff and residents in decision making, and how the structures within the facility affect these relationships. They may also be interested in wider political and social structures and how these affect life in the facility.

Again, a postmodern researcher might be interested in how

people develop meanings and relationships and how they co-construct terms such as 'staff' and 'resident'. They might be wanting to analyse how the discourse of 'residential setting' mediates relationships. Rather than assuming power lies in social structures and roles within the organisation, they would assume that power is more fluid and a feature of relationships, meanings and language. Their methods of observation and the focus of conversations would be quite different from those of other researchers from different approaches.

Every aspect of research is influenced by our theories and values. The important point is to become aware of what our underlying theories and values are, how they influence our choice of and general approach to the topic, and to incorporate this understanding into our thinking as we develop our conceptual framework or plan for the research.

Part of deciding on the topic area involves developing a conceptual plan for how you will undertake the whole project. Usually this is not a straightforward linear process, but rather a cyclical one. As you read more, talk to different people and discover more about the topic, so your conceptual framework develops. This will include the underlying purpose of the research, the topic area, the particular questions or focus that you are most interested in, the methods you intend to use, the steps in the research process and the means by which you will analyse the data, as well as what you hope will happen as a consequence of the research. At the same time as you are working out the topic of your research, you will be formulating this conceptual plan for how you intend to investigate it. If you can be explicit about the values and theories which underlie your approach, you will be much clearer about your purpose and alert to any conflicts of interest which may occur with other players in the process.

Often funding bodies or academic institutions require a research proposal before they give their approval to a research project. Completing a research proposal can be a good start to setting out the conceptual framework for your research. Even if such a proposal is not required, it is imperative that you write down a plan of how you conceptualise your topic and the process by which you will research it, before you begin the research itself. Having a clearly defined plan will save you much time and energy later. As you begin to think about your research topic and to develop your conceptual plan, there are several people whose opinions you should take into account.

WHO DECIDES ON THE TOPIC AREA?

Whatever the path by which you become involved, it is critical that *you* are interested in the topic. Research requires much time and effort. Unless you are curious and interested in the area you are about to research, there is little point devoting your valuable time and energy (and those of other people) to it. Questions which might help you decide whether you really are interested include: What is my interest in this issue? What can I learn from it? How will it contribute to my own or others' work? What do I hope to achieve by my involvement? Will I have the time, considering my other commitments, to complete the research?

In chapter 1 we saw that there are four other types of key players, in addition to yourself, who must be taken into account when you are formulating the topic you wish to research. The first group is the *people being researched*. Who are they? What are their attitudes to the issue you are interested in? Will you be able to get access to them and if so, will they want to be involved? What's in it for them?

Second, you must consider the *organisation* paying for or sponsoring the research. Often this will be the agency where you already work. You will need to explore questions such as: What are the organisation's aims for the project? Do these conflict with the aims of the people being researched? Do they conflict with your own interest in the problem? How can you resolve such issues so that the project can go ahead? Will the organisation provide adequate resources? If not, are there other avenues of funding for the project? Will the organisation permit you the time for the project? All these issues have to be negotiated carefully as part of refining the research topic.

The third group we identified in chapter 1 was the *people who will benefit from the research*. Who are they? Will the people you are researching receive some benefits? Will your agency? Will you? Finally, you need to consider the *people who the research is aimed at convincing*. How can they be involved in the topic so that they become committed to taking the decisions or action to which your research results point?

Selecting an advisory group

One way of addressing many of these issues is to meet with members from each of these groups, in order to assess their interest and involvement and how they see the problem. A useful mechanism is a steering committee or advisory group consisting of representatives from each of the groups of key players. This group can be the 'sounding board' against which you try out your ideas, negotiate the purpose of the research, work out the questions you wish to ask and the general approaches you will take. Such a group, with the different perspectives of its members, can help you avoid many political and ethical pitfalls in the research process and ensure that your project meets the needs of the key players. It can also be a great help throughout the life of the project, not just at the problem formulation stage.

Of course, forming this advisory group is not without its challenges. Each of the members must feel that they have sufficient respect and influence that they are not intimidated into silence. A representative from the group who is being researched should be someone who is used to being on committees and working with welfare professionals, or at least someone who is not afraid to offer their opinion in such a group. Having a 'token' member on an advisory group, who feels unable to speak up, is pointless, and sometimes destructive. It can give the impression that there is support from the group being researched when this is not the case at all. Even if it is not possible to form a group such as this, it is most important that you identify the key players and consult with people from each of the four categories about how they see the topic, as part of the process of defining the problem that you will be researching.

Criteria for defining the research topic

Four criteria must be met before you finalise your research topic (Williams, Tutty & Grinnell 1995). Together, these criteria address many of the questions raised in this introductory discussion.

Criteria for choosing the research problem

- Is it relevant?
- Is it researchable?
- Is it feasible?
- Is it ethical?

Adapted from Williams, Tutty & Grinnell (1995)

Unless the problem you choose is *relevant* to the social welfare industry, that is, unless it will lead to 'making a decision or taking some action', as we have specified in our definition of research in chapter 1, there is no point in proceeding. Research topics can be either 'pure' or 'applied', although these terms are really ideal types at each end of a continuum. *Applied research* is directly related to organisational or program goals and is often seen as being immediately 'useful'—for example, evaluating the effect of a living skills program on residents' quality of life. *Pure research* topics, on the other hand, involve theoretical development, or exploring more general issues that affect social welfare—for example: What are the factors that contribute most to good quality of life? While not as immediately useful as the first 'applied' topic, this more 'pure' topic is still relevant since many services aim to improve quality of life. Whether your topic is at the applied or pure end of the research continuum, it must be relevant or the interest and resources will not be available.

Some problem areas are simply not amenable to methods of social research. Ethical questions, which are extremely relevant to welfare policies and people working in social welfare, may not be *researchable*. For example, the topic, 'Should homosexual and lesbian couples be allowed to foster children?', is not researchable using the methods of social research. This question is a problem of values or ethics rather than one of systematically finding 'patterns' in the social world, as specified in our definition in the Introduction. On the other hand, the topic, 'Are there different outcomes for children fostered by homosexual and lesbian couples compared to children fostered by heterosexual couples?', is theoretically researchable because it involves a search for patterns and the systematic collection of information.

Once you have established that your problem area is both *relevant* and *researchable,* you need to ensure that it is also *feasible.* Feasibility is about whether it is possible for you to actually do the research. Your topic needs to be manageable and possible within the resources you have. In the example above, if agency policies have only recently included homosexual and lesbian couples as foster parents, it will be impossible to study the long-term outcomes for children, no matter how relevant and researchable the issue. Similarly, if your topic is too broad, it will not be feasible. Even if homosexual and lesbian couples have been fostering children for some time, few researchers would be able to examine a large topic such as comparing all the issues affecting foster children's quality of life and how these relate to whether their foster parents were in homosexual, lesbian or heterosexual relationships. However, researchers might be able to investigate smaller, more manageable questions such as the length of time the foster placements lasted, children's ability to form friends at school, academic performance and emotional security.

Narrowing the topic even further from these four issues to just one (for example, emotional security) may transform your study into a feasible project within the resource limitations you and your organisation have. When considering feasibility, you must also consider the time and costs involved. A research project will not be feasible unless it is affordable. It is very easy to underestimate costs. Ex-foster children and parents may have scattered widely. How long will it take to locate them? How much will phone calls, postage, printing and travel to interviews cost? Another aspect of feasibility is making sure that you are collecting information in a form that you, or someone you can afford to pay, can analyse. Thus expertise, and access to expertise, is another important part of feasibility.

Feasibility involves questions of ethics as well as of resources. For example, if you wanted to research children's previous experiences of being fostered by homosexual and lesbian couples as compared with heterosexual couples, it is highly unlikely that the relevant organisation would allow you to interview the children. Similarly, schools, counselling agencies and other organisations which are involved with foster children will have policies which prevent researchers gaining access to their clients, especially about sensitive issues, in order to protect privacy and confidentiality and to prevent harm. Before you decide on your topic, it is crucial that you make sure that your topic and methods meet the ethical guidelines of the agency(ies) through which you want to contact the people you are researching, and that you will be able to collect the data you need in order to address the question.

Sometimes a topic becomes feasible by changing the focus of the question. In the example above, if the researchers amend their topic to an investigation of long-term outcomes for children who had been fostered by homosexual, lesbian and heterosexual couples five to ten years ago, they may be permitted to review case histories from client records, with proper safeguards in place to protect privacy and confidentiality. In some circumstances, the agency may also be willing to approach ex-clients and foster parents on behalf of the researchers, to gain permission for the researchers to contact them to discuss becoming involved in the research.

The fourth and final criteria which must be met before your topic is finalised is that it must meet general *ethical criteria* for research. In chapter 1 we reviewed five major summarising principles which must be followed in order to conduct ethically acceptable research, as well as the sorts of guidelines for ethical research set down in social work codes around the world. It is most important to check that your topic meets these criteria. Ask yourself the three questions which were also listed to help you further think through the ethical implications of your topic area. In most instances you will have to submit your research proposal to an ethics committee, as we discussed in the previous chapter, so it is important to think through these issues as part of formulating your research topic.

PURPOSE OF RESEARCH AND YOUR TOPIC

The purpose of your research also affects how you view your topic. There are three broad types of research purposes.

The three main purposes of research

- Exploring social phenomena or theories (exploratory research)

- Describing various aspects of the social world (descriptive research)
- Explaining social phenomena (explanatory research)

The three purposes of research are part of a continuum (Grinnell 1993, Williams, Tutty & Grinnell 1995), and in fact most studies contain elements of all three (Babbie 2001). For example, the first part of a study may begin with a concern to describe a particular phenomenon such as juvenile delinquency, including a description of who juvenile offenders are most likely to be, what their backgrounds are, and what sort of offences they commit (descriptive research). The study may also include a goal of examining various causes of juvenile delinquency (explanatory research).

Exploratory research is undertaken when little is known about an area. Often exploratory research is the prelude to a more detailed study, but it is also an important form of research in its own right. Imagine that youth violence has been the source of newspaper headlines in a major regional city recently. Gangs of unemployed youths are being blamed in the media for all sorts of crimes, from a recent outbreak of robberies of small businesses to attacks on old-age pensioners, break-and-enters into private dwellings and an increase in assaults on public transport. The local council employs you as a researcher to find out more about youth violence. Let us assume that the purpose of your research is exploratory. You may interview a wide range of people to gain an understanding of how violence, and especially youth violence, is perceived in that city. You may talk to professionals such as teachers, police, court officials, health centre and hospital personnel, local counsellors, juvenile justice workers, youth workers, refuge workers and ministers. You may also talk to members of local youth groups and clubs, churches, publicans, high schools, centres for unemployed youth, or security officers who patrol the city at night. If you have the trust of health workers or victims' groups, you may be able to interview or meet people or groups of people who have been identified as having experienced youth violence. In this way the researcher gathers information and gains insights into how youth violence is perceived (or not perceived) in the city by the different groups. Usually exploratory studies identify the general terrain of a topic or problem area, and the important themes and issues which arise within this area.

If, on the other hand, the purpose of the study into youth violence is *descriptive*, the researcher usually already knows, or has found out, much of the information that an exploratory study provides. In descriptive research, the researcher's aim would be to describe more specific details and patterns of youth violence. The researcher may be finding out the types of violence which have been recorded by the various agencies, the number of assaults reported, the categories of people who have been assaulted and the ages of people who have been identified as perpetrators. If she finds that youth violence is indeed a problem for the city discussed above, the researcher may look for descriptions of the patterns of events leading up to and following incidents of this violence, for the 'typical' story of what occurs, how it is reported, and what happens after violence has been reported. With the right methodology she may also be able to investigate the types of violence which are not reported, and the stories surrounding such events. Thus, descriptive research aims to find out in more precise detail than exploratory research the *what* of social phenomena.

In contrast to descriptive and exploratory research, the purpose of *explanatory research* is to investigate the *why* of social phenomena— that is, to answer questions about their causes. Thus, an explanatory study stemming from newspaper articles on youth violence in the city may endeavour to explain why youth violence occurs in this particular city, or particular areas of this city, or what factors are associated with its increase. It may attempt to explain what causes young people rather than other age groups to become violent. If the method used is quantitative, hypotheses about what causes youth violence and its increase in this setting may be developed and then statistically tested. If the methodology is qualitative, hypotheses about the causes of youth violence and its increase will be developed during the course of the study, as data are collected and the literature searched for theoretical explanations.

As you can see from these brief examples, research with exploratory, descriptive and explanatory purposes can use either quantitative or qualitative approaches or a multimethod mixture of both. Whatever approach you use, it is most important that you are clear about the purpose or purposes of your research, and what you hope to achieve from your study of the topic.

Summary

As you begin to formulate your research topic, you will also begin to develop a conceptual framework or plan for the research which includes the purpose of the research, specific questions, methodologies, structure for carrying out the research and data analysis. As far as possible, you need to clarify your own and others' theoretical/ value positions, as an important prelude to establishing the broad purpose of the study. Generally, research projects have exploratory, descriptive or explanatory purposes. It is essential that your research questions and methodologies reflect these purposes. Several issues arise when you are choosing your research topic, even before you have defined your research problems or questions, all of which require clear and careful thought. Having established the general territory of the problem, it is important to identify who the key players are, what they want to achieve and whether the problem itself is relevant, researchable, feasible and ethical.

QUESTIONS

1 What is 'decidophobia' and how might it be overcome?
2 Whose views should be considered when you are developing your research topic?
3 What are the four criteria for choosing a research topic?
4 'Under what conditions do women have the right to choose abortions?' Is this a researchable topic?
5 An article appears in the local paper debating whether discipline in schools is declining. Give some examples of the different sorts of questions that research with exploratory, descriptive and explanatory purposes might generate.

EXERCISES

You are a university student on placement at the local council in a small rural town. You have been given the newspaper article on page 70 about domestic violence and are asked to research it.

1 Who would be the key players from each of the four groups whom you could consult about this topic?
2 What might be the underlying theories and values which influence this research topic?
3 What exploratory questions could you ask about this topic?
4 What descriptive research questions could you ask about this topic?
5 What explanatory research questions could you ask about this topic?
6 Is this topic:
   (a) relevant?
   (b) feasible?
   (c) researchable?
   (d) ethical?

FURTHER READING

Cournoyer, D. E. & Klein, W. C. 2000, *Research Methods for Social Work*, Allyn & Bacon, Boston. Chapter 3 covers developing research questions, including a discussion of the influence of theory and values from a sociocultural perspective.

de Vaus, D. A. 2001, *Research Design in Social Research*, Sage, London. The whole book is devoted to a detailed and clear discussion of research design. Chapter 2 specifically examines formulating research questions and internal and external validity. Highly recommended.

——2002, *Surveys in Social Research*, 5th edn, Allen & Unwin, Sydney. Chapter 3 provides a clear discussion of formulating research questions and how this process is related to the design of the study

Kumar, R. 1996, *Research Methodology*, Longman, Melbourne. Chapter 4 contains an interesting model for formulating topic areas and research problems.

Marlow, C. 1998, *Research Methods for Generalist Social Work*, 2nd edn, Brooks/Cole Publishing Co., Pacific Grove. Chapter 3 provides many good examples of defining research problems and questions in different types of social work research. It also focuses on issues of multiculturalism in defining research topics.

Rothery, M. 1993b, 'Problems, questions and hypotheses', in *Social Work Research and Evaluation*, 4th edn, R. M. Grinnell Jr (ed.), Peacock Publishers, Itasca Ill (chapter 2).

Yegidis, B. L., Weinbach, W. W. & Morrison-Rodriguez, B. 1999, *Research Methods for Social Workers*, 3rd edn, Allyn & Bacon, Boston. Chapter 3 contains a thorough examination of how social workers develop useful research questions.

3 Developing research questions

In chapter 2 we discussed some of the issues involved in choosing your research topic. We now go into more detail about how to transform your general research topic into researchable questions. Qualitative and quantitative approaches do this in different ways and from different directions.

Developing quantitative research questions

In chapter 1 we discussed how the quantitative approach begins with theories and questions which are examined in carefully designed studies. Researchers using this approach must work out how they are going to test their ideas in the social world. Developing your research questions is important in quantitative research, because the types of questions asked heavily influence the whole design of your study and the sorts of data analysis you will be able to perform.

The process of thinking through research questions from the level of ideas or theory to measurable indicators (called variables) which can be used in social research is called 'operationalisation'. This has been described as 'descending the ladder of abstraction' (de Vaus 2002), because researchers transform a problem or topic area that is in their heads into something that they can see or touch or measure out in the 'real world'.

The ladder of abstraction has several 'rungs' which must be negotiated on your way to transforming your ideas into measurable variables. In fact, you will find that rather than being a ladder, the structure you are descending is actually more like a playground 'pyramid'. In quantitative research, you begin at the top, the narrowest point of the pyramid (the initial concepts), and climb down, instead of standing on the ground and climbing upwards. As you descend, each layer becomes wider and wider so that there are increasingly more choices and pathways you could take, the closer you get to the ground.

While there are many possible rungs (levels of abstraction) in the pyramid, we will discuss four, to demonstrate how the initial topic or problem area can be transformed into researchable questions as you descend the pyramid to the 'ground' of actually doing the research. The four rungs are: *concepts, dimensions* (or constructs), *indicators* and *variables*. We will use a study by Sarantakos (1994) to show how an experienced researcher has operationalised a research topic, starting with his initial conceptual questions and transforming them down through the 'pyramid of abstraction' into measurable variables.

Concepts

The top rung of our pyramid is the concept. Concepts are just the ideas or theories with which you begin; they are terms which usually summarise clusters of related elements. For example, most people understand and use the concept 'happy marriage' in daily conversation. When discussing whether or not a neighbour's marriage is 'happy', however, the people in the conversation may or may not be referring to the same things. First, this is because the idea of 'happy marriage' could have many aspects. Second, people have different views about what is important in making a relationship 'happy'. Some people may emphasise the amount of time spent together, others shared interests, others may consider the sexual side, the presence or absence of children, or the quality of communication. Some may consider a marriage to be happy if there are regular opportunities for 'vigorous discussion' of differences. Others may view the same behaviour as 'fighting' and see this as an indication that the marriage is unhappy. Thus, concepts are 'summary ideas' which may mean different things to different people. It is important to define concepts clearly so that, even if they do not agree with our definitions, people reading about and involved in our research know what *we* mean by the concepts we use.

Usually there are at least two major concepts in each research topic, and most often these are expressed as a question about how the concepts are related. For example, Sarantakos (1994) was interested in the popular phenomenon of people living together before marriage ('trial cohabitation'). He wanted to know whether trial cohabitation leads to better marriages and more successful relationships, as is popularly believed. The way he expressed this problem (Sarantakos 1994) was:

> Do married couples with premarital cohabital experience have better chances for establishing a happy and rewarding marital life than those without such an experience? Is such a cohabital 'practice' really significant? Does 'practice make perfect'? Or is it perhaps so that 'practice makes imperfect' as some writers prefer to put it (p. 13)?

There are two major concepts involved in these questions. First, there is the concept or idea of 'married couples' and, within this, the idea that couples either do or do not have experiences of 'premarital cohabital experience'. There is also the concept of a 'happy and rewarding marital life'. At first glance the marriage concept is relatively simple, while the second one, 'marital life', is more complex. Because it is more abstract, the concept of 'marital life' is actually higher on the pyramid of abstraction than the concept of 'married couples with or without cohabital experience'. To discuss both these concepts in more detail, we need to descend to the next rung in our pyramid: the level of dimensions.

Dimensions

The elements or aspects that go together to make up concepts are called 'dimensions'. There may be differing numbers of dimensions in each concept, although there would seem to be only one dimension to the concept of 'married couples with or without cohabital experience'; that is, whether couples who are married have experienced living together before they were married. However, we shall see that even translating this one dimension into indicators is not as simple as it first appears.

In contrast, there are many possible dimensions to the concept of 'happy and rewarding marital life'. Some of these dimensions we listed in our discussion of what could be involved in the concept of a happy marriage. In his study, out of all the myriad possibilities, Sarantakos (1994, p. 15) chose three dimensions by which to assess the happiness of marriages:

- Quality of marital selection
- Quality of marital life
- Marital stability

Already we can see how the pyramid broadens as we descend each rung to make our definitions of the problem clearer and more specific. From one concept (marital life) we now have three dimensions. Many others could have been selected. However, at least for this study, we are beginning to know the grounds on which this researcher has assessed whether marriages are 'effective' or 'happy'.

Indicators

Indicators are measurable aspects of dimensions, usually expressed in observable or behavioural terms. In defining dimensions in this way, it is clear exactly what is being measured and how concepts are being defined. By describing indicators in behavioural or measurable terms, quantitative researchers also hope to enable others to measure the same phenomena, perhaps under different circumstances, in order to expand knowledge in the particular area of interest. Thus, with his clear definitions, Sarantakos has allowed other researchers the possibility of replicating his study and expanding or commenting on his findings, in other situations. Whereas he studied couples in Australia, other researchers may wish to study couples from different countries or cultures, or of different age groups.

Just as there can be many dimensions to a single concept, so there can be many indicators created to measure one dimension. (Remember, as we descend the pyramid, the layers become ever broader.) Many quantitative researchers advocate using a range of indicators to measure a single dimension, especially if the dimension is complex. As one example, let us see how Sarantakos operationalised the dimension 'quality of marital life' into measurable indicators.

In fact, Sarantakos chose twelve indicators by which to measure the single dimension, 'quality of marital life'. These included (Sarantakos 1994, p. 15): marital success, competence, happiness, freedom, independence, respect, communication, commitment, emotional expression, violence, conflict and sexual experience. These indicators were selected on the basis of extensive reading of the literature and previous research experience of the researcher. The indicators were measured by asking respondents to rate each indicator on a scale. How these scales were measured, and what information they could provide, is discussed on our next rung of the pyramid, 'variables'.

Before discussing variables, let us consider how the relatively simple dimension, 'marriage with or without prior cohabitation', was defined. First, it appears to have been assumed in the study that 'marriage' meant legal marriage and that cohabitation meant living together. Further definitions were not given, since the study had a large qualitative element. In a 'pure' quantitative study, both 'marriage' and 'cohabitation' would have been more explicitly defined. For example, there are many variations of 'living together'. Would two people living as a couple within a household of a group of adults be defined as 'cohabiting'? Some couples maintain separate houses/apartments but spend each night together. Would these couples be cohabiting? What about couples who spend some nights but not every night together? At what point is a not-married couple considered to be cohabiting? These are questions that would be addressed in operational definitions in a strictly quantitative study.

Another issue which arises is how to 'count' prior cohabitation in married couples. Should we consider those who lived with the person to whom they are now married separately from those who lived with a different partner before they were married to their current spouse? Should we count how many previous cohabitation partners each spouse had? What about couples in which one person has experienced 'prior cohabitation' but the other partner has not? Are marriage patterns different for these people? Such questions raise an important issue which must be considered when we are operationalising research questions: the *unit of analysis*.

Units of analysis

The unit of analysis is the unit we study, or the unit from which we gather the information we need (de Vaus 2002). In social work research, the unit of analysis is usually an individual, a group or a social artifact (Marlow 1998). In Sarantakos' (1994) study, the major unit of analysis was the couple, rather than the individual people making up the couple. Sarantakos described three basic types of couples: couples where both parties had experienced cohabitation before marriage, couples where one member had, and couples where neither member had experienced prior cohabitation. Studies can use more than one unit of analysis. Sarantakos also collected information about men and women and about individuals. Thus, there were really three units of analysis in his study, but the primary one, the one about which most of his conclusions dealt, was the couple.

From these examples, it can be seen that even apparently simple concepts require careful thought and definition if they are to be transformed into measurable indicators for quantitative social research. Defining the unit of analysis is an important part of this process.

Variables

The bottom rung of the 'pyramid of abstraction', the level before we reach the 'ground' and start actually doing the research, is specifying just how we will measure our indicators and what 'level of measurement' we will use. Variables are indicators expressed in measurable terms, with the form of measurement made explicit. Variables must vary; that is, they must have more than one value. For example, in the case of prior cohabitation, Sarantakos measured how many different experiences people had, and for how long they had cohabited before marriage (two variables). For the 12 indicators making up the dimension 'quality of marital life', Sarantakos used 5-point scales, with (5) being 'very high' or 'very satisfied' and (1) being 'very low' or 'very dissatisfied', to create variables. He could then discuss the quality of marital life in terms of the individual indicators within this dimension, or in summary form, by putting each person's scores on all the variables together into one single 'quality of marital life' score.

Dependent and independent variables

In explanatory research, researchers explore questions about how one variable affects another, or about the causes behind some social phenomenon. The terms 'dependent' and 'independent' are used to describe pairs of variables which are in relationship with each other. The *dependent variable*, symbolised by a Y in research texts, is the one that researchers are most interested in understanding or explaining why it varies (Yegidis et al. 1999). Yegidis et al. describe the independent variable (symbolised by an X) as one that the researcher believes may produce at least some of the variation in the dependent variable. Another way of expressing this is that the value of Y is dependent, to some extent at least, on the value of X.

In Sarantakos' study there were many dependent variables, developed to measure the concept of 'marital life', which Sarantakos wanted to understand. Premarital cohabitation was the independent variable; that is, Sarantakos wanted to know whether the quality of marriages was affected by premarital cohabitation.

There are other kinds of variables as well as dependent and independent variables. We will discuss these in greater detail in chapter 6.

Hypotheses

Once variables have been defined, many quantitative researchers go on to develop hypotheses about their variables. Hypotheses are *statements about variables* and the relationships between them. They are derived from the research questions about concepts which began the process of operationalisation. Hypotheses are important in quantitative research because they clarify and guide the research process, including how the data will be analysed. There are many forms of hypotheses: they may be descriptive ('premarital cohabitation is increasing in the 1990s'), or relational ('marital satisfaction is related to the number of premarital cohabitation experiences'), directional ('marital satisfaction increases with the number of premarital cohabitation experiences') or non-directional ('there is a relationship between marital satisfaction and number of premarital cohabitation experiences').

In social research we can never actually *prove* that there is a relationship between two variables. The closest we can get is to disprove the hypothesis that there is no relationship. The hypothesis which states that there is no relationship between two variables is called the *null hypothesis*. Most statistical tests aim to reject the null hypothesis. If we can be fairly sure that there is evidence of a relationship then we reject the null hypothesis and accept the alternative or research hypothesis. These days null hypotheses are rarely stated in research reports. However, it is important to know that 'rejecting the null hypothesis' is the basis of most statistical tests which provide support for the existence of a relationship.

Hypotheses may be explicit or implicit. In Sarantakos' study of how premarital cohabitation affects marital life, there were several implied hypotheses; for example, 'number of premarital cohabitation experiences affects perceived stability of marriages' and 'there is a relationship between premarital cohabitation and rates of marital violence'. Because his study was largely descriptive and contained many qualitative aspects, Sarantakos did not need to state the various hypotheses which emerged in the way he discussed the topic. We will discuss how qualitative researchers develop hypotheses after mentioning levels of measurement and their importance. It is a useful exercise for beginning researchers using quantitative approaches to try to formulate hypotheses using the variables they have operationalised, as a way of clarifying exactly what they are researching.

In summary, as quantitative researchers descend the 'pyramid of abstraction', they transform general research questions about concepts into specific hypotheses about variables. In the summary below, we have traced how two concepts from Sarantakos' study were operationalised, selecting only one example from each 'rung' of the pyramid to take down to the next rung at each stage. If we included all the options on each rung, the pyramid would not fit on the page! We will discuss some of the different variables that Sarantakos developed in more detail in the next section on levels of measurement. Chapter 5 of Sarantakos (1998) and chapter 5 of Williams, Tutty and Grinnell (1995) provide more detailed discussions of hypotheses.

EXAMPLE OF DESCENDING THE PYRAMID OF ABSTRACTION

Research question
Do married couples with premarital cohabital experience have better chances for establishing a happy and rewarding marital life than those without such an experience?

Concepts
Premarital cohabital experience
Marital life

Dimensions
Premarital cohabital experience

Marital life
- Quality of marital selection
- Quality of marriage
- Marital stability

Example of indicators
Premarital cohabital experience
- Length of cohabitation
- Number of cohabital experiences

Quality of marriage
- Marital success, competence, happiness, freedom, independence, respect, communication, commitment, emotional expression, violence, conflict and sexual experience

Examples of variables
Length of cohabitation
- Number of years and/or months respondent has lived as a couple outside marriage

Marital satisfaction
- Five-point self-rating scale: Very satisfied (5), Satisfied (4), OK (3), Dissatisfied (2), Very dissatisfied (1)

Example of hypothesis
There is a relationship between marital satisfaction as self-rated on a five-point scale and the number of years and/or months partners have lived as a couple (either with each other or another person) before they were married

Sarantakos (1994)

Levels of measurement

An important aspect of specifying variables is determining the level of measurement they will have. This in turn affects the kinds of statistical procedures that can be performed (see chapter 14). There are four levels at which variables may be measured. Each level provides different kinds of information.

Nominal level

Nominal level is the simplest level of measurement. It sorts variables into categories. For example, the categories for the variable 'gender' are 'male' and 'female'. These are usually assigned numbers, so that they can be coded for analysis. However, the numbers do not imply order or magnitude. If 'female' is coded '1' and 'male' is coded '2', we are not assigning females more value, or a higher score, than males! We are simply differentiating them.

Ordinal level

Ordinal level of measurement is the next level of measurement above nominal. As well as being able to divide a variable into categories, at the ordinal level we can rank the categories from high to low, or from best to worst. In Sarantakos' study, the 5-point scale measuring marital satisfaction is an example of an ordinal level variable. Note that while we know that a score of (5) means that someone is more satisfied than someone who has scored (4), we do not know how much more satisfied the first person is, or whether there would be the same amount of difference between two people who scored (3) and (4), as between two people who rated their satisfaction at (4) and (5).

Interval level

In addition to the properties of nominal and ordinal level measurement, interval level measurement is distinguished by there being equal intervals between the ranks or ordered categories. This means that we can add and subtract—a useful function for summarising large amounts of information. An example of an interval measurement is the IQ scale (Marlow 1998). While the difference between an IQ of 80 and 90 is supposed to be the same as the difference between an IQ of 160 and 170, it is not possible to claim that someone with an IQ of 160 has twice the IQ of someone with an IQ of 80.

Ratio level of measurement

The ratio level of measurement is the closest level to numbers or mathematics. Not only do measurements at this level include all the properties of the previous three levels, but at this level there is also an absolute zero point. This permits us to multiply and divide results—another very useful property for summarising large amounts of information to give us a typical 'picture' of the issue we are studying. Examples of variables at ratio levels of measurement include age, height, time span in years or in minutes. In practice, many interval level measurements are also at the ratio level, but it is important to understand the difference between the two.

There are four rules that must be followed in all measurement of variables. First, variables must have at least two categories (they must *vary*). Second, categories must be distinct (that is, different). Third, categories must be mutually exclusive (the same person should not be able to fit into two categories of the one variable). Finally, categories must be exhaustive (all the people being studied must fit into one of the categories; even if the category is 'other', every person should be assigned to a category).

CHECKING THE EFFECTIVENESS OF MEASUREMENT: RELIABILITY AND VALIDITY

Having operationalised our research questions down to measurable hypotheses involving variables, including specifying the level of measurement of each of our variables, we must consider how effective our variables actually are. There are two main ways of evaluating the usefulness of our variables: checking their validity and reliability. Reliability and validity are treated differently in quantitative and qualitative research. We will discuss both in this section, as a prelude to examining how research questions are formulated in each.

Validity in quantitative research

The first important test of whether variables are effective in quantitative research is whether they are actually measuring what the researcher wants to measure. This is termed 'validity'. Ultimately, the validity of a variable depends on how we have defined the concept it is intended to measure (de Vaus 2002). There are two main aspects of validity (Bostwick & Kyte 1993):

- The extent to which a variable measures what it is supposed to measure
- The extent to which a variable is an accurate measurement

Different texts deal with quantitative validity in slightly different ways. We refer you to some of these different discussions at the end of this chapter. Basically, there are three main ways to assess validity in quantitative research (Bostwick & Kyte 1993, Babbie 2001, de Vaus 2002). Each method assesses a different aspect of validity. No one method is perfect. Which method you choose will depend on the purpose of your measurement and what sort of evidence of validity is most important.

Content validity

Content validity refers to the extent to which variables cover the whole content, or all the major dimensions, of the concept being measured. For example, do the 12 indicators chosen by Sarantakos (1994) really capture the full extent of quality of marital life, or has something crucial been omitted? Of course, it is never possible to cover all the meanings of a concept, but variables can be more or less successful in covering the content of a concept. *Face validity* is a term sometimes used interchangeably with content validity (Bostwick &

Kyte 1993), which means the degree to which a measurement appears, on the face of it, to measure what it is supposed to measure. Cournoyer and Klein (2000) distinguish face validity as the weakest, 'skin deep' form of validity based on the notion of whether a measurement appears to be what it claims to measure.

Criterion validity

To establish criterion validity you would compare the results from your measuring instrument with results from some outside criteria or 'gold standard', such as other well-accepted methods of measurement. For example, do the couples who score highly on Sarantakos' quality of marital life dimension also score highly on other tests of good marriages? There are several kinds of criterion validity including *concurrent validity* (for example, the ability to predict accurately a couple's current marital quality) and *predictive validity* (for example, the ability to predict how happy a couple will be two years from now).

Construct validity

Construct validity is concerned with how well a measure conforms to theoretical expectations (de Vaus 2002), or how well it measures a theoretical construct (Bostwick & Kyte 1993). Suppose, for example, that there was a well-accepted theory that says that marital happiness is related to self-fulfilment of the partners. If we measured self-fulfilment of the partners as well as marital happiness, and found that our measure of marital happiness increased with increasing self-fulfilment, we could say that our measure of marital happiness had construct validity.

Remember that there is no ideal way of establishing validity. Which method you choose will depend on your purpose and what is available. De Vaus (2002) recommends that if a good external criterion exists, use this; if the definition of the concept is well accepted, use content validity; and if there are well accepted theories which use your concept, use construct validity.

Validity in qualitative research

Qualitative researchers view validity differently from quantitative researchers. Rather than beginning by making sure that their variables are accurately operationalised, qualitative researchers ensure validity through their methods of data collection and analysis. One way of ensuring validity of findings in qualitative research is to re-check findings with respondents to make sure the researcher 'got it right'. Qualitative researchers Kirk and Miller (1986, pp. 30–1) have argued that qualitative research has an 'in-built sensitivity' which creates a kind of 'automatic validity' because, being out in the field 'in territory controlled by the investigatees rather than the investigator . . . the researcher is at the mercy of the world view of his or her subjects'. Similarly, Belcher (1994, p. 129) lists 'prolonged engagement and persistent observation' as two important methods of validation in his study of homelessness and 'social drift'.

Possibly the most important way that qualitative researchers ensure that their findings are valid is called 'triangulation' (Belcher 1994, Davis (1994), Berg 1995, Sarantakos 1998). Triangulation is the use of a variety of methods and also sometimes researchers, theories, data collection technologies or a combination of these (see Davis 1994, Berg 1995).

In fact, many qualitative researchers claim that because their methods and data collection procedures are closer to reality and more flexible than those used in quantitative research, because they communicate about the nature of their research and its findings with the people involved, and because they have the opportunity of going back or expanding their research if their findings are found not to be valid in the first place, they have better ways of ensuring validity than quantitative researchers. (Read Kirk & Miller's [1986] account of validity and reliability in qualitative research and Berg's [1995] discussion of triangulation.)

Reliability in quantitative research

Testing for reliability is the other way that researchers have of evaluating whether their variables and findings are effective. Reliability is about consistency. A variable is reliable if someone else who uses it gets very similar results to the original researcher, or if the original researcher uses the measure at a later time, or with a similar group of people, and similar results appear.

There are several types of reliability in quantitative research as well as different ways of assessing whether research results are consistent. Reliability can refer to results being consistent over time, with groups of different respondents, or across different variables; the latter may also be called 'interchangeability of indicators' (Cournoyer & Klein 2000).

The most common method of testing reliability is to use the same instrument on several occasions with the same group of people (called the *test–retest* method). This has many problems, in that differences in measurement could indicate real differences in the way the people feel over time or reflect some 'interference' effect of the previous test, which may have raised awareness of the issue in the people being researched. However, it is the major method of testing reliability which can be applied to single questions, as well as to scales (de Vaus 2002).

Another method is the *split-half* method, whereby the variables or scales in an instrument are divided into two halves and administered separately. If the scores are similar, the instrument is considered to be reliable. There are several other methods of testing reliability, most of which also apply to scales (de Vaus 2002). For further reading, see Bostwick & Kyte (1993), Sarantakos (1998) or de Vaus (2002).

Reliability in qualitative research

Qualitative researchers do not use the methods of controlling variables and manipulating the environment described above for quantitative researchers, and in fact are quite critical of these approaches. (For example, Pieper [1994] argues that it is better to focus on credibility rather than on reliability in social work research. She writes that just because many people report the same thing, that does not mean it is credible.) Instead, qualitative researchers try to ensure reliability or consistency by trying to find exceptions to their results, or to consciously list all possible sources of error.

Several writers (for example, Kirk & Miller 1986, Sarantakos 1998) have acknowledged that whereas qualitative research has paid detailed attention to questions of validity, it has tended to ignore issues of reliability. Kirk and Miller (1986) suggest that qualitative researchers should be more vigorous in the way they take field notes, and be prepared to share these with other qualitative researchers as a way of ensuring reliability. More recent accounts of qualitative research set out methods of ensuring reliability such as: using extra questions which are worded slightly differently, using a systematic and consistent line of questions with different interviewees, and carefully setting out how data were collected so that the research can be replicated (Berg 1995).

Validity and reliability

Validity and reliability are different but related concepts. In quantitative research, 'reliability is a necessary but not sufficient precondition for all forms of validity' (Cournoyer & Klein 2000). It is possible for research questions to be quite reliable but not valid. For example, the everyday question, 'How are you?' is likely to reliably get the reply, 'Well thanks', but the response does not necessarily indicate how a person is really feeling. Thus it is reliable, but not valid. On the other hand, quantitative research questions which are valid are necessarily reliable because accuracy is an essential part of validity in this approach.

Having briefly noted how quantitative and qualitative researchers try to ensure that the variables they develop are effective by being concerned about validity and reliability, we conclude this chapter with an examination of how qualitative researchers develop research questions. We use as an example a qualitative evaluation of some support groups for women suffering from postnatal depression, which was conducted by two health workers (a social worker and a nurse) in a rural area of Australia (Purches & Jaeger 1994).

DEVELOPING QUALITATIVE QUESTIONS

Whereas quantitative research begins at the top of the 'pyramid of abstraction' and involves careful thinking through of research questions before the research is begun, qualitative research begins as close to the ground as possible, and gradually works upwards through the rungs of the pyramid, developing questions and hypotheses as it goes. Some qualitative researchers claim to actually start on the 'ground' with no initial ideas at all, but we have seen that it is really impossible for researchers to begin with 'empty heads'. A more accurate picture is given by Kirk and Miller (1986, p. 30): 'Typically the qualitative researcher arrives on the scene with considerable theoretical baggage and very little idea of what will happen next.'

When thinking through their general topic, researchers from both qualitative and quantitative perspectives must take into account the issues that we discussed in the first half of this chapter. However, having decided on their general topic area, researchers using predominantly qualitative methods try not to define their concepts too clearly before they have talked to or observed the people whom they are researching. Qualitative research will involve the research subjects in the process of defining the topic, to a greater or lesser extent, depending on the researcher's theoretical approach. The concepts with which qualitative researchers begin their inquiries have been termed 'sensitising concepts' (Sarantakos 1998, p. 105).

Lee Purches (social worker) and Frances Jaeger (nurse) were two rural health workers who wanted to evaluate some support groups for women which Frances had set up in several small townships in a rural region. The support groups had initially been formed because workers at the local family care cottage had noticed that a large number of mothers with babies and small children were being referred to them with symptoms of postnatal depression. About one year after the groups began, the workers felt it was time to evaluate the groups.

With an egalitarian, feminist rationale, the groups had been set up as independent, self-help units in different towns, with each group developing its own aims, objectives and methodology. In line with this basic philosophy, the evaluators decided to involve the women in developing the approach to the evaluation, the aims of the evaluation and the questions that would be asked. Thus they went into the planning stages of the evaluation with an explicitly feminist approach, whereby the research would be *for* the women, not just *about* women.

First, the evaluators met with members from the original postnatal depression group from the family care cottage to discuss the aims of the evaluation, and to invite the women's participation. They then consulted with leaders from the various groups to discuss what questions and approaches the women would find most useful. The leaders in turn consulted with their groups and reported back to the researchers.

To the evaluators' surprise (and initial dismay), the women wanted a much broader approach to the research than the evaluators' original idea (or 'sensitising concept'). Instead of just an evaluation, the women wanted a more general inquiry about postnatal depression and its impact on women's lives, and to explore issues of community awareness. Following further discussions with the women and local health workers, the topic of how living in a rural area affects the experience of postnatal depression was also included.

Throughout this discussion phase, research questions were being worked and re-worked with the women and other interested people. The participants decided to design a questionnaire which would be posted to the members of the support groups in the various towns. A questionnaire was chosen rather than interviews or group discussion because of the distances involved, and also because it was hoped that the women would be able to be more honest if they could write their thoughts anonymously. Note that the questionnaire has traditionally been associated with quantitative research, yet in this case it was being used in a qualitative framework (with some quantitative questions being included as well).

The questionnaire turned out to be much longer than the evaluators would have liked, due to all the questions that the women wanted to be included. In addition, in the tradition of qualitative research, the researchers were then overwhelmed with an enormous amount of information in response to the questionnaire. Women wrote extra pages and described their thoughts and feelings in great detail in response to the open-ended qualitative questions that were asked. More detail on these sorts of questions will be provided in chapter 6.

From this brief introduction to formulating research questions in qualitative research, you can see how the researcher begins at the opposite end of the 'pyramid of abstraction' from the quantitative researcher. Rather than beginning at the top of the pyramid, qualitative researchers attempt to begin as close to the ground as possible, and then to allow their questions and hypotheses to emerge from their observations, discussions or 'immersion in the field'.

In the example of the rural women's support groups evaluation (Purches & Jaeger 1994), we have seen how the researchers circled between the bottom rungs of the pyramid, beginning with a general idea for the research (evaluation), which was slowly refined as the researchers gradually developed their questions, always returning to the 'ground' to check with the people they were researching that this was the approach that was wanted. By the end of this process, the research questions had significantly changed from the researchers' original ideas for an evaluation into a study about postnatal depression in rural areas as well as the evaluation. From the discussions with the group and the group leaders, a hypothesis about rural areas affecting the experience of postnatal depression also emerged. These three ideas (the group evaluation, experiences of postnatal depression and influence of rural lifestyle) were then further examined in a qualitative questionnaire.

Variables at different levels of measurement were used in this study. However, the emphasis was on qualitative, open-ended questions and thus the major level of measurement was nominal.

SUMMARY

In this chapter we have discussed how general ideas or problem areas for research are transformed into researchable questions. From our discussion of the factors involved in choosing the general area for the research, we examined how quantitative and qualitative research questions are developed, beginning at different ends of the 'pyramid of abstraction'. In both the examples of research that were used to demonstrate this process, we have shown how research questions and designs are, in fact, often a mixture of qualitative and quantitative approaches. These days quantitative researchers often begin with qualitative-type inquiries as they develop and test their concepts, dimensions, indicators and variables, to make sure that they are valid and relevant to the people who are being researched. We have also seen how qualitative researchers can use quantitative methods, such as questionnaires, to refine their questions with the people they are researching.

The important lesson from this discussion is to understand that clear and careful thought about your research topic is an integral part of the research process, and not something that can be rushed through so that you can 'get on with asking people questions'. If you are doing quantitative research, it is vital that you operationalise your concepts and dimensions properly, because once these are set, you are committed to a particular course of action and it is difficult to correct mistakes. In qualitative research there is more flexibility, because qualitative researchers can alter their questions and directions as they go. However, qualitative researchers need to end up with results that are valid and reliable, and careful thinking about their research questions during the process of their research is just as important as it is for quantitative researchers at the beginning of theirs.

QUESTIONS

1 A study appears comparing the average income between countries. What is the unit of analysis?

2 What is wrong with this question?
Please place a tick against the box which indicates your weekly income:

$10–$20	☐
$20–$50	☐
$50–$300	☐
$300–$1,000	☐

3 What level of measurements are the following?
(a) Marital status:
- Single
- Married
- Living with partner, not married
- Divorced
- Widowed
- Separated

(b) Age expressed in years
(c) Number of children
(d) Satisfaction rating of a movie on a scale of 1–10 where 1 = not at all satisfied and 10 = very satisfied.

4 What is the difference between a hypothesis and a research question?

5 Read the following statements. Name the variables and their probable level of measurement. Indicate whether there are dependent or independent variables in each statement and, if so, label them accordingly:
'The price of wheat increases with the annual yearly rainfall.'
'The longer the marriage, the more satisfied are the partners.'
'Women have lower incomes than men.'
'Increasing blood alcohol levels cause increasingly serious car accidents.'

6 A researcher into youth culture is repeatedly told during her time with a gang that they are not involved in hard drugs, only 'soft' drugs. Shortly after her research is written up, members of the gang are arrested for heroin trafficking. What could be said about the reliability and validity of her results?

7 The researcher from the previous question is beginning her research and has decided to use a qualitative approach. How might she go about defining her research questions?

EXERCISES

1 Operationalise the questions from the descriptive topic that you devised in the exercise in chapter 2, into a researchable form for a quantitative researcher. List the concepts, dimensions, indicators and variables that could be involved, including more than one dimension for each concept, and more than one indicator for each dimension.
2 Specify the level of measurement of each of your variables.
3 Formulate a number of hypotheses from your variables.
4 What are the independent and dependent variables?
5 What is the unit of analysis for your study?
6 Is this topic relevant, feasible, researchable and ethical?

FURTHER READING

Conceptualising and operationalising quantitative research including measurement, validity and reliability

Babbie, E. 2001, *The Practice of Social Research*, 9th edn, Wadsworth, California. Part 2: chapters 4 (on research design) and 5 ('Conceptualisation, Operationalization and Measurement').

Bostwick, G. J. & Kyte, N. S. 1993, 'Measurement in research' in *Social Work Research and Evaluation*, 4th edn, R. M. Grinnell Jr (ed.), Peacock Publishers, Itasca, Ill. (chapter 9).

Cournoyer, D. E. & Klein, W. C. 2000, *Research Methods for Social Work*, Allyn & Bacon, Boston. Chapter 4 covers measurement, including a detailed discussion of reliability co-efficients.

Gibbs, L. E. 1991, *Scientific Reasoning for Social Workers: Bridging the Gap Between Research and Practice*, Macmillan, New York. Chapter 7 provides an interesting approach to validity and reliability.

Royse, D. 1999, *Research Methods in Social Work*, 3rd edn, Nelson Hall, Chicago. Chapter 5 contains a comprehensive review of reliability and validity as including presentation of a number of measurement instruments.

Sarantakos, S. 1998, *Social Research*, 2nd edn, Macmillan, Melbourne. Chapters 3, 4 and 5.

Williams, M., Tutty, L. M. & Grinnell, R. M. Jr, 1995, *Research in Social Work: An Introduction*, 2nd edn, Peacock Publishers, Itasca, Ill. Part 2 Problem formulation (*Note:* has a different treatment of validity).

Yegidis, B. L., Weinbach, W. W. & Morrison-Rodriguez, B. 1999, *Research Methods for Social Workers*, 3rd edn, Allyn & Bacon, Boston. Chapter 10 covers the issues dealt with in this chapter in more detail.

Conceptualising and operationalising qualitative research, measurement issues

Berg, B. L. 1995, *Qualitative Research Methods for the Social Sciences*, 2nd edn, Allyn & Bacon, Boston. Chapter 2, section on operationalisation and conceptualisation; also discussion of triangulation in the Introduction.

Kirk, J. & Miller, M. L. 1986, 'Reliability and validity in qualitative research', in *Qualitative Research Methods*, vol. 1, Sage, Newbury Park, California.

Sarantakos, S. 1998, *Social Research*, 2nd edn, Macmillan, Melbourne. Chapters 3, 4 and 5.

4 STEPS IN THE RESEARCH PROCESS

Measuring Poverty.

You have begun with a situation that perplexes, excites or alarms you. You must now decide on which aspect of the problem you wish to focus and what it is you hope to achieve. You will have decided on the methodology or combination of methodologies which best suit your purposes. This chapter, which focuses on the steps you must now undertake to complete a piece of research, is designed to demystify the research process by breaking it into a series of comfortable stages that you can use as a model for future research projects. Your research plan will act as a blueprint guiding you through the project. We have also included examples of research plans to familiarise you with the process of turning an idea into a recognisable research design. You should remember that the stages outlined here are not meant to be rigidly followed in each research project but should act as a flexible guide to your work.

If you are conducting a study you should always begin by making a flexible, conceptual plan outlining the process you will follow. Your plan should include the stages below.

Research steps

- Defining the problem
- Choosing the methodology

- Reviewing the literature
- Preparation
- Research design:
    Sampling
    Data collection
    Administration
    Data analysis
    Reporting

- Conducting the research
- Disseminating the findings

FACTORS INFLUENCING THE NATURE AND SUCCESS OF YOUR RESEARCH

Research projects are not developed in a vacuum. A variety of factors will influence the content of your research design—its subject matter, scope, methodology; and so on. For social workers these factors also include the agency in which you work, your professional background, and your own limitations of time and expertise (Williams, Tutty & Grinnell Jr 1995). It will also include your theoretical orientation, the social and political context of the work and your need to meet ethical requirements (Fortune & Reid 1999; see also chapter 1). The prospects that your research will attract funding (its competitiveness) will also be influenced by a variety of factors such as the currency of the issue. It is important that you understand these when preparing your research.

Agency context

As we have noted in chapter 2, your agency will necessarily influence the type of research you are able to do, and hence the type of research proposal you are able to draft. Some agencies are more committed to research than others and will influence your ability to act as researchers. Some agencies provide support and seed funding for small research projects which, while they may be small, are excellent sources of funds for 'learner' researchers. If funding is available for a small project, there may also be the opportunity within the agency to discuss your project with more experienced researchers. Take advantage of internal funding and support and the possibility to learn all you can before entering the competitive, cut-throat world of external funding.

Where agencies do not provide research funding and support, you may need to convince your employers about the potential value of research. In the present tight economic environment, agencies may be happy to discuss an evaluation study, for example, which will show that they take seriously their responsibility to be accountable to external funding sources and to clientele. Shared projects between groups of agencies are also a possibility. Such projects provide excellent collegial experiences as well as allowing enhanced inter-agency cooperation. If you are daunted by the prospect of conducting your own research, seek collaboration with other workers in your region or in your speciality.

You should also bear in mind that the agency you work for will have a distinct philosophy that will influence the type of research you can undertake. Some private welfare agencies, which operate from a well-defined religious framework, will circumscribe the types of research that they will support. However, you should bear in mind that all agencies, public and private, operate from a framework which will influence the operations of their workers. What research is, and is not, possible will be influenced, sometimes powerfully and sometimes subtly, by the philosophy of the agency for which you work.

You should not ignore the organisational culture of your agency, a factor that will have a telling influence on potential research projects. How does the chain of management work? In other words, who has the power to endorse or influence your research proposal? How are decisions approved? What are the practices traditionally supported by your agency? Taking time to note the culture of your organisation may facilitate your research agenda.

Additionally, agency resources will have an impact on the scope of the research you may be able to undertake. The availability of advanced computer systems and administrative support staff will allow you to complete more detailed and complex research. The possibilities of research within your agency or within a group of agencies will also be influenced by the type of clientele, the size of the agency and the type of client files kept as ready sources of data. The availability of client files may negate the necessity for collecting new data. However, you and your agency must deal with ethical issues of confidentiality before you decide whether this is a viable alternative.

Agency influences on social work research

- Availability of seed funding
- Importance of proposed research to agency accountability
- Agency philosophy
- Organisational culture
- Agency resources
- Agency clientele

Theoretical and sociopolitical context

Your research project will be influenced by a number of very evident factors, such as the agency setting and the professional and practical issues that shape your work. Less evident will be the factors that implicitly influence the type of research you undertake and the way that you carry it out. Chief among these is the theoretical background and orientation you bring to your work. Think about the way you practise social work. Do you operate from a psychotherapeutic framework? Maybe you favour systems theory or narrative therapy. In any case you will no doubt be able to identify your practice orientation. In conducting research you will have a similar distinct focus that shapes the way you 'practise' research—the way you identify a problem, the way you gather data about that problem and the way you interpret the data. For example, a feminist researcher examining the over-representation of children of single mothers in juvenile justice may seek to empower the women involved rather than categorise them, creating a quite different interpretation of a problem (see chapter 2).

Another no less influential factor in the shaping of your research project is the sociopolitical context in which it takes place. What social issues are on the agenda? Think about the change in the welfare agenda during the 1990s and into the twenty-first century. Many Western countries have moved from a position where social justice and community responsibility for the vulnerable was actively fostered to a new era where the welfare state is in decline and individuals are often held responsible for their poverty. Think about the change of focus and note how this may affect the type of research conducted and the research agenda favoured by funding bodies. More recently there has been a great deal of research on the best ways to get the unemployed to work but far less on the factors that create poverty traps. You should take time to be a 'conscientious consumer' in your reading of newspapers and analysis of government ministerial priorities. What are the trends and the 'hot topics'? How is the discourse of disadvantage being shaped and by whom? Is your research of advantage to the vulnerable? Be 'reflective researchers' (Fook 1997), consciously focusing on the context of your research practice.

Theoretical, social and political context

- Your theoretical and practice position
- What are the 'hot' social issues?
- What is the political agenda of the funders?
- Who is shaping the agenda?
- Is your research empowering the disadvantaged?

Professional context

The social work industry, and its ethical position, will critically affect the type of research we might undertake. Specifically, there are some types of research that our profession will not sanction. These would include the possibility of inflicting harm on clients or withdrawing services in order to examine the consequences. We should also protect research subjects from any harm that may arise from the publication of results, obtain informed consent and ensure that insensitivity and bias are not part of our practice (Fortune & Reid 1999). You should also note that research is often directed at assessing the most vulnerable. For example, we know far more about juvenile crime than we do about white-collar crime. Are vulnerable populations too easy a target and too powerless to direct the shape of research conducted around their circumstances? Our work requires a strong worker–client relationship and we must not jeopardise this relationship by our research. The need for this confidential relationship may also prevent us being able to observe other social workers at work for the purposes of collecting data.

Finally, your research proposals will be influenced by the emerging social work research culture, your professional background, and by your own values and ethical position.

Professional influences on social work research

- Professional code of ethics
- Protection from harm
- Confidentiality
- Informed consent
- Research focus
- Social/welfare work research culture
- Developing professionalisation

Personal context

Your research will be shaped not only by agency and professional concerns but also by the personal issues that affect you as a practitioner. These include your background, your workload and resources, and your track record.

Important issues you should consider are workload factors and the time you have available to conduct research. These issues may require some negotiation on your part with your employers. It is important that you, together with your agencies, recognise that research is 'real' work and work that can have a lasting impact on policy development, professional practice and agency resourcing. As such it should be deemed to be part of your workload and not something you do in your spare time.

Your track record in research is important to the way your proposal to undertake research will be assessed. If you have experience as a researcher this will improve your chances of success in a competitive round. You might ask, 'How does a beginning researcher achieve a track record?' The best way to gain experience is to be a junior partner in a research project with others who have the necessary skills to pass on valuable knowledge and insights. Do not be afraid to put up your hand and volunteer to help in a large project.

Personal influences on social work research

- Research background
- Workload and time pressures
- Track record

Practical issues

To be successful, research projects must be manageable. In defining the limits of your research, be aware that you cannot change the world with $10 000 (or whatever sum you are seeking), so do not try. Turning your research problem into a project which has a reasonable chance of success is a skill with which beginning researchers have a great deal of difficulty. To do this properly you must devote an adequate amount of time to developing your proposal.

Note that your proposal must be clear and concise. The problem must be explained so that the assessor of your proposal knows exactly what the problem entails, why it requires researching and how you as the researcher propose to do just that. In putting a proposal into a competitive environment, a potential researcher must be aware that they are competing for scarce funds. It is important that you do not waste your own time and that of the assessors with a poorly constructed proposal. The funding body or the agency in which you work has to be convinced that this problem, which has excited you as a worker, is worth its time and investment. Consequently, research proposals should be developed with the same attention to detail and respect with which one would prepare a curriculum vitae. For a detailed summary of the items to include in a research proposal see Appendix A.

Practical issues affecting social work research

- Ensure the proposed research is manageable

- Consult with colleagues and experts
- Ensure the proposal is written clearly and concisely
- Ensure it is properly costed
- Is the proposal well presented?
- Have you checked for spelling errors?

Having considered the factors that may influence your research, let's now turn to the important steps in the process of research.

DEFINING THE PROBLEM

In chapters 2 and 3 we learned how to turn a puzzling situation into a researchable question. In any research you must define your problem, note the dimensions of the issue, the target group affected, the political context, and the anticipated outcomes. Decide whether your research is to be exploratory, descriptive or explanatory. Remember that your topic must be relevant, researchable, feasible and ethical.

Mark (1996) suggests that we follow these steps when conceptualising the research problem:

- Select a topic
- Brainstorm a list of things we might want to know about the topic
- Select a focus for the problem
- Relate the focus of the problem to existing knowledge
- State the specific research question or problems
- If quantitative, operationalise the concepts and variables

Yegidis, Weinbach and Morrison-Rodriguez (1999) also note you should decide where the research is to take place, when, what data you wish to collect, from whom, how you will collect the data, what variables you wish to measure, how you will analyse the data and how the findings will be disseminated.

This process is facilitated if you carefully outline your objectives in undertaking the study. While there are no limitations on the number of your objectives, you should be careful not to take on more than you can handle comfortably. Beginning researchers have a tendency to try to solve the big-picture issues when they really only have the resources and expertise to concentrate on a small study. Limit your objectives based on the constraints that bind you.

If your study is to be predominantly quantitative, you will need to define accurately the research problem, and this will involve operationalising the variables as outlined in chapter 3. Qualitative-based research allows a much looser conceptual understanding of the research question at the beginning of the process.

METHODOLOGY

We discussed different methodological choices in chapter 1. You will remember that these include quantitative and qualitative approaches. A quantitative methodology would be most useful where you have extensive knowledge of the environment or situation you wish to study and are looking to test hypotheses about relationships between variables and to make statistical inferences from your quantifiable data. Quantitative research is generally about testing theory.

A qualitative methodology enables you to further your knowledge of the situation when seeking to describe social reality. An emancipatory approach, using quantitative and/or qualitative methodologies, would be appropriate if you wish to conduct research that centralises the concerns of marginalised or disempowered people.

You should be aware that you might choose a combination of approaches if this best suits your study. A combination of methods, also called triangulation, is useful for obtaining a wide range of information on an issue. Think carefully about your study and determine what it is you wish to achieve from the research and then select an appropriate framework. Remember, it is not a political statement to choose one or other methodology and, in fact, you would demonstrate naiveté if you were to declare, 'I am always and only a quantitative [or any other] researcher'. It is better to be pragmatic and to decide on the basis of the constraints you face. Decide carefully, because your research plan is determined by the choice you make.

LITERATURE REVIEW

Conducting a literature review is a vital part of your research. If you have prepared a research proposal you will have already read widely. A literature review allows you to discover what knowledge is already available about the issue you wish to investigate, to determine how your study will differ from existing work and hence add to our knowledge in the area, and it enables you to conceptually frame your work. Some researchers find themselves overwhelmed by the amount of literature available on a given topic. If you find yourself in this situation, you should selectively choose works which:

1 Represent the argument of a larger body of works
2 Present opposing views
3 Reflect current debate, legislation and policy

Older works are not necessarily inferior and you should consider references which are classical representations of new ideas or groundbreaking developments. Essentially, your literature review should indicate that you are up-to-date with current thinking in the area of study.

A review of literature is a far simpler proposition now than even five years ago. On-line computer catalogues exist in most libraries that allow you to conduct keyword searches of large data banks. There are now many journals available on-line, allowing you to get complete articles. There are also very sophisticated websites available with a great deal of information to assist you. For example, many government departments have detailed websites containing policy documents, media statements and other useful material and links. Ask your librarian to help you scan both national and international literature and resources in your chosen area.

Read these references carefully and critically analyse the existing studies to determine what you can best do to extend your understanding of the issue. You might decide to research the issue in a new context, or with a previously unresearched group. For example, if your research topic is child protection, you might study the implications of established practices in a rural situation or with an ethnic population. Your literature review should be thorough so that you are sure that what you propose to do is original research. As you further refine your topic, your reading will become more focused and specialised. It is a good idea to summarise the literature at this stage because this will form part of your final research report.

PREPARATION

Once you have defined your topic and analysed and reviewed the literature, you have a number of tasks to undertake before you can launch into the research. Funding the project will be an issue for any piece of research. You should develop a research proposal for your agency or for a funding body, following the outline in Appendix A. A further issue which must be dealt with during this preparatory stage is seeking ethics approval from the ethics committee at your agency, your university or the funding body. You should also spend some time discussing the proposed research with experienced researchers, colleagues and friends in order to help you develop a suitable design and to gain the benefit of others' experience.

RESEARCH DESIGN

Having defined your problem, chosen your methodology, reviewed the literature and completed the preparatory stages, you must now develop an appropriate research design. A research design indicates how your data will be collected, analysed and reported and includes the types of sampling, methods of data collection and analysis to be used. Your design is a plan of action which indicates how you propose to research the defined problem and is necessarily shaped by the problem and the methodology. For instance, if your study is qualitative and largely exploratory, you will have a more flexible design. During the course of the study, the questions are refined and clarified and the researcher chooses the subjects as the research progresses. A quantitative study, on the other hand, will be far more precise, with a definite plan of action at the beginning of the study.

Sampling

Both qualitative and quantitative researchers employ sampling techniques. However, quantitative researchers employ probability sampling and so claim representativeness. Qualitative researchers eschew representativeness, claiming that non-probability techniques are more useful for assessing the social reality in which they are interested. Types of sampling will be outlined in chapter 5. What you must ask yourself is whether your sample is truly adequate for the problem being studied. If you are conducting quantitative research, is your sample representative of the target group or is it biased in some way? For example, if you propose to study attitudes to euthanasia, would it be appropriate to survey university students only? Students may be largely responding to such an issue in an impersonal and non-reflective way. A sample should include those directly involved in the problem being investigated, in this case terminal patients, relatives, doctors and nurses.

A qualitative sample is usually chosen purposively to reflect the situation under review. For example, Oakley, a feminist researcher, conducted a groundbreaking study of housework in the 1970s that fundamentally altered the notion that housework was not 'work' (Oakley 1985). It still surprises many to learn that she interviewed only 40 women for this study. However, her sample was chosen purposively to reflect women working full time in the home in working-class London; it was small and she was not claiming that it was representative of all women. Her work was so well crafted that she influenced a generation of feminist researchers. Choose your sample to reflect accurately the problem you wish to study or the area you wish to explore.

Data collection

The way you go about collecting your data is equally as important as the way you draw up your sample. While data collection methods will vary according to the type of information you are seeking, the research question and the resources at your disposal, there are no right or wrong methods for a given situation or a given methodology.

66

As Sarantakos (1998) notes, methods are the tools of trade for the social scientist and each method is used where and when it proves the most suitable. We should, however, choose methods that are the best ways of obtaining the information required. For example, questionnaire data will tell us how people felt about a particular issue at a given point of time, but may not be consistent with how they actually behave when the situation in question arises. A good example might be a survey of a group of nurses in nursing homes that finds that they are adamant that the elderly in their care deserve the best quality of life that can be provided. A study using observation methods may, however, have revealed that nursing homes are under-staffed and that patients may not always be fed and showered on time, and may be left sitting alone in their rooms for long periods of time. The nurses have not necessarily lied during their survey. The researcher has simply used an inadequate method for collecting the data.

Methods employed in quantitative and qualitative research often overlap. For example, you might use interviews, surveys, unobtrusive methods or content analysis in either—the methods are merely the instruments used to elicit the desired information. What differs is the purpose for which they are used (or the theoretical perspective of the researcher) and the way they are used (or the implementation of the methods).

Quantitative methods are more precisely implemented. They are carefully developed and tested prior to the commencement of the study to determine the suitability of the chosen methods. For instance, if the instrument is to be a questionnaire aimed at determining the cause and effect links between variables, it must be carefully tested to determine whether the questions relate to the chosen variables. Qualitative methods are far more flexible and allow the researcher to change and develop the methods employed. For example, survey methods may be unstructured or semi-structured, with topic areas specified and questions varying depending on the issues being explored. This allows the researcher to move into new areas of inquiry and to better understand the perspectives and priorities of the subject. Thus, while methods may be similar, the way they are used by a quantitative or qualitative researcher may vary. As a researcher you must be clear about your own perspective and what it is you are seeking to know. Based on this information, your plan will specify the method/s you have chosen.

Administration

Conducting any piece of research creates a significant amount of administrative work. Your plan should note the administrative arrangements that will be put in place to ensure the success of your method/s. If you have chosen to survey 1000 people, for example, what materials will you need? Will you need research assistants? How will they be recruited/paid? How will they be trained? Where will interviews take place and how will you set them up? What ethical clearances do you need to obtain prior to commencement? What will you do about non-response? Where will data be stored securely while awaiting processing? If you have chosen to do a qualitative study you might have decided to use participant observation or un-structured interviewing as your method. How will you gain entry to the situation? Have you thought through the ethical issues? Have you the time and resources to spend a great deal of time in the research situation? For any method there will be a multiplicity of administrative issues to be sorted out and documented in your plan.

Administrative tasks

- Materials organised
- Access to equipment arranged
- Assistants recruited and trained
- Interviews or access to the situation organised
- Travel and accommodation booked
- Data storage security arranged
- Ethical issues resolved

Data analysis

Richards and Richards (1990, p. 5) note that 'theories are not little lizards waiting under rocks to be uncovered; but webs of under-standing constructed by the researcher, and used actively to make sense of the data'. The success or failure of any research endeavour lies in the researcher's ability to work with the data and to actively generate understandable theoretical arguments. (This will be more fully discussed in chapters 12, 13 and 14.) What have you discovered that you did not know before? How can you document these findings to clearly indicate the new information you have generated? This process is, perhaps, the most daunting for new researchers but also the most exciting, because you have made discoveries and have created a new understanding of the research issue. Once you have undertaken this process of analysis, you will find that the research process is demystified, understandable and challenging.

The way your data are to be analysed is an integral stage of any research and should be planned carefully. If you have conducted a quantitative survey and have data requiring statistical analysis, you may need to employ an analyst or purchase appropriate computer software and seek relevant training. A qualitative research study produces vast amounts of new data, often unstructured, which must be coded, categorised and analysed. This can be usefully done by computer. Whatever means you choose, you must incorporate this into your plan and allow time and resources for training or employing others to do the analysis.

Reporting

The final section of your plan will detail how you propose to report your findings. What is the most appropriate medium to allow you to widely disseminate your findings so that they have maximum impact on the situation which led you to do the research in the first place? You might decide that this is an interdepartmental report, a conference paper, a journal article, a book or a newspaper article. You should see this stage as crucial to the resolution of the problem and make resources available. You may need to contact agencies, editors or publishers before you commence your research so that no time is lost and your research findings do not become dated. Chapter 15 expands on this topic area.

Reporting your research

- Interdepartmental report
- Conference paper
- Journal article
- Book or book chapter
- Newspaper
- Pamphlet or flyer

CONDUCTING THE RESEARCH

Your plan acts like a roadmap that indicates how your study will be conducted. It should be comprehensive so that no surprises emerge during the execution phase. When conducting the research you should follow the plan you have developed, allowing some flexibility for the unforeseen issues that may arise. The execution phase takes a great deal of time and represents the major commitment in terms of time, energy and focus. Do not be discouraged if your data do not support your position or if your research plan must be reassessed. Negative or non-significant findings are just as valuable as findings showing a significant relationship or positive effect. If people do not publicise such findings, the research community and the profession may be left with a distorted picture of the existing situation. The experience you gain is important, and your findings will contribute to the knowledge base of our profession regardless of whether or not they are earth-shattering revelations.

Disseminating the findings

Research should be viewed as having three equally important stages: the preparation phase, the execution phase and the dissemination stage. Your research findings may have the potential to completely change our thinking on a particular issue. However, unless you first communicate your findings effectively by writing them in a way that is clear and intelligible and, second, disseminate those findings widely, your research will merely gather dust on your bookshelf. Research reports should be written clearly and concisely in a way that interests the audience by avoiding jargon and masses of superfluous information. Take careful note of the points outlined in chapter 15 when presenting your findings.

Research in action

To further your understanding of the differences between qualitative and quantitative methodologies and the different types of research plans they generate, let us examine some examples. In 1995 the article below appeared in an Australian rural newspaper.

THURSDAY, 16th NOVEMBER, 1995

DOMESTIC VIOLENCE COMMITTEE

—— newly formed Domestic Violence Committee will meet for the first time today following the issue of a record number of domestic violence orders following Monday's —— Local Court sitting.

Fourteen domestic violence restraining orders were issued after Monday's court.

It was the largest number ever issued here.

A committee to formulate effective response systems to the problem, and to follow up progress in individual cases has been formed.

The article details a significant increase in the number of local women appearing before the local court seeking protection orders from their violent partners. It was sent to us by a colleague in the area. As researchers in the welfare field, we are alarmed by the social problems in the town that underlie these bald facts. You might ask yourself, if you were a member of the newly formed Domestic Violence Committee, how would you best go about finding out more about the situation in order to formulate an effective response?

The first issue is problem definition. What are your objectives?

What is it we wish to find out? Are we interested in quantifying the problem or seeking to explore and understand the experiences of the women or the perpetrators in the town? Are we interested in how the police and legal systems are responding to the situation? What programs or actions have proved effective? Is this an historically isolated experience for this town, or is it a common feature of the gender dynamics in rural communities? Is this town any different from other small rural towns and how does it compare to coastal towns or cities? These questions illustrate how difficult it is to decide what you might fruitfully explore through your research.

To help define the problem, outline your objectives carefully. Do you want facts about the numbers of victims coming before the courts? Are you more interested in understanding the experiences of the women so that you can develop programs? Are you interested in the possible link between poverty/unemployment and violence? Your ultimate concern will no doubt be to influence programs and policy so that violence is no longer a feature of your town.

Let us examine some different approaches, one quantitative and one qualitative, the qualitative example having a feminist orientation.

QUANTITATIVE STUDY OF VIOLENCE AGAINST WOMEN IN RURAL AREAS

Definition of the problem

From the newspaper report you have determined that violence is possibly an emerging and increasing problem in small towns. You have, therefore, decided to test this hypothesis and to determine whether there is a link with high unemployment levels. Your hypothesis acts like a guess or tentative answer to a perplexing problem. Your hypothesis is: 'Violence against women is increasing in small rural towns as unemployment levels increase'.

Note that you will need to operationally define certain terms in your hypothesis. Violence against women has been variously defined over history. However, there is now consensus that violence should be more broadly defined than overt physical violence and include emotional, psychological and spiritual violence (National Committee on Violence Against Women 1992). This definition is comprehensive but, in turn, difficult to research because many women do not report their experiences of violence. When they do, it is more likely that they will report physical rather than non-physical forms of violence. You might choose, then, to operationally define violence against women as 'cases reported to police and to social/welfare workers in local agencies'. Small rural towns might be operationally defined as towns with 5000 or less. 'Unemployment levels' are operationally defined as government unemployment statistics for the areas studied.

71

Operationally defined, your hypothesis now reads: 'Violence against women, as evidenced by reports to police and social/welfare workers, is increasing in rural towns of 5000 or less as official unemployment figures increase'. As a social worker, you are concerned to incorporate into your study an examination of treatment procedures and effective programs. Your study will have a further aim to examine the responses of the helping professions in the towns surveyed.

Literature review

You must read widely to determine what studies have already been done in this area and to help you to further define your approach to your research. There is a great deal of literature conceptualising and contextualising violence and you should read as much as you can so that you are aware of the theoretical work in the area you are researching. Many researchers are so keen to get into the field and to begin collecting data that they may ignore the value of existing literature in helping to develop an efficient and sound study.

Preparation

Funding research is a constant problem for researchers and workers in the welfare field. You might seek funding from your agency, or from a combination of the services represented on the steering committee. Alternatively, the committee might choose to make a joint submission to an external funding body. In any case, cost your plan carefully so that you are not disadvantaged by a shortfall in funding.

In any research, particularly in an area as sensitive as violence, you should make sure you have ethical clearance from your own agency and/or the funding body's ethics committee. In this case, issues of confidentiality, privacy, access to counselling for interviewees, and security for those taking part are all relevant ethical issues.

Research design

How to gather data that accurately reflects the defined problem is a skill that must be learned. To assist with this, a carefully developed research design is vital. Your design reflects the ideal sampling, data collection and data analysis methods chosen. You must draw up a careful plan to test your hypothesis, always bearing in mind that your plan will be limited by your funding and time constraints. Despite these, ensure that it retains its focus on the research problem. Let us assume that you have adequate funding and have permission to spend one day a week for six months on this study.

Sampling

The committee decides to restrict the study to ten rural towns with populations of less than 5000 in the state where you are working. Your sample of towns might be chosen randomly, or be determined by distance constraints so that the ten closest to your home form the basis of your study, or you might look at towns across a number of regions including coastal and inland areas. Within the ten towns, the committee decides to survey a representative sample of local police and social/welfare workers. Your first task is to seek the names and addresses of these service providers so that your sample is complete.

Data collection

Your methods must be chosen well to gather the required data and adequately test your hypothesis. In this case, you are seeking reported cases of violence as well as unemployment figures and information on response mechanisms. Because you are looking for a link between the two variables your data must span a specified period (say two to five years) to determine fluctuations. Collecting data on employment figures will be relatively easy as these can be obtained through the government employment services. These data will be broken down by local areas and will allow you to note fluctuations.

Collecting data on reported cases of violence will be more difficult as you will need to survey a number of people to gather the required information. You might choose to draw up a questionnaire or interview schedule for the police and service providers in the selected towns. With a sensitive issue such as this, face-to-face interviews, although time consuming, will allow you to gather the information more successfully than mailed questionnaires. Your interview should cover issues dealing with historical trends in the reporting of violence, but should also examine a number of other issues that might affect reporting in order that you may determine whether any factors not related to unemployment are affecting the results. Issues such as changes in legislation, new services which make it easier for women to seek help, community education and community changes in attitude will have an impact on the reporting of violence, and may have a greater effect on results than unemployment. You will also include questions on types of service responses and effective programs.

Before entering the field you should test your questionnaire by pretesting questions and by conducting a pilot program in a town not in your sample. Piloting allows you to refine your questions to ensure that they are not ambiguous and are focused on the issue in question. With a quantitative study, your interviews will be standardised so that each person is asked the same series of questions.

Administration

The administration issues involved with this study will depend on the funds available. If you have sufficient funds to employ a research assistant who can conduct the interviews for you, you will need to allow time to draft the questions, to train the assistant, to conduct the interviews and to analyse the responses. You may also need to allot funds for travel and accommodation in the various towns to be visited. Most importantly, you need to be sure your interview appointments have been made well in advance.

Data analysis

Once the interviews are completed your analysis of the collected data will necessarily take a great deal of time. This is where you determine whether the evidence supports your hypothesis, or whether other variables have had a greater influence on reported violence. There are several quantitative data analysis computer programs available that will assist you at this stage of your research—these will be further discussed in chapter 13.

Reporting results

Your results may indicate that increasing reports of violence are linked to increasing unemployment figures. They may also indicate a number of other issues that influence violence in the community. You may also have a great deal of valuable information on effective programs. Whatever the case, you should not lose sight of the original reason for conducting the study—your alarm at the numbers of women reporting violence in the newspaper story. Your report of the study should illuminate this issue and carefully present your findings. If your results are being published in a newspaper, there is little need to do more than report the issues. If you are writing a report, a paper or a book, you should write about any additions to the conceptual understanding of the problem that you are able to make. Your work is useful regardless of how conclusive your findings are because it adds knowledge and informs others about your methodology and the application of methods to achieve the stated results.

QUALITATIVE STUDY OF VIOLENCE AGAINST WOMEN

Because qualitative researchers are concerned to understand the lived reality of people's experience, such a study will necessarily be different to a quantitative study. In this case, the committee may decide that a qualitative study is essential to understand what is happening in the town. Qualitative research does not need a clearly defined research hypothesis but it does require you to clearly state the research problem. The committee may decide that the problem is essentially to find out more about violence in the town, what strategies women employ to deal with the situation, whether current responses are seen as acceptable, and what changes might be made to deal more effectively with violence. In this case the plan is more flexible and will be shaped by the emerging data. Regardless of the methodology employed, a literature review remains an essential element of any piece of research. Your reading should help to shape your thinking and alert you to the issues that should be incorporated into the study.

Research design

Sampling

In qualitative studies, there is no claim that the sample is representative of the whole population, and little attempt to claim that findings are generalisable beyond the study population. Qualitative researchers are less interested in recognising patterns of behaviour, attitudes or other phenomena than they are in *understanding* social reality; therefore the sampling technique employed will be non-probability based, or purposive, because subjects will be chosen for a *purpose*. In this case, the committee decides to seek permission to speak with women who are seeking protection orders to find out what is happening to them, where they are seeking help, whether this is effective and what can be done to prevent violence. The committee also decides to speak with service providers in the town to find an effective response, to coordinate community education activities, to maximise protection for women and to undertake preventive measures against violence. Thus, the sample might comprise women who have sought protection orders during the past two years and all service providers in the town.

Preparation

To undertake such a study the committee must clarify where funds will be obtained, who is to do the work and how the committee will oversee the project. Most importantly, the committee must address the ethical issues involved in the proposed study. How will victims of violence be approached to participate in the study, and what strategies will be put in place to ensure confidentiality is maintained? Clearance must be sought from relevant ethics committees so that those participants approached are not compromised. In this case, the local police officer and the magistrate are part of the newly formed committee. One of these officials might be asked to contact women who have come to the court for assistance over the last two years to request their participation in the study. In this way, a purposive sample of women might be developed.

Data collection

Effective methods for this piece of research would be semi-structured interviews with the women and focused discussion groups with the service providers. Semi-structured interviews allow certain desig-nated areas of inquiry to be explored with the interviewees. Focused discussion groups with service providers will allow information to be collected from all providers and for response strategies to be 'brainstormed' in the group situation. This method will save time and money. Data from both chosen methods are most effectively gathered via tape recording. Permission must be sought from participants to allow taping, and confidentiality of such highly sensitive material must be ensured. We have found it effective to use no identifying family names during interviews; this protects the confidentiality of informants when tapes are being transcribed by assistants.

Because qualitative interviews usually take more time than quan-titative interviews, and elicit a great deal of rich data, researchers tend to do a smaller number of interviews. Students often ask, 'How many should I do?' The best response is that you should continue until no new data is emerging.

Data analysis

Once tapes are transcribed you will find yourself with piles of print-outs and, no doubt, a huge sense of uncertainty! However, you will have a sense of the key issues from your interviews. This is why qualitative researchers usually prefer to collect and analyse their own data. The research is an emerging process which you should signpost by writing memos to alert you to significant features of the data. During the analysis phase these memos form an important part of the coding process.

Your data should be coded around key issues and recurring themes. In this case, key issues might be the significant factors which have led to the violence, coping strategies, sources of help, issues of rurality that aid or constrain help, legal responses, effectiveness of protection orders, and suggested changes in response systems. The qualitative analyst looks for patterns of response around such themes to determine their findings.

Analysis of data from the focused groups should be a process shared and developed by the group. The group might have a series of meetings focusing firstly on what is happening now and what are the current responses. Further meetings might develop strategies for change to address the problem.

Reporting findings

The data gathered in a qualitative study is no less important than that gathered through quantitative research. Although this research has looked only at the town itself, it is also important for workers in other areas who may be facing similar issues and it is vital for policy development because it may have identified issues which must be addressed at policy level. Your research should be widely disseminated through newspapers, journals, conferences or a book chapter.

A FINAL WORD

In these examples we have made a clear distinction between qualitative and quantitative methodologies for the purpose of illustrating and highlighting differences. Many researchers now incorporate both qualitative and quantitative aspects into a study in order to obtain a comprehensive understanding of issues. Thus, in this example, the committee might choose some quantitative analysis—analysing trends in violence—and some qualitative analysis—assessing the reality and impact of violence.

SUMMARY

This chapter has identified the steps you should undertake to conduct a piece of research. Although these steps may vary by methodology, they generally include problem definition, literature review and research design stages of sampling, data collection, data analysis and reporting.

The stages in the research process have been illustrated by reference to research aimed at examining violence against women in rural areas. What is important to note is the way qualitative research seeks to discover and explore issues in a different way to quantitative research. While quantitative research seeks to tabulate, quantify and discover cause-and-effect variables, qualitative research seeks to understand a situation from the inside by investigating the lived experience of research subjects. These are important concepts for beginning researchers to understand. Equally important is the fact that research projects may contain both quantitative and qualitative elements. In fact, we have often found that this may produce the most comprehensive results. Furthermore, despite any claims to methodological purity, experienced researchers will tell you that the type of research you choose to conduct is often determined more by pragmatic considerations such as time and resources than by any overriding methodological orientation.

QUESTIONS

1 What factors might influence your research?
2 What are the steps in the research process?
3 How does the process of quantitative research differ from qualitative research?
4 How do methods of data collection differ in quantitative and qualitative research?
5 What means of data analysis would you use in qualitative research?
6 How might you analyse quantitative data?
7 What administrative arrangements should you make in order to conduct your research successfully?
8 What is the purpose of a literature review?
9 How and why should you report your research findings?

EXERCISES

1 In your work as a hospital social worker you have become aware of an increasing number of patients presenting with AIDS-related illnesses. Consider how:
   ■ a quantitative study could add to our knowledge of the problem
   ■ a qualitative study might assist us to develop an understanding of the area.
   Outline the steps in your research process.

2 Part of your work in a local community centre is to construct a day care program for the aged. You have become conscious of the difficulties experienced by carers. How might you:
   ■ develop a quantitative study?
   ■ develop a qualitative piece of research?
   Outline the steps in your research process.

FURTHER READING

Fortune, A. E. & Reid, W. J. 1999, *Research in Social Work*, 3rd edn, Columbia University Press, New York.
Herbert, M. 1990, *Planning a Research Project*, Cassell, London. An easy-to-read guide to the stages in a research project.
Mark, R. 1996, *Research Made Simple: A Handbook for Social Workers*, Sage Publications, London. This is a step-by-step guide to the research process.
Rogers, G. & Bouey, E. 1996, 'Reviewing the literature', in *Social Work*

Research and Evaluation, R. M. Grinnell Jr (ed.), 4th edn, F. E. Peacock Publishers, Itasca, Ill. Appendix A provides a useful examination of the process of reviewing literature.

Sarantakos, S. 1998. *Social Research*, 2nd edn, Macmillan, Melbourne.

Yegidis, B. L., Weinbach, R. W. & Morrison-Rodriguez, B. 1999, *Research Methods for Social Workers*, Allyn & Bacon, Boston.

5 SAMPLING

Sampling is about choosing who or what we wish to study in order to answer our research question. Sometimes these units of study are chosen randomly (more typically for quantitative research) and sometimes they are purposively selected (more typically for qualitative research). In any case the way we choose the units of study will have a major impact on our results and should, therefore, be done thoughtfully and with a clear rationale.

QUANTITATIVE AND QUALITATIVE RESEARCH SAMPLES

It is important to note that quantitative researchers use probability sampling while qualitative researchers will more often opt for non-probability sampling. Quantitative researchers require a random or probability sample for the statistical processes they undertake (see chapter 14). Qualitative researchers, on the other hand, use non-probability sampling because of the nature of their research which is largely exploratory. Researcher bias is unavoidable but the process allows a significant sample to be generated quickly.

Qualitative researchers often seek typical cases. Sometimes, however, they deliberately seek atypical, extreme or deviant cases, as a means of shedding light on the typical or for their own intrinsic interest. Often sampling in qualitative research is controlled not by a need for statistical rigour but by the developing theoretical argument, and so the sampling paradigm is sometimes referred to as *theoretical sampling*. In other words, the sample is chosen to assist the researcher to understand the phenomena under study and to illuminate the researcher's emerging theory. Because the type of research undertaken by quantitative and qualitative researchers is different, neither probability nor non-probability sampling is superior to the others, or necessarily more effective.

Quantitative versus qualitative sampling

Quantitative	*Qualitative*
■ Probability sampling	■ Non-probability sampling
■ Objectivity	■ Subjectivity
■ Representative	■ Non-representative
■ Results generalisable	■ Results not generalisable
■ Statistically rigorous	■ Not statistically rigorous
■ Random sampling	■ Theoretical sampling
■ Claims no researcher bias	■ Researcher is integral to sample selection
■ All units equal or known chance of selection	■ No attempt to give units an equal chance of selection

---

WHAT IS A SAMPLE?

Thus once we have decided on our research question and other aspects of our research design, some thought must be given to the subjects, cases or events we wish to study. In order to be completely accurate, every person (or case or event) in the population under study would need to be surveyed. This is called a *saturation sample* or *census*. In practice, saturation sampling is rarely possible because of the nature of the study question, the size of the population and because of time and resource constraints. Instead, we select a *sample* from the total population under study. In quantitative research, this sample is ideally chosen at random. As a result, researchers can claim that results are generalisable because inferences can be drawn from the research about the wider population (that is, the results from the sample are representative of results in the population).

For a sample to be representative, it must be chosen in such a way that subjects or cases have beliefs, attitudes or experiences which are similar to the population being investigated. Conventional social science wisdom suggests that a random sample drawn from the study population and selected according to sampling theory will reflect the characteristics of the entire population. In this way, the researcher is able to make informed statements about the group under study.

Let us look at an example to allow us to better understand the concept of sampling. Imagine yourself an employee of a government income-support organisation that provides payments for people who are unemployed, ill or unable to work due to disabilities. It also pays pensions to people of retirement age and income supplements to people caring for others full time, or for children with disabilities.

You are interested in examining the attitudes and experiences of clients coming to your agency for the first time. You are concerned that clients may find the experience humiliating and confronting. Your ultimate aim with such a study might be to make this experience easier for clients. To study such an issue affecting a very large group you must draw a sample. First-time clients will represent at least several thousand people each week. Ideally you would study all first-time clients in every office of the income-support organisation across the country over a specific period of time. Pragmatically, you might choose a sample that is localised (first-time clients in your own office) and time-defined (in a one-week period). Such a sample may allow you to generalise beyond the subjects of the study but with a large degree of caution.

No doubt you have noted that drawing such a sample will have serious limitations. Can you generalise beyond the local area? Do your findings reflect the experiences of clients in branches in other locality areas? Will clients in small communities find the experience more difficult than those in larger, more impersonal offices? By confining your time frame to one week, are you picking up on seasonal variations in the workforce? Are recent school leavers, for example, a part of your sample?

As you can see from this example, drawing a sample that accurately reflects the study population requires a great deal of thought. Because of pragmatic concerns such as time and resource constraints, you may have to make trade-offs that reduce the generalisability of your findings. This is not to say that you should not undertake the proposed study. Your findings, and particularly any strategies you develop which improve client service, will be useful to workers in offices across the country.

Let us examine some of the most common types of sampling. First, you should note that sampling can be categorised as either *probability* or *non-probability* sampling.

PROBABILITY SAMPLING

Probability sampling refers to sampling in which each unit of the population has an equal (as in the case of simple random sampling) or known chance of being selected for study. The units of the population under study are referred to as the *sampling frame*. The sample is chosen from the sampling frame in an unbiased and rigorous way, allowing a small sample to be used to assess or predict the studied behaviour in the larger population. Probability sampling is favoured by quantitative researchers as it allows a high degree of representativeness from which results can be generalised. The four main types of probability sampling are:

1 Simple random sampling
2 Systematic random sampling
3 Stratified random sampling
4 Cluster random sampling

Probability sampling

- Each population unit has an equal, or known, chance of selection
- High degree of representativeness
- Allows researchers to generalise results
- Favoured by quantitative researchers
- Four main types:
    Simple random sampling
    Systematic random sampling
    Stratified random sampling
    Cluster random sampling

Simple random sampling

Simple random sampling is the most common form of probability sampling. There are several methods we might choose to select a simple random sample.

Let us use another example to illustrate the process of simple random sampling. Imagine you are working on a government policy research team and you are interested in assessing the effects of a new policy to move previously institutionalised people with psychiatric problems into group homes in the community. Your study is motivated by a number of violent incidents reported by police and causing community concern. Your sampling frame represents the entire population of people who have moved from institutions to group homes in the five years since the policy was adopted. Suppose that you find that there are 10 000 people in your sampling frame and you choose to sample 1000 of them. We might first allot a number to each person on the list from 1 to 10 000. Numbers from 1 to 10 000 are then placed in a container and are selected (without replacement) until 1000 numbers have been drawn. Referring to your list, the numbers are related to the people in the sampling frame. These 1000 are then used as subjects for your study.

Alternatively, you might use a table of random numbers; these are readily available in many research methods textbooks or can be generated by a computer. Begin at a randomly selected point in the table and choose the first number on the table between 1 and 10 000. Work your way up (or down) the column selecting numbers and relating them to your list of names. In this way you can generate your sample of 1000.

Table of random numbers

1986	3067	1309
2254	5321	0532
4763	9854	5643
1589	8623	2875
7415	9792	3261

A simple random sample may be chosen in a number of other ways, including by dates of birth or by initials. Any randomised technique is suitable.

Simple random sampling

- Sampling frame is identified
- Desired sample number identified
- Numbers assigned to subjects in sampling frame
- Random numbers selected in some way
- Numbers related to list of subjects
- Sample generated

Systematic random sampling

Systematic random sampling varies from simple random sampling in that the chosen units are not independent of each other. For instance, you might decide to select every tenth person in order to generate your sample.

The size of the interval between chosen units is decided by dividing the total population, or sampling frame, by the desired sample size. Thus, using our previous example of previously insti-tutionalised people (10 000) and our desired sample (1000) we decide the interval (x) in the following way:

$$x = \frac{\text{total sampling frame}}{\text{desired sampling}}$$

$$x = \frac{10\,000}{1000} = 10$$

The first name on our list is chosen at random from those numbered from 1 to 10. Thereafter, we choose every tenth person. We will generate a sample list of 1000 using this method.

When using this method, we need to be careful that no unintended bias creeps into the sample. For example, by choosing every tenth name, we might be missing residents in smaller communities and in certain types of group housing. (If the initial list is randomly generated this should not be an issue.) Once your sample is selected, carefully check that you have generated a sample that is not biased on certain variables that may be important to your study.

Systematic random sampling

- Sampling frame identified
- Desired sample number identified
- Numbers assigned to each subject in sampling frame
- Sampling interval (x) identified
- First subject randomly chosen
- Every xth subject chosen
- Sample generated

Stratified random sampling

Stratified random sampling allows us to divide our sampling frame into various strata or groups before selecting our sample. This allows us to ensure that each group is represented proportionately or disproportionately to their numbers in the overall population. For example, we might decide that it is important to assess how the effects of group home living vary by gender. We divide our frame by gender and select a random sample of 500 from each group.

Alternatively we might decide that age is a critical factor. We thus divide our sampling frame by age and select from each group. If we are to select a proportionate sample then we choose a sample from the subgroup that reflects their numbers in the total sampling frame. If we choose to sample disproportionately, then we choose equal numbers from each group regardless of their relative proportions. Table 5.1 illustrates the way we might select a stratified random sample by age.

Whether you choose a proportionate or disproportionate sample depends on how valuable you feel the information from each group might be and what it is you wish to find out. For example, reported incidents of violence among deinstitutionalised people might be related disproportionately to the older age groups, in which case you might feel a disproportionate sample will be more valuable. To choose

Table 5.1   Selection of a stratified random sample by age

Strata	Number in sampling frame	1/10 proportionate sample	Disproportionate sample
Age 20–29	4 000	400	250 (1/16)
Age 30–39	2 500	250	250 (1/10)
Age 40–49	2 000	200	250 (1/8)
Age 50 +	1 500	150	250 (1/6)
	10 000	1 000	1 000

a disproportionate sample the sampling frame is divided into age groups. The sampling fraction is used to decide the interval between chosen subjects. For example, in the 20–29-year age group every 16th person is chosen, in the 30–39-year age group every 10th, in the 40–49-age group every 8th and in the 50+ age group every 6th.

A proportionate sample, on the other hand, is selected by choosing every tenth person in each group.

Stratified random sampling

- Sample frame identified
- Desired sample identified
- Strata or groups identified
- Proportionate or disproportionate sample numbers identified
- Sampling interval (x) identified for each strata or group
- First name in each group randomly selected
- Every xth person chosen from each group
- Sample generated

Cluster random sampling

The final type of random sampling to be discussed here is cluster random sampling. Cluster random sampling is generally used when there is no sampling frame available; that is, we do not know who is in the group from which we are sampling as there is no readily available list of subjects. We also use this type of sampling when we are limited by resource constraints. Suppose, for example, that we wish to survey homeless street kids. We do not have access to a convenient list of names from which to draw our sample. What we can do is randomly select certain areas or *clusters* that are relevant to our research problem. For example, we might choose to survey kids in youth refuges in both city and country areas. While we cannot hope to survey all homeless youth in all areas we can choose the areas or *clusters* that represent the sample under study. To reduce the possibility of sampling bias, it is a good idea to increase the number of clusters surveyed. In our homeless youth study we might reduce bias by surveying in inner-city areas and in outer suburbs with high ethnic populations. We might also survey in regional cities and a selection of country areas, making sure we sample coastal as well as inland regions. Once our clusters or areas are identified, we then randomly choose our desired sample from the current population in the identified youth refuges.

Cluster random sampling allows us to systematically sample a population which is not readily identified. While it allows us to work within budgetary limits and other constraints, it does increase the possibility of sampling error. The only way to minimise this problem is to increase the number of clusters surveyed.

Cluster random sampling

- Sampling frame unknown
- Desired sample identified
- Clusters identified
- Random sample drawn from clusters
- Sample generated

NON-PROBABILITY SAMPLING

The second major category of sampling is non-probability sampling. Non-probability sampling is generally used in exploratory research and by qualitative researchers. It does not make any claims to be representative of the population under study and therefore the generalisability of results is limited. This, however, is not the point of the research.

Non-probability sampling is very useful and justifiable when the researcher is seeking information in a new area and targets subjects or cases who typify the issue to be studied. Suppose, for example, you are working in a respite unit and you wish to examine the pressures facing carers of AIDS patients. Because AIDS is a relatively new disease, little is known about the unique issues facing carers. To explore this new area of investigation you select a small sample (for example, ten) of carers known to you through your position in the respite unit. You will note that these ten cases will not be representative of all carers of AIDS patients because of the small sample number and because they are limited by locality. However, this sample will give insights into a previously unexplored area and will provide a qualitative researcher with a rich source of data.

The four most common types of non-probability sampling are:

1 Accidental (sometimes called convenience or availability) sampling

2 Quota sampling
3 Purposive sampling
4 Snowball sampling

Non-probability sampling

■ Each population unit does not have an equal chance of selection
■ No claim to be representative
■ Does not necessarily allow the researcher to generalise results
■ Favoured by qualitative researchers
■ Four main types:
    Accidental sampling
    Quota sampling
    Purposive sampling
    Snowball sampling

Accidental sampling

Accidental sampling is, as the name implies, a sample you chance upon by accident. The sample is convenient or available to you for some reason. The most common form of accidental sampling is standing in a public place such as a supermarket or railway station for a certain period of time and interviewing people who walk by. For workers in the welfare industry an accidental sample might be drawn from a worker's caseload or from clients coming to the agency. Suppose you are working in a women's refuge and you wish to understand more about the difficulties women have seeking court protection orders. You might choose a sample from your case records or, alternatively, you might sample all new residents over a two-week period. In either case, your sample is not representative of the entire population of women seeking protection orders but it will give you valuable insights into the legal and court process and allow you to explore the problems facing women in this situation.

Accidental sampling

■ Sample drawn from available or convenient group
■ Sample reflects the problem being investigated
■ Number of subjects determined by access and availability
■ Sample generated

Quota sampling

Quota sampling allows us to set quotas for subgroups of our sample. Suppose, for instance, that we believe from our experience in the women's refuge that women with ethnic backgrounds find it more difficult to obtain protection orders because they are reluctant to approach the court system. We might then choose to study women from a non-English speaking background as well as English speaking women. We might also decide that it is important to survey women with children under five as well as those with no children or older children. We can draw up a matrix that will allow us to categorise women in the study.

Children under 5	Non-English speaking background	English speaking background
Yes	A	B
No	C	D

We must now decide how many women in each category will be surveyed. If we decide all categories are important, we may seek equal numbers of subjects for each category. For example, should we seek a sample of 20, our matrix will look like this:

Children under 5	Non-English speaking background	English speaking background
Yes	5	5
No	5	5

Quota sampling allows us to target certain characteristics that are important to our research problem. Because it is a type of non-probability sampling technique, it does not claim to be representative of the population being studied. While it does allow us to make observations about particular subgroups of the population, these results cannot be generalised with any degree of certainty.

Quota sampling

- Significant categories determined
- Quota determined for each category
- Quota selected
- Sample selected for each category
- Sample generated

Purposive sampling

This sampling technique allows us to select the sample for our study for a *purpose*. We may have prior knowledge that indicates that a particular group is important to our study or we select those subjects who we feel are 'typical' examples of the issue we wish to study. In our study of women seeking protection orders, we might decide that women from rural areas or outlying metropolitan areas appear to have more serious problems and so we choose a sample from these clients in order to determine why the system appears to be letting them down. Alternatively, we might choose a sample of experienced women who work in refuges in these areas to allow us a different perspective to aid our understanding of the issues involved.

Purposive sampling

- Sample is chosen for a particular purpose
- Sample gives insights into a particular issue related to the study area
- Number determined by the research topic, availability
- Sample generated

Snowball sampling

Snowball sampling is used when we have no knowledge of the sampling frame and limited access to subjects who may meet the criteria for our research. Suppose we do not have access to women seeking protection orders as we do not have access to a refuge. However, we do know a woman who has taken out an order. We might approach her for an interview and ask her to nominate other women she might know in the same circumstances. We contact these women for interviews and they nominate further women. We continue collecting our sample in this way until we feel we have reached the stage where our sample is *saturated*. In other words, no new information is emerging from our research and so we determine our sample is complete.

Snowball sampling

- Contact a 'typical' case
- Ask this person to recommend further cases
- Continue until sample is complete and saturated

HOW BIG SHOULD MY SAMPLE BE?

One of the most often asked questions is about sample size. Students and beginning researchers often beg for a magic sample size number.

Research, however, is not as simple as that. Sample size depends on what it is we wish to know, how certain we want to be about our findings, the resources we have available, the research design and its purpose, the type of statistical analysis required and the degree of representativeness we consider desirable (Yegidis, Weinbach & Morrison-Rodriguez 1999). Naturally, to be entirely accurate we would need to survey the entire sampling frame. As this is rarely possible, you should note that, in general, the larger the sample the more accurate will be your findings. Of course, you should also note that a small representative sample may be more accurate than a large unrepresentative one. It depends on the accuracy of the sampling technique. For small populations you should choose proportionately more for your sample than for samples drawn from larger populations.

With quantitative research, sample size is related to the type of statistical analysis you may wish to undertake. A minimum size for adequate statistical analysis would be 30, although many texts suggest your sample should be at least 100 or 120 (see, for example, Williams, Tutty & Grinnell, 1995, p. 233).

It is important that you understand the concept of *sampling error* in relation to sampling in quantitative research. We will explain this concept in detail in chapter 14, once we have explained some basic statistical concepts. For now, it is important to know that sampling error is an estimate of the amount of error you could make if you use just one sample of a certain size from a population to estimate the results for the whole population. In chapter 14 we show you that standard error or sampling error is inversely proportional to the size of your sample—hence you will have more confidence that your sample statistics will be closer to those of the population if you use a larger sample. The general principle is to take the largest representative sample you can.

Experienced statisticians have developed ways of estimating sample sizes that will give you a fairly accurate result based on the size of the population. One such table is reproduced here (Table 5.2) for your consideration. Note that the ideal sample size varies according to the confidence level required.

Confidence level (or confidence interval) refers to the level of confidence we have that the results accurately reflect the views of the population. A 95 per cent confidence level means that our results could occur by chance only 5 times in 100 trials. You should aim to have a 95 per cent confidence level with a 5 per cent standard error, meaning that the results will be out by 5 per cent only 5 times in 100 (Royse 1999).We will discuss confidence intervals in more detail in chapter 14.

Using Table 5.2, you can see that should you wish to sample a population group of 100 with a 95 per cent confidence level and a 5 per cent margin of error, you would need to draw 79 of the

Table 5.2 Appropriate sizes of simple random samples for specific permissible errors expressed as absolute proportions when the confidence level is 95 per cent

	Sample size for permissible error				
Population size	0.05	0.04	0.03	0.02	0.01
100	79	86	91	96	99
200	132	150	168	185	196
300	168	200	234	267	291
400	196	240	291	343	384
500	217	273	340	414	475
600	234	300	384	480	565
700	248	323	423	542	652
800	260	343	457	600	738
900	269	360	488	655	823
1000	278	375	516	706	906
2000	322	462	696	1091	1655
3000	341	500	787	1334	2286
4000	350	522	842	1500	2824
5000	357	536	879	1622	3288
6000	361	546	906	1715	3693
7000	364	553	926	1788	4049
8000	367	556	942	1847	4364
9000	368	563	954	1895	4646
10000	370	566	964	1936	4899
15000	375	577	996	2070	5855
20000	377	583	1013	2144	6488
25000	378	586	1023	2191	6938
30000	379	588	1030	2223	7275
40000	381	591	1039	2265	7745
50000	381	593	1045	2291	8056
75000	382	595	1052	2327	8514
100000	383	597	1056	2345	8762
500000	384	600	1065	2390	9423
1000000	384	600	1066	2395	9513
2000000	384	600	1067	2398	9558

Note: This table was calculated for binomial distributions.
Source: *Research Methods in Social Work*, 3rd edn, David Royse, Nelson-Hall Publishers, Chicago.

members of that group into your research sample. If the population is 1 000 000, your sample size should be 384.

Social work students frequently do qualitative research where sample size is not such a big issue and relates more to convenience and availability. With qualitative research you tend to continue to sample until no new information is emerging. Once you get to the point where you feel you've heard it all before you know your sample size is complete.

Size of sample is also guided by the diversity of the population you are studying. If your target group is heterogeneous you will need a larger sample size than if it were homogeneous. For example, if the target group is white, anglo-saxon and middle class you will achieve a high level of accuracy with a small sample. If the target group includes several ethnic groups, and diverse income levels, you will need a much larger sample.

Summary

When we conduct a piece of research we are interested in a particular target group or population. It is rarely possible to survey the entire population so, using sampling techniques, we select a sample of this target group. This chapter has examined the types of sampling techniques we can use to generate an adequate sample. We have seen how a sample can be developed using either probability or non-probability techniques. Probability sampling is a more precise or non-biased method which allows a representative sample to be selected, and results to be generalised. In order to use probability sampling we should have access to the entire target group—this is called the sampling frame. Four types of probability sampling have been discussed in this chapter. They are simple random sampling, systematic random sampling, stratified random sampling and cluster random sampling.

Non-probability sampling, on the other hand, is less precise and involves researcher bias. It allows the researcher to carefully select the sample for a particular, usually theoretical, purpose. Non-probability sampling techniques are used for exploratory, qualitative and often feminist research. They include accidental sampling, purposive sampling, quota sampling and snowball sampling.

Decisions on sample size, which are particularly critical in quantitative sampling, are governed by the accuracy we desire and the degree of homogeneity of the group. In general, the larger the sample the more confident we can feel about the generalisability of our findings. However, if the group is homogeneous we can feel confident about limiting sample size.

Non-probability sample sizes are not as critical as they are for probability sampling, as sample size is governed by the emerging data such that a researcher should continue sampling until no new data is emerging.

Questions

1 Why can't I make it easy on myself and do a saturation sample?
2 What is the difference between probability and non-probability sampling?
3 Outline the four main types of probability sampling and provide an example for each of when they would be an appropriate choice.
4 Outline the four main types of non-probability sampling and provide an example for each when they would be the most appropriate choice.
5 What issues affect the size of the sample you should take?

EXERCISES

1 Go to the library and find three social work research articles. List the article and the sampling technique used for each. Note whether you feel the sample is adequate for the research problem discussed.
2 Go to the library or a government department. Locate a government report based on research which lists policy recommendations. Assess whether the report is based on an appropriate sample and whether the recommendations are well-grounded in the research.
3 How would you develop a sample to study the employment status of graduates of your social work course?
4 How would you develop a sample to study the opinions of people about euthanasia?

FURTHER READING

You will find that most research textbooks have a detailed section on sampling techniques. Select those that support your methodological position and review the discussion on sampling.

6 SURVEYS AND INTERVIEWS

Having decided on your research questions, the basic design of your research (whether qualitative, quantitative or multimethod design) and who will be researched (your sample), the next step is to create your research instrument. In this chapter we will consider the two most common forms of research instrument: surveys (or questionnaires) and interviews.

Surveys and interviews generally lie on a continuum, with surveys being at the more structured end and interviews at the less structured. Usually, surveys are the research tools for quantitative methodology, with the design and questions being prepared well before the research subjects are contacted. Interviews, on the other hand, can be more flexible and are often the tools of qualitative research. Sometimes, however, surveys may be administered by an interviewer (structured interviews), and qualitative researchers can use surveys. We have already seen one example of how a mailed questionnaire was used in qualitative research in chapter 3, in the evaluation of rural postnatal depression groups. Keeping these things in mind, the continuum of research tools from surveys to interviews is as shown in Table 6.1.

Interviews can also be held with groups of people. Such interviews are often called focus groups and will be discussed at the end of this chapter.

Of course, there are many other research instruments as well as surveys and interviews, some of which are covered in later chapters.

Table 6.1   Continuum of research tools

Structured, pre-planned, quantitative					Unstructured, spontaneous, qualitative
mailed surveys	survey personally delivered	telephone interview	structured interview	semi-structured interview	in-depth interview

Nevertheless, surveys and interviews are still the most commonly used tools in social research and it is important to understand some basic principles for using them. In this chapter we will first discuss surveys, including issues common to both surveys and interviews. We will deal mainly with quantitative surveys in this section. We provide some tips on how to construct a questionnaire, then we discuss the sorts of questions you might include in your survey. The third section summarises the process of conducting a survey. Following this we review different styles of interviews, including handy hints on interviewing, in-depth interviews and focus groups.

SURVEYS

On designing surveys for quantitative research, most of the hard work is done before you conduct the interviews or mail the questionnaires to the people you are researching. For the purposes of this chapter, we will assume that you have thought about your research topic and its general design, read about it and discussed it widely with key stakeholders and interested people, perhaps formed a steering committee or advisory group, and formulated your research questions (including transforming them from concepts into measurable variables). We will also assume that you have decided what the unit of study is to be, who the population is, and how you will design and find your sample.

Constructing your questionnaire

There are five aspects which you need to address when constructing your questionnaire. These are: the cover letter, the instructions, the structure of the questionnaire itself, layout and follow-up procedures.

Cover letter

The cover letter is essential and needs to be carefully planned if you want people to take your survey seriously and be willing to participate. The cover letter can make the difference between whether people will return their survey, or agree to a telephone or personal

Figure 6.1   Cover letter

Consumer Consultancies Inc.
PO Box 54 Country Gardens Inland City Australia 8276
Telephone 09 333221 Fax 09 333222

February 1998

Dear Citizen

I am part of a group of independent consultants who have been employed by the government income support agency. We are conducting research on how people found their first visit to an office of this organisation.

Please fill in the enclosed questionnaire. Everyone who visited the agency for the first time this week has been given a copy. Your response will provide valuable information about the operation of the organisation. Answering the survey is entirely voluntary—you are not required to fill it in. However, if you do, you will help us improve the quality of service the agency provides.

You will see that although personal questions are asked, you do not identify yourself. The information you provide is completely confidential. Only your postcode, age and gender are requested so that comparisons can be made between regions, age groups and men and women. The agecny will **not** know who answered the survey—it is sent to us, not the agency.

Please ring me on the above number if you have any questions about the survey.

Your time in filling in the questionnaire is greatly appreciated. It should not take longer than half an hour. When you have completed the questionnaire please post it, in the Freepost envelope provided, by the end of the week. No stamp is needed.

Thank you for your time and cooperation
Yours sincerely

Miranda Bloggs
Principal Researcher

interview. Be prepared for many drafts to get the right tone and form for your cover letter!

Your cover letter should include a number of elements. Explain who you are, which agency you represent, what the survey is about and what it is aiming to achieve. It is also important to reassure people about their anonymity and confidentiality, and about their right not to participate. If you are using an identity number to follow up non-respondents, you need to explain its purpose, how it is used and how privacy will be protected. In mailed questionnaires a reply-by date (usually two weeks) should be specified and a reply-paid or freepost envelope included. For interviews, the next stage of contact is explained. The cover letter must be as brief as possible, never more than a page. Your aim is to arouse people's curiosity and motivate them to become involved.

Sometimes the cover letter doubles as a consent form, especially in mailed surveys where consent is implied if people return the

Figure 6.2   Consent protocol

This research project on sports reporting is being conducted by the Associate Director of the Centre for Rural Social Research.

The purpose of the research is to assess the extent of women's involvement in sport in rural areas and to examine the portrayal of women's sport in rural media. Sporting representatives will be interviewed in three different rural areas. They will be asked about women's involvement in their sport and about their perceptions of sports reporting. Media representatives will also be interviewed. Questionnaires will be used for the initial interviews. In-depth interviews will also be held with selected sporting representatives and media personnel. These will be taped, transcribed and analysed via computer.

In order to ensure confidentiality, no person will be identified on tape, and names will be changed where any reference is made to informants in the final report. Tapes will remain the property of the researcher and no other persons (other than the research assistant and the transcriber) will have access to the tapes.

Please note that, should you have any complaints about the conduct of the research, you may contact the Executive Officer, Ethics in Human Research Committee on 099 654321.

Consent Form
Research Project: Women and Sport in Rural Areas
Principal Investigator:
Dr Miranda Bloggs
Centre for Rural Social Research
099 654321

I am willing to participate in this research project. I understand that I am free to withdraw my participation in the research at any time.

The purpose of the research has been explained to me and I have been given the opportunity to ask questions about the research.

I understand that any information or personal details gathered in the course of this research about me are confidential and that neither my name nor any other identifying information will be used or published without my written permission.

I understand that if I have any complaints or concerns about this research I can contact the Executive Officer of the Ethics in Human Research Committee on 099 654321.

Signed:
Date:

questionnaires. At other times it is necessary to include a separate consent form with your covering letter, and to make sure that respondents have read it and signed it (that is, given their informed consent to participate in your study), before you proceed with any form of interview or questionnaire completion. Figures 6.1 and 6.2 contain examples of a cover letter and consent protocol.

What to include in your cover letter

- Official letterhead of sponsoring organisation
- Introduction to yourself and your role in the study
- What the survey is for and why it is important
- How the person was chosen and why their response is important
- Measures to protect confidentiality or anonymity (explain identifying number if using one)
- Right to refuse
- General information about the research procedure (whether they will be contacted again, who will interview them, reply dates, etc.)
- Contact phone number for further questions

Instructions

There are three types of instructions that you need to give when sending a mailed survey or conducting a structured interview. The *first type* involves general instructions about the whole survey. These are usually in the cover letter with the most important instructions sometimes repeated in an introductory paragraph at the beginning of the survey itself. General instructions include: who should complete the survey, how you want the questions answered and in what order, that there are no right and wrong answers, that all questions should be attempted and how to return the questionnaire by what date.

The *second type* of instructions introduce different parts of the survey. These instructions also act as signposts and punctuate the 'flow' of the questionnaire (for example, 'In this section you are asked to answer some background questions so that we will know how different people think about this issue'). Remember to thank respondents at the end of the survey and to provide a contact number for further questions or information, if this is possible.

The *third type* of instructions are specific guidelines to answering different questions (for example, 'Please tick the box which corresponds most closely to your employment situation at present. Choose one option only from the following list . . .').

Simple, clear instructions are vital to the success of your survey, both in relation to the accuracy of people's answers and also to the response rate. If people are confused about what is expected of them and the general reasons for it, they may give up and not return the survey at all, perhaps only partially complete it, or answer a different question from the one you intended. Figure 6.3 provides an example

---

Figure 6.3 Example of questionnaire (page 1 only)

QUESTIONNAIRE ON QUALITY OF LIFE

Introduction

This questionnaire deals with quality of life and access to education. You are asked questions about various areas of life including your housing, health, education, work, transport and leisure.

Most questions just require you to tick or circle the answer which applies to you. Please write 'don't know' if you do not know the answer to any question, and 'N/A' if it is not applicable. Leave blank any questions you do not wish to answer.

The information you provide is completely confidential. Only your postcode, age and gender are requested so that comparisons can be made between regions, age groups and men and women.

The questionnaire should take no more than half an hour of your time. Thank you for your assistance. The first section is about your housing and household.

Housing and Household

1. Is your home in a:
    ☐ City ☐ Large town ☐ Small town ☐ Isolated dwelling ☐ Other

2. Your postcode is: _____ (for regional comparisons)

3. Are you living in a:

☐ Caravan	☐ Flat/apartment	☐ Townhouse
☐ House	☐ Farm	☐ Hostel
☐ Institution	☐ Retirement village	☐ Boarding house
☐ College	☐ Nursing home	☐ Hospital
☐ Training facility	☐ Other (e.g. rehab centre) _____	

4. Please tick whether you own, rent, pay board for your home, or whether it is free:

☐ Owned by self/spouse	☐ Owned by self and others
☐ Privately rented	☐ Public rent: Department of Housing
☐ Rented through organisation	☐ Pay board to relatives
☐ Pay board to others	☐ Free
☐ Other_____	

5. How long have you lived here?
    _____ years _____ months

---

of the first page of a survey, showing introductory and specific instructions.

Questionnaire structure

Good questionnaires are structured similarly to good conversations. Initially it is important to establish rapport with the respondent by asking enjoyable, interesting questions which are not too difficult, challenging or personal. The researcher then 'takes the respondent by the hand' and guides them through a series of questions which are grouped into topics or sections, providing brief rationales and clear instructions as discussed. Thus, it is important that the sections or topics are meaningful, following a logical or sensible sequence, and that within each section, questions follow a logical order.

Usually it is best to move from concrete to abstract, from easy to hard, from simple to complex, from impersonal to more personal or sensitive questions. This allows respondents who may not have thought about issues in detail to think through the topic as they go. Respondents are more likely to answer personal questions, including background information such as age, gender, employment or marital status, if these arise further into the questionnaire when they have become more comfortable with the process.

It is important not to waste respondents' time by asking them questions which are irrelevant to their situation. Written surveys and structured interviews avoid this by using filter and contingency questions which direct respondents to other parts of the survey if a particular topic does not apply to them. These questions will be discussed in the next section.

Try to finish the interview or survey on a high note, leaving people feeling a little better than when they began the process. As most respondents volunteer their time to complete surveys or interviews, this is the least researchers can do. Asking people's advice about a particular topic and acknowledging their contribution are two ways to achieve this. Remember to thank them for participating. A reminder to post the questionnaire at the end of the last page is also a good idea.

Layout

In these days of computers and a discerning public, the layout and presentation of your questionnaire are increasingly important, especially for mailed surveys. It is now accepted that the presentation of your questionnaire, even down to the type of envelopes and colour of the paper, will affect your response rate. Paying attention to detail and presenting your survey as an important document that is worthy of the respondents' involvement (and also reflects the hard work you have put into it) has become a vital prerequisite for a successful survey.

Most researchers advise printing one side of each page only, because people often miss the second page on the back of another. Having only one side of the page printed also allows room for extra notes to be made on the blank side. Take advantage of the different fonts now available to distinguish between instructions and questions. Make sure that filter questions and instructions about where to go in the questionnaire can be seen at a glance. Space the questions so that the page does not look crowded, leaving adequate room for answers to open-ended questions. Also, remember to leave a column on one side of the page for computer coding.

Layout is not so important for interview schedules, as these are usually for the interviewer's eyes only. However, it is important to leave plenty of room for comments and, where possible, guides to directly computer-code the respondents' answers onto the form. Spacing needs to be clear so that interviewers can find their place easily. On interview schedules it is also possible to include extra suggestions about prompts and, in more qualitative, semi-structured interviews, probes to explore topics further.

Follow-up procedures

Whether interviewing or sending mailed questionnaires, you need to plan what to do in case of non-response. Many researchers label each of their mailed questionnaires with an identity number so that they can keep track of who has replied. Some researchers send a reminder postcard to all people in the sample a week after the survey was due, thanking those who replied and reminding those who have not. A week or so later, another copy of the questionnaire and a new cover letter is sent to non-respondents. Sometimes researchers also use follow-up reminder telephone calls. Of course, it is important to respect people's right not to participate in the study, and not to harass non-respondents who are actually refusals.

In the case of interviews, researchers often contact potential respondents by telephone soon after the initial letter or approach is made, to seek consent and arrange a time for the interview. Follow-up procedures for people who are not at home when the researcher calls, or who are not on the phone, also need to be planned.

Survey questions

Survey questions can be about *facts, knowledge, attitudes, beliefs, motivation, behaviour* and many other aspects of life. When formulating your questions, it is important to be clear which of these you wish to collect information about and word your questions accordingly.

Types of questions

Questions in surveys can be broadly divided into two categories: *open-ended* and *closed-ended*. In *closed-ended* questions, a range of answers are set out for the respondent: either a yes/no, or multiple choice, or a scale showing a range of responses. From the example of the government organisation providing income support in the previous chapter, some examples of closed-ended questions are provided.

Devising closed-ended questions is difficult and requires much work to make sure that a wide enough range of options is provided not to prejudice the results. Sometimes the options for closed-ended questions are created after extensive pretesting and pilot testing (see

Examples of closed-ended questions, including scaled questions

1 Please tick the box which describes the social security payments you were receiving when you first visited the office of the Department of Social Security:

Sole parent Pension ☐
Young Homeless Allowance ☐
Aged Pension ☐
Disability Support Payment ☐
Special Benefit ☐
Unemployment Benefit ☐
Other ☐
Not receiving payments at the time ☐

2 Please indicate how you felt about your first interview with departmental staff by circling a rating out of 5 for the following statements. On the scales, 1 = strongly disagree and 5 = strongly agree.

From my first interview at the Department of Social Security I would say:

a. staff listened carefully to what I had to say:

1_____2_____3_____4_____5
strongly   neutral   strongly
disagree   agree

b. staff acted as though I was lying:

1_____2_____3_____4_____5
strongly   neutral   strongly
disagree   agree

c. staff treated me with respect:

1_____2_____3_____4_____5
strongly   neutral   strongly
disagree   agree

d. staff attitudes need to improve:

1_____2_____3_____4_____5
strongly   neutral   strongly
disagree   agree

e. staff provided me with the information I required:

1_____2_____3_____4_____5
strongly   neutral   strongly
disagree   agree

f. staff understood my situation

1_____2_____3_____4_____5

strongly   neutral   strongly

disagree   agree

3   Were you told of your right to appeal decisions made by the Department during your first interview?

Yes   ☐

No   ☐

---

next section) and are based on the results from earlier open-ended questions. One advantage of closed-ended questions is that respondents may be more inclined to circle a point on a scale, or to tick a box, than to take the time to write sentences or comments, especially about sensitive issues. A disadvantage is that closed-ended questions could reflect the reality of the researcher rather than the people being researched.

When creating the options for closed-ended questions, three rules must be kept. First, the options listed must cover all the possibilities so that all respondents can choose an answer (thus, sets of options are said to be *exhaustive*). The second rule is that each category must not overlap with any other (this is called having categories which are *mutually exclusive*). Lastly, each set of categories should refer to only one dimension (this is called *unidimensionality*). For example, a scale referring to the agency's staff would *not* be: 'rude—aloof—courteous—punctual'. Note that when using scales it is best to alternate between positive and negative statements to avoid 'response bias' (respondents selecting answers in a set pattern).

Open-ended questions invite comments or opinions without anticipating the results. They are used extensively in qualitative research, especially in interviews. Open-ended questions in mailed surveys are best placed towards the end of the survey, and should be used sparingly as they require more time and effort on the part of the respondent than closed-ended questions. Prompts can be added to clarify open-ended questions in mailed surveys. In interviews, the interviewer can clarify, probe and prompt respondents about open-ended questions. The advantages of open-ended questions include that they make no assumptions about how the respondent will reply (allowing for surprises that you may not have anticipated), and that they provide much more scope for the respondent to express their thoughts and feelings.

Two other types of questions that are important in questionnaires are *filter questions* and *contingency questions*. These questions help respondents to avoid topics that do not apply to them and to move on to relevant parts of the questionnaire. In the income support

Examples of open-ended questions

1   What happened the first time you visited an agency office?

_____

_____

_____

2   Please describe how the staff behaved towards you during your first interview at the agency.

_____

_____

_____

3   How would you describe the attitude of agency staff towards you?

_____

_____

_____

agency survey a filter question might be: 'Do you have young children?' (followed by instructions such as: 'If yes, please answer the following questions, if no, please turn to Section Two of this questionnaire.') The contingency questions following the filter question might be about taking children into an agency office, for example: 'Would you feel comfortable taking your children with you to an interview at the agency?' 'Could you suggest improvements we could make so that our office is more friendly to parents and children?'

Tips on wording questions

- Use plain, simple English; avoid jargon, acronyms and initials
- Make questions as short as possible
- Be clear and avoid ambiguity (check the cultural meaning of terms as well)
- Avoid double-barrelled questions (e.g. ask about mother and father separately, not parents)
- Beware of leading questions (e.g. 'Wouldn't you agree that all people on the dole are lazy?')
- Beware of the word 'not' (avoid negatives, especially in closed-ended questions—they can be very confusing)

- Beware of artificially creating an opinion (allow for the options of 'don't know' or 'no opinion'. Use filter questions to check if people know about the topic you are researching)
- Decide if wording should be direct or indirect ('Have you ever been unemployed?' versus 'Please list your employment history.')
- Decide if wording should be personal or impersonal

Adapted from de Vaus (2002, pp. 97–9)

Steps in conducting your survey

There are several steps in designing a survey or questionnaire. Note that they overlap, and that many will be carried out concurrently. For example, as you design your sample you will also need to have in mind the method for your survey (mailed questionnaire, telephone interview or face-to-face interview) and your research topic. When you are constructing the survey and the questions you will ask, you will also be planning your data analysis.

1 Define the research topic

See chapters 2 and 3. Think about the problem, consult and read widely, formulate your research topic, decide on qualitative, quantitative or mixed design, formulate questions and hypotheses and operationally define variables (if quantitative).

2 Choose the research instrument

Decide on the form your survey will take. Will you choose to mail out a questionnaire, personally deliver the questionnaire to individuals or a group, conduct a telephone survey or undertake structured interviews? Your decision will rest upon the aims of your project, the resources at your disposal, the sample of people you aim to research, and the types of information you are seeking.

Generally if you are aiming to reach a large number of people and have well-thought-out research questions which have been operationalised into indicators, a mailed survey will be the most convenient and possibly most effective research instrument. On the other hand, for exploratory research on sensitive or complex issues, or for research with populations who have difficulty with written English, face-to-face interviews may be the most effective method. Telephone interviews can also be a useful strategy. Costing somewhere between interviews and mailed surveys, and allowing more flexibility than written surveys though less than face-to-face interviews, they are also well worth consideration. However, if doing telephone surveys, your questions must be kept simple unless you also mail people a copy of the questionnaire to look at during the interview. Another limitation of telephone interviews is that you will

Table 6.2   Comparison of three survey research instruments

	Mail survey	Telephone survey	Face-to-face interview
cost	lowest cost	middle cost	highest cost
response rate	lowest response rate	moderate response rate	highest response rate
coverage	reaches greatest number of people yet only those with good literacy skills and motivation respond	reaches respondents with poor literacy skills but only those who have telephones	reaches smaller numbers but wide range of people whether illiterate, low income, without phone
convenience	respondent can complete in own time, at own pace	can be completed quickly	time-consuming for interviewer and respondent
	quick results ready for computer entry	direct computer entry of results possible	more time-consuming to code and enter data
accuracy and type of information	visual layout can help comprehension	can clarify questions	can clarify questions, probe and prompt
	cannot clarify confusion, probe or prompt	limited opportunity to probe and prompt	can record nonverbal and other responses
	cannot check if right person answered the questions	misses nonverbal responses	can ensure the right respondent answers questions in right order
	cannot check if questions were answered in the right order	ensures questions answered in right order	interviewer may misrecord response
	partial response possible	can't always ensure the right person answers the questions	most likely that survey will be completed
	needs to be short to ensure response rate	more chance that survey is completed fully	allows for longer, more open-ended responses
	least chance of bias caused by interviewer attitudes, presence	must use simple questions moderate chance of interviewer bias	highest chance of interviewer bias
anonymity	highest level of anonymity/ confidentiality	less assurance of anonymity	less assurance of anonymity

only be able to interview people who have a telephone. As you can see from this very brief discussion, there are advantages and disadvantages of each method. These are summarised in Table 6.2.

3 Identify population and sample

Review chapter 5. In defining your population and the units of study, it is most important that you know who is included within the scope of your definitions—who is in and who is out. It can be easy to exclude people who should have been included and thus weaken the impact of your results. As you design your sample and work out sampling procedures, you will also be thinking about the most effective research method.

4 Construct draft questionnaire

Develop your questions, keeping in mind the objectives of your study and the research questions and indicators you have created as you operationalised your variables. As you work out the questions, you will also be thinking about how you will analyse the data you collect. *All* the variables you have come up with will need corresponding questions.

A good idea at this early stage is to draw up 'dummy tables' of the results you expect to get, to make sure that you are collecting the right information to explore the relationship between the variables that are most important for your study. Dummy tables are most helpful in explanatory research. They can assist you to think through whether your questions are at the right level of measurement, and have the right amount of detail, for the purposes of your study. Dummy tables are also useful in descriptive and exploratory research for checking that the questions you ask will provide the information you need to address your research questions.

Taking the income support agency example from the previous chapter, suppose that you want to know whether clients have different experiences of the agency depending on whether they live in the country or city. At this stage you are interested in whether the clients' experience was good, satisfactory or bad. In this case, it is implied that coming from the country or city will be the *independent* variable and clients' experiences the *dependent* variable. The first dummy table could look like this:

	Location	
	Rural	City
Experience at agency	%	%
Good		
Satisfactory		
Bad		
Total	100	100
	(n=)	(n=)

You will need to work out questions which measure whether respondents come from the country or city, and whether their experience of the agency is good, satisfactory or bad. The series of scales described in the section on question formulation can be transformed into a summary measure to suit this table.

Perhaps you suspect that the length of time people have been unemployed may also affect clients' treatment when they visit the agency's office. Length of time of unemployment would then be an 'interfering' or 'test' variable, because it may 'interfere' in the relationship you are investigating between living in the country or city and people's experience of the Department. The dummy table for the interfering variable 'length of time unemployed' could look like this:

Experience at agency	Long term unemployed		Short term unemployed	
	Rural %	City %	Rural %	City %
Good				
Satisfactory				
Bad				
Total	100 (n=)	100 (n=)	100 (n=)	100 (n=)

As well as including questions about all the variables you have devised for your research topic (*independent*, *dependent* and *interfering* or *test* variables in the case of explanatory research), surveys include questions on *background* information such as gender, age, education, employment, marital status and ethnic background, depending on the nature of the research. Such issues may affect the relationships you are investigating and also provide a baseline of information about the characteristics of your sample, which you can compare with the population you are studying. Generally you should include questions about these four types of variables in your draft questionnaire. At this draft stage, it is wise to have a few extra questions about each variable to try out during the next step of survey design.

Four aspects to include in questionnaire design

- Independent variables
- Dependent variables
- Interfering or test variables
- Background variables

---

5 Pretest questionnaire

Once you have your first draft of questions, including questions relating to each of the major variables and background variables, it is time to pretest your questionnaire. Try out sections of it, or the whole thing, on friends, family, colleagues, experts and non-experts in the area of your research, to see if the questions you have devised really elicit the information you want. Ask people if the questions could be improved and generally obtain as much feedback as possible.

This is one of the most important stages in the process. It can be very embarrassing to have the final version of the survey returned, only to find that the majority of respondents ticked the 'other' category for an important question. You would still be none the wiser as to what people thought about the issue! Thorough pretesting will help you to pick up such difficulties early in the process.

Pretesting also assists you to discard poorly worded or confusing questions, and questions which are repetitive or boring. During the pretest you may also discover that some of the language is offensive to the people you are researching. If so, change it immediately. It is important that only the most effective questions end up in the questionnaire, and that the survey itself is not too long, while covering the essential aspects of the topic.

6 Revise questionnaire

While you are pretesting the questionnaire on a wide range of people, revise it and make changes, testing the new or revised questions as you go. At the same time as you are pretesting the questionnaire, you will probably be working out how you will select your sample for the study. Once you are satisfied that the questions seem to work, and that you have drawn the sample you hope to interview or send the questionnaire to, it is time for the next step.

7 Pilot the questionnaire

This is an important stage, particularly for written questionnaires. To pilot the questionnaire, you literally give the survey a 'test run', under the same conditions in which you intend to conduct the whole survey. Thus, you use the sampling procedures you have worked out to try out the survey on a small group of respondents just as though it were the 'real thing'.

During the pilot you have the opportunity to fine-tune three main areas of the survey. *First*, you are checking the questionnaire design itself, including the wording of questions and scales, and the 'flow' of the questionnaire. *Second*, this is your chance to finalise field procedures, such as the number of call-backs you will make if the people you are interviewing are not at home when you call, or people do not respond to mailed surveys. The pilot may also allow you to gain an idea of how many refusals (to participate in your study) you can expect, and to form ground rules about how you will deal with this. Will you select a larger sample to begin with, to account for refusals? While all researchers would welcome a 100 per cent response rate, refusals indicate that respondents have genuinely been given a choice about being involved, and that those who do participate have given their informed consent. You also need to ensure that you only survey people once and don't double-count people in your sample. This can be a problem in large surveys or when you are constructing a sample from multiple lists of names, and is known as the issue of *coverage*.

Third, during the pilot you can test your definitions of population and sampling procedures to ensure that your sampling frame has allowed for all the people who should be included. You need to include enough cases in the pilot to cover the variability which exists in the total population. For example: Is the gender balance right? Is there provision for people from non-English speaking backgrounds to be included? Is the right age range covered? This is called attending to the *scope* of the survey. Often researchers nominate a referee (it could be your advisory committee) to make decisions about problems of scope and coverage.

Another function of the pilot can be to test your tools for data analysis and make sure the questions provide answers with the right level of detail and measurement for analytical purposes. Thus, you could use the data from the pilot to fill in the dummy tables and check if the information gained will be sufficient for the statistics you wish to perform. You also trial your coding procedures at this time.

During the period of the pilot test, training for interviewers often takes place, if there is to be more than one interviewer in your study. Feedback from interviewers during the pilot as to how the survey is received is invaluable. Many researchers devise evaluation sheets for their interviewers' comments during the pilot test (a survey within a survey!).

If the pilot test shows that there are only a few minor changes to be made (that is, if your pretesting was thorough enough), then you can keep your pilot test results to include in your data analysis. If major changes are made to the questionnaire or sampling procedures, however, you may not be able to include pilot results in your final data analysis.

8–11 Data collection, coding and data entry, data analysis and interpretation, publication

These last four steps are covered in chapters 12, 13, 14 and 15.

Further references on surveys are provided at the end of this chapter.

INTERVIEWS

As we have seen, interviews are more flexible research instruments than questionnaires. They can be used for a wide range of re-search purposes: from very structured settings (literally as 'spoken questionnaires') through to unstructured in-depth interviews, and for both quantitative and qualitative research designs. In this section we will examine some of the extra features of interviews that are different from surveys and provide some handy hints for conducting interviews. Note that many of the general principles identified for surveys, such as establishing rapport, and being clear about your expectations, also apply to interviews and will not be repeated in detail here. The chapter concludes with a brief look at focus groups and other types of group interviews.

THE CONTEXT OF SOCIAL WORK RESEARCH INTERVIEWS

Before discussing the various types of research interviews you could use, we raise some of the issues social workers must engage with when they are doing research interviews.

Your role as interviewer—researcher or social worker?

Social workers undertaking research interviews face an interesting lot of challenges—particularly if they are doing research as one of their work roles in an organisation in which they also do face-to-face or other client work. On one hand they can use their communication skills to assist interviewees to feel comfortable, to be open and to explore in depth their feelings about a research issue. On the other hand, social workers must be very careful how they use their skills so that they do not 'lead the witness' in any way.

Social workers interviewing people with whom they have other relationships (for example, clients, relatives of clients, colleagues, supervisees or supervisors) must be aware of the power and the political and ethical implications of their research and its effects on the people they are interviewing. If you have something your interviewee wants, such as access to resources, or if they just want to please you because you are their counsellor and they like you, they are likely to tell you what they think you want to hear rather than their actual opinion about an issue. This applies particularly to social workers attempting internal evaluations of their own services. In such cases other methods, such as anonymous questionnaires or using interviewers from outside your service who can guarantee some protection or privacy, are preferable to you doing your own interviews.

The ethical issues raised throughout this book are especially pertinent to social workers undertaking research interviews, particularly when they are in the dual roles of researcher and service provider. You must be sure that interviewees are not exposed to additional risks as a result of being part of the research. For example, how will you deal with a situation where an interviewee reveals something confidential during a research interview which directly impacts on whether they will continue to receive a service? In such cases the issues of privacy, confidentiality, protection from harm and informed consent are of paramount importance. It is part of your duty of care as both a social worker and a researcher to have thought through such issues well in advance and to have worked out strategies which will protect the interests of all the players. Many of these dilemmas can be solved in advance, particularly if representatives of the people you are interviewing are also involved in designing the research (for example, being on the advisory committee). Another important way of preventing the dilemmas arising in the first place is to develop clear role delineations with your supervisors about the separate roles of practitioner and researcher.

A related dilemma social work researchers face when they are interviewing people is drawing the line between helping and research roles during the interview. Of course, this dilemma is not limited to social work researchers! Researchers doing qualitative research, for example, talk of the times when the people they are interviewing become emotional about a topic, or it becomes obvious that they need some assistance or information that the interviewer has. At this point, you the interviewer may decide to 'turn off the tape' and switch roles, becoming a social worker for a while, then returning to the research interview when it is appropriate. If such a situation arises, it is important to be clear with your interviewee what you are doing and what role you are undertaking at the time.

Researching sensitive issues

Most social work research which is relevant involves sensitive issues. Usually these issues affect the people you interview, so the communication skills you have as a professional are particularly important. Just as we noted for surveys, it is best to locate discussion of sensitive issues around the middle of an interview. This gives you and the interviewee time to develop some trust and rapport to be able to discuss such topics, and also allows time for you to deal with any unexpected outcomes.

It would be disastrous to raise an emotionally laden topic towards the end of an interview, then finish abruptly leaving the interviewee distressed. Remember that as most research participants are voluntary, the least you can do is leave them feeling a little better at the end of the interview than they did at the beginning.

Diversity and interviewees in social work research

Because social work directs much of its effort towards improving conditions for people who are disadvantaged and disempowered, it is to be hoped that much of your research will include people from a wide range of backgrounds. An essential social work skill which is also a research skill is the ability to work with a diverse range of people, including people who come from different backgrounds from your own.

While we mention various aspects relating to differences between interviewers and interviewees throughout the rest of this chapter, we thought it would be useful to include a checklist of 'respectful communication' hints. This checklist was devised by Cindy Lesley, an indigenous advocate for people with disabilities. Originally created as a tool for teaching students how to enter indigenous communities and work with indigenous people with disabilities, it is also useful as a checklist for respectful communication generally. It is relevant to situations in which the people you are interviewing are different from you and may have different assumptions about the world, and/or ways of talking about things. This includes differences such as culture, language, disability, sexual preference, age or gender. You will notice that it is as much about homework and preparing for the interview beforehand, as it is about your behaviour during the interview itself.

Guidelines for interviewing people from backgrounds different from your own.

Note: As each situation is different, this is a list of questions and things to be aware of, rather than rules!

When entering a new community
- Know the country/community you are visiting.
- How do the people of the community refer to themselves?
- Do you have permission to enter the community?

Dress sense
- What is respectful and appropriate dress for this community?
- As a general rule, don't wear glitz and glitter—usually basic wear causes less offence.
- Do not wear clothes that could be seen as sexually provocative.

Non-verbal communication skills
- Find out what is appropriate: should you use eye contact or not? How is other body language used (for example, head gestures)?
- What is respectful nonverbal communication?

Verbal communication
When people are from non-English speaking backgrounds

(including deaf people using sign language), or have learning disabilities, it is important to:

- Use an interpreter whenever possible.
- Speak in plain English.
- Use minimal written material unless in the person's language.
- Use simple words without being patronising.
- Find out about and use respectful verbal communication.

Concepts and language about sensitive concepts

- Build trust and rapport before launching into delicate issues.
- What words do people use about concepts such as 'disability' or 'poverty'?
- How do they refer to these concepts within their community?
- Do you need to go around the issue rather than ask directly?

Gender

- What are the usual rules for speaking with people from your own and different genders?
- Do you need to take special measures in this community as a result of your gender?

Cindy Lesley, Northwest Regional Advocate, Disability Service Aboriginal Corporation, personal communication (2002).

Structured interviews

Structured interviews are usually questionnaires which are conducted by an interviewer. In the strictest quantitative tradition, interviewers working with quantitative interview schedules try to use exactly the same wording, prompts and tone of voice for each interview, to ensure that every interview is conducted as similarly as possible. Nowadays computer interviews provide the closest approximation to this ideal. In an interview situation with two human beings involved, it is virtually impossible to make each interview the same. This has its advantages, even in quantitative designs. The added flexibility of an interview allows misunderstandings to be clarified, and enables the researcher to ensure that the right person answers the questions in the right order. None of these advantages are available in mailed questionnaires.

The general rules for structured interviews follow the same principles as for questionnaires. Go over the section on surveys carefully if you are planning a structured interview as your research instrument. Depending on the design of the study, it is often possible to include more open-ended questions in structured interviews than in mailed questionnaires, as the interviewer can prompt the respondent, probe for more information, and clarify what the questions mean.

Structured interviews can also be longer than mailed surveys, as respondents will be more motivated to talk with interviewers than to complete lengthy pen and paper exercises, and there is less concentration involved if the interviewer is recording the answers.

Semi-structured interviews

As their name implies, semi-structured interviews fall somewhere between structured and in-depth interviews. Usually semi-structured interviews follow a set outline of topics with some pretested questions and prompts in each section. These are the triggers for the main directions of the interview and interviewers are mostly required to at least ask the questions on the schedule as they appear. However, having asked a particular question and recorded the answer/s, the interviewer is often allowed to explore additional information that the respondent has raised, to ask other questions, or to follow up issues that were not originally included in the interview schedule.

Thus, the interviewer is allowed more initiative and has more ability to respond to the perceptions and priorities of the respondent. Semi-structured interviews vary enormously in the degree of structure and amount of initiative which is given to the interviewer. They can be ideal research instruments for exploratory and descriptive designs in which the researcher is finding out about a topic and/or has little prior knowledge of what the respondents think about it. Skilled interviewers are needed for semi-structured interviews because so much depends on the interviewer's ability to pick up, explore and accurately record additional information.

Typically, semi-structured interview schedules contain many open-ended questions, with lots of suggestions for prompts and probes. Probes can include *summary techniques*, in which you summarise what the person has said (checking that you understood in the process) and *controlled non-directive probing* (Sarantakos 1998, p. 263) in which you ask further questions (for example, 'Can you tell me more about that?', 'What do you mean?', 'Can you give me an example?'). It is important to leave plenty of room on the page under appropriate headings for the extra information interviewers may collect. Sometimes semi-structured interviews are audio-recorded but, due to the costs of transcription, it is more usual for the interviewers to record the responses on the interview schedule.

Interviewers using a semi-structured approach need careful training about the aims of the research and the stance of the researcher, and to be skilled in interviewing techniques. The gender, age, class and ethnicity of interviewers can heavily influence how the respondent answers questions. This is more of an issue in face-to-face interviews than in mailed surveys or telephone interviews in which the characteristics of the interviewer may not be as obvious. Sometimes feminist and other researchers deliberately match such interviewer characteristics with respondents, believing that respondents will be more open and honest with interviewers who are similar to themselves. This is an area of debate, as other feminist researchers believe that respondents are more likely to be honest with strangers or people who are different from them.

Depending on the ideology of the researcher, the ability of the interviewer to maintain 'objectivity' or 'neutrality' is considered to be more or less important, and more or less possible (see chapter 1). Whatever the researcher's position on this, throughout the process of data collection regular checks with interviewers are needed to keep track of how the interview process is developing. After a few interviews it can be tempting for different interviewers to develop their own hypotheses about the topic, which they may indirectly 'suggest' to respondents. In some designs this may be acceptable and even encouraged and shared with other interviewers, in others not. In any case the researcher should be aware of what is happening and be guiding the overall process. One way of achieving this is by holding regular group meetings with the interviewers during which they discuss how the interviews are going.

In-depth interviews

In-depth interviews are the most flexible type of research instrument and are used in qualitative research. Generally the researcher/s conduct in-depth interviews themselves rather than employing other interviewers. This is because the quality of data collected depends so much on the skill of the interviewer and their developing understanding of the issues which they are researching. Whereas semi-structured interviews include many open-ended questions, in-depth interviews are often seen as being more of a discussion, and ideally are guided by the respondent rather than the interviewer.

Some feminist researchers try to develop an 'equal' relationship with the people they are interviewing, rather than the traditional relationship of 'expert researcher' interviewing a subject or respondent. These researchers may include personal self-disclosure, provide information and answer questions as part of the discussion process. They may also conduct multiple interviews with respondents, using subsequent interviews to check the accuracy of their impressions and information, and to discuss the results and their meaning. Such researchers see themselves as being in partnership with the respondents (also called 'participants') and may make conscious efforts to share control and ownership of the research process and results with them.

The structure of in-depth interviews depends on the nature of the topic, the context of the interview and the personality and skills of the researcher and the respondent. Although at one end of the spectrum of in-depth interviews it is theoretically possible to begin with absolutely no structure other than a general topic, most researchers arrive at in-depth interviews with a number of topics or areas that they wish to cover and a loose structure for how they anticipate the interview unfolding. This enables some comparison of what different respondents think about the same issues. It is also important, for ethical reasons, to be able to foreshadow the general content of the interview and the way it will be conducted, in order for the respondent to give their informed consent to the research.

During an in-depth interview and in follow-up interviews, new issues which emerge can be fully explored. The aim of an in-depth interview is to see the world from the eyes of the respondent as much as possible, to explore with them their thoughts and feelings and to thoroughly understand their point of view. Whatever structure is planned before the interview is less important than capturing the 'reality' of the person being interviewed, including their own language and use of words.

A critical skill in in-depth interviewing is the ability to establish a relationship with the respondent in which they feel free to openly express their inner thoughts and feelings. The social work skill of demonstrating *empathy*, in which the person being interviewed feels heard, accepted and understood, is vital to in-depth interviewing. Empathy is a complex skill which involves the researcher's own characteristics (age, gender, socioeconomic status, etc.) as well as learned communication skills. As Reinharz (1992, p. 26) has commented: 'every aspect of the researcher's identity can impede or enhance empathy'. Communication skills involved in empathy include attending to the respondent's verbal and non-verbal messages, displaying attentive, respectful listening, and accurately reflecting back the content and feeling of what has been said, including the 'message beneath the message'. Accurate empathic listening is a powerful way to help respondents clarify what they think and feel, to explore it in more detail and to become more specific. Empathy can be built up over several interviews.

Generally, due to their flexibility and the huge amount of information which is collected (typically an interview will last from one to three hours), in-depth interviews are audiotaped by the interviewer. This allows the interviewer to focus on the respondent and the interview process, rather than having to attempt to record data at the same time. Questions have been raised about the effects of the microphone on the respondent and the data collected. In reply, qualitative researchers maintain that they have effective techniques for overcoming reticence on the part of the respondent, and that once the interview is underway most people forget about the microphone.

Clearly, given the nature of in-depth interviews, the researcher must have exceptionally good interviewing skills, a highly developed theoretical understanding of research methodology, and considerable experience in this method before they attempt it without close supervision. Researchers using in-depth interviews can experience high levels of stress, which can adversely affect the quality of the data they collect. For example, some researchers find themselves avoiding painful issues with respondents, cutting them off with comments such as 'I know what you mean' because they cannot cope with the distress or painful nature of the material being discussed. Interviewers must be aware of their own sensitivities and responses, and how these are affecting the interview process, if they wish to use in-depth interview techniques.

This section on interviews concludes with a list of 'handy hints' for interviewers. These hints apply to all forms of interviews, although obviously some will be more important in structured, and others in unstructured, formats.

Handy hints for interviewers

Arranging the interview
Send introductory letter covering the same issues as for a survey cover letter. Follow up with a phone call. Sometimes you need to obtain prior written consent before further contact; sometimes a phone call is made to explain the purpose of the research, obtain consent and organise the interview. Make sure that interviewer and respondent are clear about the place, time, purpose and approximate length of the interview, and that these are at the respondent's convenience. Try to organise a time and place that will be private and have minimum interruptions.

Beginning the interview
Dress in a culturally appropriate manner to show respect and avoid offence. Introduce yourself. Begin with a clear (re)statement of purpose, time frame, general outline of process and content of interview, confidentiality precautions. Make sure appropriate consents have been signed, including the way in which the data will be recorded (notes, tape-recording, video, etc.). Establish rapport, perhaps begin with some small talk. Same principles as for surveys: easy, interesting questions assist in developing motivation and trust at the beginning of an interview.

During the interview
Be sensitive to respondent's state of mind. You have an ethical duty of care not to upset or cause distress to respondents. Have open-ended questions, prompts and probes prepared. Place difficult or potentially sensitive questions in the middle of the

---

interview so that there is time to deal with any repercussions before the end of the interview time.

Closing the interview
Finish on a high note. Clarify permission for follow-up procedures, further interviews, call-backs, etc. Tell the respondent how they can contact the researcher for more information, or for anything further they wish to say. Arrange for other follow-up such as results to be sent. Don't make promises you can't keep. Thank the respondent.

Focus groups

Interviews can also be conducted with groups of people. Focus groups are groups that parallel the range of interviews, from semi-structured to in-depth interviews. Structured interviews are also often administered in groups, but these are not focus groups because the role of the interviewer is to administer the questions on the questionnaire, and the role of the respondents is to answer the questions as presented.

In focus groups the researcher is usually prepared with some structure, a list of topics and trigger questions, but also aims to use the group discussion to explore the topic further. People in the focus group are often specially chosen because of their interest, involvement or knowledge in relation to the research issue. The group process during the discussion allows people to develop their ideas with each other, and to 'brainstorm' different options or opinions. With skilled facilitation, focus groups can come up with ideas and solutions which none of the individual members had thought about beforehand. Focus groups can be an economical means of gathering data. On the one hand, they can produce creative ideas; on the other, 'group think' can operate so that individual members feel afraid to voice their true opinions and diversity is lost. Much depends on the skill of the group facilitator.

Summary

In this chapter we have considered a range of research tools, beginning with more structured quantitative surveys and moving through a range of research formats, finishing with in-depth interviews. The advantages and disadvantages of each method have been discussed, along with key techniques and handy hints. Of course, it is possible to mix these methods. Combining methods, if approached thoughtfully, can lead to much better results. For example, focus groups can be used following individual in-depth interviews to report back results and discuss their meaning. Your choice of research tool will largely depend on the topic, the design of your study and the type of sample you are using.

QUESTIONS

1 What are the three types of instructions that are used in surveys?
2 What are the two broadest categories of questions in survey research? Give examples of each.
3 What is wrong with the following questions?
   (a) Please tick the box which corresponds most closely to your marital status:

Single	☐
Married	☐
Living alone	☐
Cohabiting with a partner	☐
Other	☐

   (b) Please indicate your opinion of the government's actions to cut interest rates on the following scale:

1	2	3
bad	very bad	terrible

   (c) Wouldn't you agree that the savage beating of innocent children should be punished by more than a 'holiday at the taxpayers' expense' (i.e. prison)?

Yes	☐
No	☐

   (d) When you last visited a police station, was the duty officer polite and did he or she deal with your request to your satisfaction?
4 List four advantages/disadvantages comparing mailed questionnaires, telephone interviews and structured interviews as methods of conducting surveys.
5 What is the difference between a pretest and a pilot test?
6 When would you use structured compared to in-depth interviews?
7 How would you record information from an in-depth interview?
8 What are some of the differences between semi-structured and in-depth interviews?
9 Give some examples of non-directive probes which could be used in interviews.
10 List some of the ways in which you could establish rapport with an interviewee.
11 What is empathy? In which types of interview is it most frequently used? What is its purpose?

Exercises

1 Devise a questionnaire to examine the influence of media on the body image of teenagers. Assuming that this is an explanatory study, write questions around the following variables:
   - Dependent variable
   - Independent variable
   - Interfering or test variables
   - Background variables

   Include examples of open, closed and scaled questions and at least one example of a filter and contingent question.
2 List some strategies for pretesting this questionnaire.
3 Draw some dummy tables to show the relationships you are investigating.
4 Write a cover letter of no more than one page, including the aspects listed on page 99.
5 How will you pilot this survey?
6 What ethical issues are raised in this study?

Further Reading

Alreck, P. L. & Settle, R. B. 1995, *The Survey Research Handbook*, 2nd edn, Irwin, Burr Ridge, Ill. Chapter 6 offers a comprehensive guide to contstructing questionnaires.

Babbie, E. 1990, *Survey Research Methods*, 2nd edn, Wadsworth, California. See Chapters 7 and 9 on surveys, and chapter 10 on interview surveys.

Berg, B. L. 1995, *Qualitative Research Methods for the Social Sciences*, 2nd edn, Allyn & Bacon, Boston. Chapter 3 is a thorough treatment of qualitative interviews.

de Vaus, D. A. 2002, *Surveys in Social Research*, 5th edn, Allen & Unwin, Sydney. Chapters 7 and 8 provide an excellent guide to designing and administering questionnaires.

McMurty, S. L. 1993, 'Survey research', in *Social Work Research and Evaluation*, R. M. Grinnell Jr (ed.), 4th edn, Peacock Publishers, Itasca, Ill. Chapter 13 provides a comprehensive coverage of surveys.

Rogers, G. & Bouey, E. 1996, 'Phase two: collecting your data', in *Qualitative Research for Social Workers*, L. M. Tutty, M. A. Rothery & R. M. Grinnell Jr (eds), 4th edn, Allyn & Bacon, Boston. Offers a detailed account of qualitative interviews from structured through to unstructured interviews.

Sarantakos, S. 1998, *Social Research*, 2nd edn, Macmillan, Melbourne. Chapters 10 and 11 cover surveys and interviews in qualitative and/or quantitative designs.

7 NEEDS IDENTIFICATION AND ANALYSIS

In this and the following four chapters, we introduce you to methods that will be useful for you as a social work practitioner. We begin with needs identification and analysis. Part of your role as a community social worker may be to identify the needs of your community or target group, and to analyse and rank these needs with a view to determining gaps in service provision. While needs identification and analysis can be seen as a legitimate research activity in its own right, it can be viewed as a first stage in a five-step process of program evaluation. While program evaluation is discussed more fully in the next chapter, you should be aware that needs identification and analysis leads to the development of new programs or the overhaul of existing programs and services which may be further evaluated using the strategies discussed in chapter 8.

Before we attempt to define needs analysis, you should also note that the process of identifying and analysing needs is an implicitly value-laden and non-objective task that has the potential to disempower the very group or community for whom you are working. Providing a needs analysis implies that you, as a professional, have made a value judgement that a group has an inadequate service or a less than acceptable standard of wellbeing. As Ife (1995, p. 67) notes: 'A statement of need, then is both a narrative and a descriptive statement reflecting both the values/ideology and knowledge/expertise of the said definer'. He uses the example of a community with a high rate of juvenile delinquency and crime. A professional may define this as a 'need' for more policing whereas the community may wish to examine the cause of youth alienation. In conducting an examination of needs, then, you must be conscious that a statement of need is a judgement laden with ideological and political notions and that any identification of need should be informed by community consultation.

While social justice and values of fairness and equity should drive your analysis, be equally conscious of the potential to empower the community or group with whom you are working to define their own needs. As a community social worker, you should assist the process of allowing the community or group to ultimately define and structure their own needs. As Ife (1995, p. 225) points out, 'neither need assessment nor evaluation should themselves be defined as community work roles. Rather they are tasks for the community, and the community worker will simply facilitate the process.'

WHAT IS NEEDS IDENTIFICATION AND NEEDS ANALYSIS?

The ad hoc development of health and social services as a result of interest group lobbying, changing political priorities and an inadequate coordination of services has resulted in uneven levels of service delivery in many communities. An analysis of needs and services may be necessary to focus on an improved level of service for a particular community or group. *Need identification* is a process of identifying health and social service requirements in a geographic and social arena, whereas *needs analysis* is a process of prioritising the identified needs. This implies a two-stage process where we (in conjunction with the community or group) identify the needs and then make a value judgement about the priority of needs.

What is needs identification and analysis?

Needs identification is about collecting information about the needs of the community in order to plan for improved service delivery. Needs analysis is about evaluating and ranking those needs. Information collected will help determine:

- The nature and characteristics of the community/group
- Whether current services and initiatives are responding appropriately
- Where there is a gap in services
- Where new services are necessary to remove an existing health/service inequity

---

- What environmental changes are necessary to improve health and quality of life
- How community structures are affecting health, quality of life and service delivery
- The need for community development

Adapted from South Australian Community Health Research Unit, *Planning Healthy Communities: A Guide to Doing Community Needs Assessment*, Flinders Press, Adelaide (1991).

What do we mean by need?

To adequately identify and assess need, we must understand what it is we mean by need, and be aware that this will differ depending on who is defining need. The typology developed by Bradshaw (1977) is important in any discussion and definition of needs. He describes four types of need: *normative need*, which is the standard or expected need defined by professionals or others in authority; *felt need*, which is the 'wish list' of the target group and which equates with want; *expressed need*, which is the need of the target population expressed overtly in some form (for example, waiting lists for services); and *comparative need*, which is the need of the community or group determined through comparison with other communities or similar groups or national or state norms.

As you can see from this typology, need can be defined differently by professionals/experts (normative and comparative) and by the community (felt and expressed). Expert opinion may be misleading because it is not based on lived experience and is limited by the perspective of the expert. However, it may provide a broader view of need. Community opinion, on the other hand, will be grounded in experience but may also be unrealistic and self-serving. In any needs analysis project you should incorporate the different levels of need. Your ultimate aim is to work towards a *convergent needs analysis*, which is a comprehensive assessment of all four levels of need.

Why do we conduct a needs assessment?

Needs assessments are important for adequate planning because:

- They assess the needs of the community and, by providing a 'snapshot' of the community's needs, empower the community to seek action
- They determine if services exist
- They allow us to advocate for change and provide information about gaps in service
- They determine if enough potential clients justify a new service

- They determine who uses existing services
- They determine what barriers to service use exist
- They allow an informed allocation of resources, policy formulation and planning of services
- They assist us to evaluate whether our service is responding effectively to community needs
- They document the existence of ongoing social problems (Marlow, 1998)

Additionally, a needs assessment allows us to work for change, secure in the knowledge that we are responding to the community's needs. If the motivation for conducting the analysis has been to support or sustain a political cause rather than to bring about needed change, you should re-examine your motivation. We would caution you about the more dubious reasons for conducting a needs analysis. These include:

- Using the research as a delaying action to stall opposition
- Doing the research to use up available funds rather than from any serious motivation to assess needs
- To copy what someone in a similar position in another community is doing
- Conducting the research simply because there are experts available to assist
- To prove what everyone already knows
- As a ticket to legitimacy in our profession (South Australian Community Research Unit 1991, pp. 18–19)

Needs analysis should be motivated by a desire to empower the community and to better target resources.

Why do we conduct needs analysis?

Appropriate reasons:

- To assess community/group needs
- To empower the community/group
- To advocate for change
- To assess gaps in service
- To assist allocation of resources, policy formulation and planning
- To evaluate how effectively services are responding to community needs
- To determine barriers to effective services

Dubious reasons:

- As a delaying action

- To use up funds
- Because someone else is doing one
- Because there are experts available
- To prove what everyone knows
- As a ticket to legitimacy

Adapted from South Australian Community Health Research Unit, *Planning Healthy Communities: A Guide to Doing Community Needs Assessment*, Flinders Press, Adelaide (1991)

BEFORE YOU BEGIN

Because there is no set formula or guide to conducting a needs analysis, you must start with basic issues in order to establish what it is you wish to know and what is the most feasible way to gather that information. Your design is necessarily constrained by the resources available to you (including your time), so your methods of gathering information must fit the available funds and staff resources. Determine what resources are available to you before you design your analysis. With community involvement in your project you may be able to count on extra resourcing and help. Your first task should be to draw together a steering committee (as recommended in chapter 2) that is representative of the community, service providers and funding bodies. It is important that the community 'owns' the data produced in the needs analysis process and is therefore represented on any committee which is deciding appropriate designs of services. This committee should decide early what it is they wish to know and why, and what will become of the data.

Before you design your needs analysis, carefully assess available services—the criteria for clients to be accepted, service capacities and whether the services are locally relevant. Social plans done by local government authorities are excellent places to begin your data collection. Seek advice from others about the important issues and identify existing community strengths. This inventory of resources allows you to analyse the services currently available to the target population, who is providing them, which services are under-utilised and where gaps exist.

When you conduct a needs analysis, it is important that you assess the problem in question carefully before looking into a determination of solutions. A lack of services for the aged or the disabled does not necessarily imply a need for more residential nursing homes. Similarly, lack of services for carers of HIV/AIDS sufferers may not necessarily call for more respite services. What you should do is determine what services would *best* afford the frail aged, the disabled and carers an improved quality of life. Before you begin, then, assess and clarify the problem as defined not only by service providers but also by the target population.

Ethical considerations must be acknowledged before commencing your analysis. These include the need to ensure confidentiality for informants and the need to gain permission from agencies to examine client records if these are to be used for gathering information. In most agencies or departments you will be required to submit your needs analysis proposal to the research ethics committee for approval. Your research plan should be comprehensive, taking account of resource and time restrictions. Consequently, it will include a detailed time line that allows the steering committee and the community to understand the time commitment expected and the approximate time when findings will be released. It will also include an outline of methods and a list of responsibilities of staff and project personnel. The final step before you begin gathering data is to conduct a detailed literature review to ascertain what information is already available, where other studies have been undertaken and how these results might influence your study.

Before you begin

- Determine what resources (time, staff and funding) are available
- Draw on community resources
- Establish a steering committee
- Assess available services
- Clarify the problem in consultation with the target population
- Be conscious of ethical concerns
- Submit a proposal to the ethics committee
- Draw up a research plan (including a time line)
- Conduct a literature review

Case study one—needs of people living with HIV/AIDS

In 1995, the AIDS Council of New South Wales [Australia], Illawarra Branch, conducted a needs analysis in order to 'investigate, develop and evaluate support and education services to the HIV positive community in the Illawarra and Shoalhaven'. The project team was particularly concerned to ensure that the target group had greater access to, and a better quality of, services. They were also seeking to improve the network of support among the target group members. The team was particularly concerned 'to facilitate communities empowering themselves' and so 'the direction of the project is determined by the consumers and not by the experts'. In adopting this stance, the team ensured that the target group controlled the project and were involved from the beginning.

A Steering Committee was established and included target group representatives, service providers, a local doctor, a representative of the carers' association and a representative of the funding body. The Committee's first three meetings were spent clarifying the problems and deciding on appropriate information gathering techniques. A literature review revealed that major issues of concern were confidentiality, privacy and fear of discrimination. Further problems for the target group related to isolation, lack of transport, a limited choice of services, problems for carers and perceived attitudes of workers.

Andrée Marie and Frank Vellozzi 1995, *United Views Building a Stronger Community: HIV Community Development Project Needs Assessment Report*, Aids Council of New South Wales, Illawarra Branch, Wollongong, NSW.

Case study two—the needs of young people

In 1991, two social work students on placement with the Adult & Family Mental Health Team in a Sydney suburb were assigned the task of conducting a needs analysis of young people in the shire. The needs analysis was prompted by media reports of the high rate of youth suicide in the shire. The aims of the project were: to determine the dimensions of the problem and whether the shire had higher rates than other similar shires; to determine how to 'recognise a potentially suicidal person'; to investigate available services and gaps in service delivery; and to examine possible preventative methods.

The students devised their own plan to gather information in consultation with their superiors. A detailed literature review documented risk factors, external contributing factors, internal contributing factors and precipitating factors. Risk factors included psychiatric illness, previous suicide attempts, depression and drug/alcohol abuse and anti-social behaviour patterns. External contributing factors were revealed as a family history of suicide, exposure to another's suicide, a family history of depression, physical/sexual/emotional abuse, family discord, permissive or authoritarian parents, class factors, sibling rivalry and the lack of an extended family. Internal contributing factors included hopelessness, romanticisation of death and problems of sexuality. Finally, precipitating factors were listed as loss, unemployment, unwanted pregnancy or abortion.

University of NSW 1991, *Suicide Prevention: Sutherland Shire Needs Analysis Report*, Southern Sydney Area Health Service Health Promotion Unit, Sutherland Hospital & Health Service, State Health Publication Number (SSAHS) 91–108, Sutherland, NSW.

CONDUCTING A NEEDS ANALYSIS

When devising a plan to conduct a needs analysis you would do well to revisit Bradshaw's (1977) typology of needs discussed earlier in this chapter. In any assessment of need we should attempt to examine normative, felt, expressed and comparative levels of need. If we neglect any significant area, our results will not provide a comprehensive analysis. This section will examine methods of gathering information under three different groupings: *social indicators analysis, social area surveys* and *community group approaches* (Seigel, Attkisson & Carson 1987).

Social indicator analysis

In order to understand the nature of your target group, social indicators are used to give an overall picture of the population, its characteristics, the size of the target group in relation to the general population, the size of the potential at-risk categories and, consequently, the potential service users. Social indicators, which are available at local, state and national level, can also be used to investigate historical trends and population changes. The most accessible form of social indicator is the national census records, which can be broken down to regional level, to reveal demographic details such as age composition, ethnicity, gender, occupation, income levels, education, marital status and religion. Other types of accessible records include police crime and local court statistics, Bureau of Statistics' information on special groups, health department indicators, local government social plans and other government statistics. Government departments at local, state and national level have records and reports containing vast amounts of quantitative information which may assist you to develop an understanding of the nature of your target group. Social indicators are a useful first step in analysing your community and in identifying characteristics of the target population. This data can be used to determine risk factors within your group that may provide a preliminary indication of the potential use of services at the local level. For example, if your service deals with young people under 18 who are unemployed, social indicator analysis of census material will give you the size of this target population in your community. Members of this group are all potential users of your service.

Social indicator analysis can also be used to compare regions or communities with others to determine area variations and target group variations. This information is useful when comparing different levels of service delivery.

While social indicators provide valuable background research information, you should note that such information should be carefully scrutinised for reliability and validity. In Australia, for example, census material is collected every five years and may quickly become dated, particularly if your community has a high transient population. Also be aware that people may not be entirely accurate with the information they provide. On examination of census data from an isolated rural area of Australia, Margaret Alston noted that 6 per cent of the population had claimed that they travelled to work each day by tram. As the nearest tram was 500 kilometres away, we realised that much of the data should be treated with caution! Be cognisant of the purposes for which the data you are examining was collected. This may influence what is reported and, more importantly, what is not. Be cautious if you are relying on this information to tell you if there are enough clients for a potential new service. You should also note that social indicator analysis helps you outline the problems in a community but does nothing to assist with the development of solutions.

Social indicator analysis

Sources: census, government departments (national, state and local), police and court records.

Outlines:

- Population characteristics
- Target group size
- Characteristics of target group
- Comparisons between regions and communities
- Historical trends
- Size of potential service users

Social area surveys

Social area surveys are used to determine felt and expressed levels of need. These techniques are useful in estimating which of a range of possible solutions or services may be the most appropriate. By analysing existing services and the client demand for a range of given services, you are able to determine a desirable range of service delivery. Social area surveys include an analysis of the demand for services, an examination of the resourcing of existing services and surveys of clients.

Demand for services

In assessing needs in a particular community or target group, it is important to examine the range of existing services to ascertain: what services exist; existing service use; services which are popular; the level of inter-agency cooperation; where there is any overlapping of services and gaps in service delivery. This information is best gathered from service providers, management committee members and from agency records that may reveal historical trends in service use. Such data may be collected by interview or survey with agency personnel.

Analysis of service resources

A thorough community needs analysis will fully examine the extent of available community resources in an endeavour to provide a comprehensive human services directory for the community being examined. Information gathered from agencies will include staffing levels, ranges of services provided, client profile data, number of referrals, size of waiting lists, accessibility and availability of services and the extent of inter-agency cooperation (Seigel, Attkisson & Carson 1987, pp. 82–3). This information is used in conjunction with other assessments of need to determine the effectiveness of current services in meeting identified needs. Service resource information can usefully be gathered through interviews or through surveys of agency personnel.

Community surveys

While demand for services and analysis of agency resources are useful ways of examining the expressed needs of a community, community surveys will elicit further information about *felt* needs and about ongoing social problems. These surveys may be either random community surveys or surveys targeted specifically at an identified target group, and are designed to determine the level of need. Commmunity surveys may be conducted as mail surveys, personally administered surveys or by interview. In each case, you will need to carefully select a representative sample of the target

Table 7.1   Client users of family services program

	Clients	Census population
Clients using the service during a 12-month period	783	
Female clients	564 (72%)	51%
Clients from non-English speaking backgrounds	32 (4%)	28%
Indigenous clients	25 (3%)	19%
Low income clients	595 (76%)	28%
Aged clients	89 (11%)	15%

group. Reread chapter 5 on sampling and chapter 6 on surveys and interviews before you conduct a community survey.

Barriers

Social area surveys elicit information about the demand for, and extent of, services and the level of felt need in the community. When compared with data from social indicator analysis, this information may reveal discrepancies between the potential service users and actual service users. Consider Table 7.1, which outlines the service users of our fictitious family services program and compares this data with population statistics.

You will note from the table that the client base of the service is skewed towards women from low-income families. By comparison with the population statistics, the service is not good at reaching indigenous clients, clients from non-English speaking backgrounds and aged people. As a result of this information you may wish to examine the barriers preventing others from using the service. It may be that those on higher incomes do not realise they are eligible for assistance; there may be language barriers; transport may be a problem given the location of the service. The service may be too expensive and have long delays, making it less desirable. Additional problems may be the times and availability of the service, a lack of awareness that the service exists and even a lack of acceptability of the service because of its philosophy or service delivery style. This type of information is important in assessing who uses the service and in alerting you to potential barriers to service use.

Of course, you might also directly seek information from the community about the barriers as they perceive and experience them. In any case, your needs analysis should isolate factors which are barriers to service accessibility.

Social area surveys

- Demand for services
- Analysis of service resources

- Community surveys

Methods: interviews or surveys with agency personnel, management committee members, workers and community residents.

Determines:
- Services available
- Service use
- Interagency cooperation
- Overlap of services
- Gaps in service delivery
- Agency profiles
- Felt need
- Barriers to service use

Case study one—people living with HIV/AIDS

The Illawarra AIDS Council decided to conduct qualitative research in order to ensure that stakeholders were given the opportunity to contribute a wide variety of perspectives to the research. The steering committee developed information packages for distribution to service providers in their area. Fliers and media publicity alerted the population to the free call telephone number. People coming forward were interviewed using a semi-structured interview schedule or, for those who did not wish to be identified, a questionnaire was sent out. Service providers were also interviewed during the data collection phase. In total 73 interviews were conducted, 34 with people living with HIV/AIDS (PLWHA) and 39 with service providers. Interviews were coded into themes and priority issues identified.

The main points of concern for PLWHA were the lack of support for carers, the need for a support network for HIV people, the need for enhanced social support, better treatment and management of the disease and a need for confidentiality and a more accepting atmosphere among medical staff and the community. Many called for increased levels of community education and the development of an advisory support service.

The Illawarra needs analysis was able to identify and rank a number of gaps in service delivery as well as make recommendations for practical support for PLWHA and for community education strategies.

Andrée Marie and Frank Vellozzi 1995, *United Views Building a Stronger Community: HIV Community Development Project Needs Assessment Report*, Aids Council of New South Wales, Illawarra Branch, Wollongong, NSW.

Community group approaches

Community group approaches are useful when a rapid appraisal of community need is necessary and/or resources to conduct a needs analysis are limited. Used in conjunction with the approaches already outlined, community group approaches can give a clearer idea of a community's priority of needs because they elicit qualitative information as opposed to the quantitative data gathered through previously discussed methods.

Community forums

Community forums are open meetings of community members called to discuss a particular issue. As a tool for needs analysis, a community forum provides an opportunity to gather information about needs and desirable services. All community members are invited and meetings should be widely publicised to ensure a cross-section of the community is represented. The aim of the forum should be to identify community concerns or to seek community input into the design of services.

Seigel, Attkisson & Carson (1987) note that community forums are quick and inexpensive ways of gathering data, allow for a range of views, serve as a catalyst to action and make it possible to identify those willing to help. They can be especially effective if run by social workers with group work skills. Disadvantages include the difficulty of allowing everyone to have their say, possible lack of representativeness of forum attendees, and the possibility that community expectations will be unrealistically raised. If you are conducting a community forum, be aware of the strengths and weaknesses of this method of data collection and take steps to overcome the disadvantages. In particular, it may be more useful to use a combination of methods to ensure your data accurately reflect community needs.

Nominal groups

The nominal group approach was developed by Delbecq (Seigel, Attkisson & Carson 1987). It allows the generation and evaluation of ideas from group members while avoiding problems which may result from normal group processes. In this approach, a group of key informants (people with expertise and unique knowledge about a particular situation), clients and service providers are brought together to discuss problems and pose solutions. Nominal groups follow a highly structured format which includes breaking initially into small groups of up to ten members. Each person is given a list of questions to which they must write responses during a silent period of 10–15 minutes. These questions might include ideas about service needs and community problems. Group leaders then record answers on a flip chart with each participant giving one response in round-robin fashion until all ideas have been listed. Discussion is discouraged at this stage to ensure everyone's opinions are recorded.

A discussion period follows during which ideas are clarified, new ideas are added and others are combined. Participants are then asked to privately select five or more ideas of highest priority. These are handed in and results tabulated on a display chart. In a needs analysis the prioritised, identified needs provide a useful basis for program planning.

The nominal group method has proved a popular and useful technique for ranking needs among key stakeholders. Each member is assured that their ideas have been acknowledged and recorded.

Delphi panels

Delphi panels are a systematic, time- and cost-effective way of reaching consensus among a panel of selected key informants or experts. The group is chosen to reflect expert or key informant knowledge of a particular issue. In the case of needs analysis, the group would consist of experts, service personnel, clients and community representatives. A questionnaire is developed by the project team to gauge opinions on key issues such as service needs and use of services. The questionnaire is distributed to the Delphi panel for response. Returned questionnaires are tallied and redistributed with collated responses noted, and this process is continued until consensus is achieved and responses are no longer altered.

Delphi panels have the advantage of being quick and easy, of ensuring anonymity and of allowing consensus to develop through reasoned responses. They are a useful way of determining and ranking community need among key stakeholder groups.

Focus groups

As discussed in the previous chapter, focus groups are small, homogeneous groups representative of the target population and of key informants brought together to discuss pertinent issues. In needs analysis, focus groups are conducted to discuss community needs and priorities. Various focus group discussions, with 10–15 members, may be held with community members, with service providers, with target group members, with carers and with any other relevant group of stakeholders. The number of groups held depends on the issues and the degree of consensus achieved. Issues are recorded and collated and the degree of convergence between groups is noted.

Community group approaches

- Community forums
- Nominal groups
- Delphi panels
- Focus groups

CONVERGENT ANALYSIS

Each of the methods of gathering data about community needs discussed in this chapter is an important technique by itself. However, they all focus on a particular aspect of need and hence have some inherent bias. For example, demand for service analysis will determine the expressed community need while a focus group with service providers may determine normative need. To improve the comprehensiveness of your needs analysis, and hence to achieve a convergent analysis, you should consider using multiple methods or triangulation. Triangulation involves the use of more than one method to increase the validity of results and to synthesise results from different sources. Of course, although the use of multiple methods is inhibited by time and cost constraints, you should endeavour to ensure that your methods have determined the normative, felt, expressed and comparative needs of your community. Convergent analysis ensures that you have gathered information from a variety of sources and from various levels of government, community and services' personnel.

Case study two—the needs of young people

The students undertaking the suicide study followed a detailed plan for collecting data. The available literature, government records and interviews with key informants allowed them to identify the characteristics of the at-risk groups of young people. Using available data, the students discovered that the suicide rate in the shire was, indeed, a cause for concern when compared with other, similar shires.

Next they identified the services currently available and interviewed key staff about the service profile. Among a series of findings, the analysis of services indicated that no services dealing specifically with suicide prevention were

---

137

available in the area. This gap in service delivery meant that at-risk young people had nowhere to go and no knowledge of available services. Interviews with young people and workers allowed the students to compare the existing service profile with identified felt and normative needs to determine service gaps. Methods for prevention of suicide were evaluated from the literature reviewed and compared with available programs. Finally, the students presented their findings to the health team.

School based programs were determined as one of the most effective means of prevention, and early detection and treatment were seen as essential. The students made a number of recommendations for service provision and education to address the significant problem of youth suicide in their shire.

University of NSW 1991, *Suicide Prevention: Sutherland Shire Needs Analysis Report*, Southern Sydney Area Health Service Health Promotion Unit, Sutherland Hospital & Health Service State Health Publication Number (SSAHS) 91–108, Sutherland, NSW.

SUMMARY

This chapter has examined the processes of needs identification and analysis by focusing on the typology of need developed by Bradshaw (1977) to determine the type of information required to ensure that a comprehensive needs analysis is conducted. Three types of analysis—social indicator, social area surveys and community groups approaches, each incorporating a number of methods—have been discussed. It is important in any analysis of need to work towards a convergent analysis of the community's needs and a comprehensive understanding of the various levels of need.

Remember that needs analysis is not an end in itself; it is merely a means of gathering data to assist informed decision making. Done inappropriately, a poorly constructed needs analysis can lead to either an overestimation or an underestimation of the need for a service and, consequently, a poorly patronised or understaffed service. An effective needs analysis is essential to adequate service planning and delivery. Ultimately, however, the decision about need for services and the priority of need must be a value judgement made by the steering committee or the service planners on the basis of comprehensive data and wide consultation.

QUESTIONS

1 What is a needs analysis?
2 Why would you conduct a needs analysis?
3 What issues need to be addressed before you begin your needs analysis?
4 What are the four levels of need identified by Bradshaw?
5 What are the three approaches to needs analysis discussed in this chapter?
6 What is a social indicator analysis and what information does it provide?
7 What are the three social area surveys discussed, and what types of need do they elicit information about?
8 What are community group approaches? Describe a situation where this would be an appropriate method.
9 What is convergent analysis and why is it important?
10 What ethical considerations are important in a needs analysis?

EXERCISES

1 Examine the needs analysis conducted by social work students discussed in this chapter. How might the methods, data collection and recommendations have been different if they had involved a steering committee representing key stakeholders?
2 Go to the library and find a journal article which describes a needs analysis. Examine the methods used, the process undertaken and the final recommendations. Has the researcher used appropriate methods and are the recommendations well grounded in the data? What might have been done to improve the study?

FURTHER READING

Fortune, A. E. & Reid, W. J. 1999, *Research in Social Work*, 3rd edn, Columbia University Press, New York. Chapter 13.

Mark, R. 1996, *Research Made Simple: A Handbook for Social Workers*, Sage, London. Chapter 11.

Marlow, C. 1998, *Research Methods for Generalist Social Work*, 2nd edn, Brooks/Cole Publishing Company, Pacific Grove. Chapter 5.

Owen, J. M. & Rogers, P. 1996, *Program Evaluation: Forms and Approaches*, Allen & Unwin, Sydney.

Reinharz, S. 1992, *Feminist Methods in Social Research*, Oxford University Press, New York. Chapter 10.

8 HOW DO I EVALUATE MY PROGRAM?

Hello— do you own a telephone?

Workers in the welfare field must be accountable for the service they provide, the resources they expend and the outcomes they achieve. Accountability is expected by governments, clients and taxpayers. Evaluation and accountability have always been important concepts for social workers. Handled effectively, program evaluation gives us the means to develop techniques for ensuring our practice is enhanced and effective and allows us to incorporate accountability and transparency into our practice. Program evaluation techniques allow us to be more effective and efficient workers, which can only enhance our work with clients and the communities we serve.

However, as we head into the twenty-first century, economic rationalism and quality assurance are being emphasised as guiding principles of management. Economic rationalism is an ideology of accountability that dictates that funding be delivered efficiently and with economic benefits. This principle stands uneasily beside those of social justice and access and equity in the assessment of the delivery of welfare support. For workers in the field this change has ensured a focus on accountability for program benefits and outcomes. We concur with the assessment of Everitt and Hardiker (1996) who voice concern that

> as part of new systems of public sector management, a form of 'managerial evaluation' is developing which, at worst, serves as a mechanism to ensure that practice conforms to New Right policy

agendas, and which, at best, will be fudged and regarded with cynicism by practitioners (p. 1).

Therefore, we urge you to take special care when assessing the purpose of your evaluation. Why are you doing it? Whose interests are paramount? Will better service delivery result?

This chapter is designed to assist you to become familiar with ways and means of assessing your programs in order to determine whether they are effectively targeted, whether they are being conducted successfully, whether they are achieving quality outcomes and, finally, whether they provide an adequate cost–benefit. The chapter will equip you with skills that will enable you to produce the program evaluations required by your agency, department, funding body community or client base and enable you to critically assess evaluations conducted by external evaluators.

WHY DO WE DO PROGRAM EVALUATIONS?

Program evaluations are conducted for a variety of reasons including, chiefly, the need to be accountable for our service and our practice. This need is being driven both by the requirements of program and service funders for responsible spending and streamlined service and by the increasingly powerful consumer movement which demands adequate services and accountable providers. While some of the motivation for our acquisition of evaluation skills has come from outside the profession, much has come also from our profession's desire to deliver high quality responsive services in the most appropriate way.

We conduct program evaluations to improve the efficiency of our service and to cut out any overlapping programs. This need for efficiency of service provision can only have positive benefits for practitioners, who become more aware of the programs on offer, and for clients, who are assured of a more professional service.

Program evaluation also assists us to plan more effectively and allows us to develop programs on the basis of a well-documented need for services. Finally, and equally importantly, program evaluation is a valuable tool for improving existing programs in response to careful assessment of the delivery and response to our service.

You should note that evaluation should be embedded in your daily practice and not left to an annual review of your programs. Ideally, evaluation should include both qualitative and quantitative methodologies and involve the perspectives of all the people involved, especially the service users or clients who normally have the least power in decision making about service directions. Dullea and Mullender (1999, p. 96) exhort us to empower our clients through our evaluation practices: 'There is no excuse for not seeing people as the experts in their own lives.'

Why do we do program evaluations?

- Accountability
- Efficiency
- Planning
- Development of appropriate programs
- Improvement of existing programs

WHAT IS PROGRAM EVALUATION?

Program evaluation has been defined by Grinnell (1988, p. 402) as 'the systematic study of the operation of social action, treatment and intervention programs and their impact'. Further, it is a 'collection of methods, skills and sensitivities necessary to determine whether a human service is needed and likely to be used, whether it is conducted as planned and whether the human service actually does help people in need'. Rossi et al. (1999, p.4) define program evaluation as the use of social research procedures to systematically investigate the effectiveness of social intervention programs. Program evaluation is applied research designed not to uncover theoretical relationships but to focus on and improve human service delivery.

Program evaluation techniques can be used to assess a program, a service, an agency or even overarching policies. There are several types of program evaluation and you should note that needs analysis (covered in the previous chapter), which determines an initial need for a program or service, may be the first stage of a program evaluation leading to the development of a new program. Further types of program evaluation to be covered in this chapter include evaluability assessment, process analysis, outcome analysis and cost–benefit analysis.

Types of program evaluations

- Needs analysis
- Evaluability assessment
- Process analysis
- Outcome·analysis\
- Cost–benefit analysis

In conducting evaulations, you will find the principles for research outlined in earlier chapters can be very useful. For example, from the outset, establish a reference group or steering committee with representatives of all key stakeholders. This group can act as a communication channel about the evaluation between you and other parts of the organisation and service user groups, and help to dispel doubts and fears about the process. It will also ensure that all people affected by the evaluation have a voice in it. Plan the steps in the evaluation process in advance (see chapter 4) so that you have agreement in advance about what is happening and clarity about the aims of the evaluation.

EVALUABILITY ASSESSMENT

Evaluability assessments are carried out to determine whether, in fact, a program has been developed in such a way that it can be evaluated (Owen 1993). It involves a description of the program, its goals and objectives, an assessment of how well defined the program is and an identification of stakeholders (Rossi et al. 1999, p. 157). Sometimes services that have not been subject to quality control will develop in an ad hoc way with a poor conceptualisation of the objectives of the service and an equally poor framework for assessing outcomes. Such services are noted by a lack of clarity of objectives, by a failure to define key concepts clearly and by a lack of standardisation of treatment. Consider for a moment agencies which deal with child protection. Imagine the problems inherent in programs that do not clearly define child abuse or vary in their interpretation of what constitutes child protection. How can services be assessed if they do not have a clear conception of the problem for which the service was devised and hence lack standardised treatment procedures?

Management structures that are not clearly delineated can also lead to ad hoc service delivery. Agencies must clearly outline their management process in order that the funding body and workers are clear about who has responsibility for delivering the proposed service. Roles need to be defined so that accountability is assured.

Case study—Sexual Assault Service evaluation

The Sexual Assault Service in a regional centre [New South Wales, Australia] was established in 1986 under State Health Department guidelines covering the design and implementation of Sexual Assault Services. In this case, the service was developed from the top down, following widespread community concern about inadequate services for sexual assault victims.

Prior to the 1980s assistance to victims was provided by

volunteers at rape crisis centres and by employers in non-government women's organisations. As a result, services varied enormously, they were not organised around any set of governing principles, and they were in many cases punitive (Department of Health, NSW 1988, p. 9). The Department of Health established Sexual Assault Services with an overriding aim of providing 'adult and child victims of sexual assault and their non-offending parents or families with high quality comprehensive counselling and medical services throughout NSW' (p. 11). This aim is supported by thirteen specific objectives for service delivery. At a regional level the service is supported by state funding, staff in-service and service evaluations. The state department also provides a detailed policy and procedures manual which lists, among other things, the counselling, legal support and medical service which should be provided to clients and the reporting mechanisms that must be followed.

This example indicates the effectiveness of a well-defined conceptual framework which leads to effective and standard treatment procedures. Services across the state may be readily evaluated in relation to each other, and standard reporting mechanisms with centralised data collection allow a ready analysis of the dimensions of the problem and the effectiveness of treatment.

Garton, Leslie, Fenton, Joan & Paton, Annette 1992, *Review of Sexual Assault Services: Report on X*, Sexual Assault Service, NSW Department of Health, Sydney.

HOW DO WE CONDUCT AN EVALUABILITY ASSESSMENT?

In conducting an evaluability assessment, it is important to observe the day-to-day functioning of the agency program or service in order to determine what the agency objectives appear to be, and what are the desired client outcomes. You should also note the structure of the agency and the responsibilities of various agency personnel. This early observation is an important first step in your evaluation of the program. Further, you should be clear about the program's boundaries. For example, if you are examining the Sexual Assault Service discussed above in the case study, you would note that it is run within the Health Department but has specially designated staff and its own discrete program objectives. The boundaries of your assessment should not stray beyond the service itself.

Your next step involves analysing the policy and procedural documents, mission statements, management structure agreements and any other relevant program documents to allow you to assess whether what is being undertaken within the agency is what was originally intended. Sometimes confusion results from the different perceptions of management and staff about the intended program outcomes. Involving program staff in the evaluation process allows you to develop a model of the link between program objectives and the program as implemented.

The next stage of the evaluability assessment is interviewing key stakeholders about their perceptions of the program's objectives. You should endeavour to interview not only staff, but also members of the funding organisation and clients. These interviews allow you to assess whether the key stakeholders view the program in the same way. Conflicting expectations may mean that the program objectives are not clearly defined or that the program has not achieved its initial objectives.

Your assessment must include an examination of the ability of the agency to meet its objectives. For example, does it have sufficient resources to succeed? Finally, you should write up your evaluation report and include detailed recommendations about how the link between program objectives and implementation might be strengthened.

Stages in evaluability assessment

- Observe
- Clarify the boundaries of your evaluation
- Analyse agency documents
- Involve program staff
- Interview key stakeholders
- Assess agency resources
- Make recommendations in report

PROCESS ANALYSIS

Process analysis is undertaken at the level of practice and is used to determine whether a program is being conducted in a manner that achieves its objectives. We use process analysis to assess overall program quality, in particular to determine whether the program or service is delivered in a standard and consistent manner as originally intended (Rossi et al. 1999). The focus is on the process of the program and how it can be improved, rather than its outcomes. According to Owen (1993, p. 129) a process analysis is conducted:

a) To examine program implementation in order to improve or review outcomes

b) When developing and refining new programs
c) When practitioners are concerned about the quality of the program being provided at agency level

Process analysis works to improve practice by aiding the standardised delivery of the service and by educating those involved about the program and its optimal implementation. This phase is an integral part of any program evaluation because we need to be sure that the outcomes of a program are a result of a consistent delivery of service. If the service or the worker intervention is not standard, then we cannot be sure whether changes in the client group are a result of the program or of other factors.

Key questions

To conduct a process analysis we must be aware of key questions which relate to the effectiveness of the service or program being analysed. In particular we must note the target group for whom the program was intended and ask who is using the service and why? Who is being excluded and why? Who is failing to return and why? These questions will allow us to assess how effectively the program is targeted.

We need also to consider the service delivery itself by noting who is delivering the service, how effective they are and what the program actually involves. Is it being conducted in a specified manner and is it effective? In particular we should look at the costs and resourcing of the program.

How do we conduct a process analysis?

One of the optimal techniques involved in process analysis is observation. Observation allows the evaluator to examine the program or service in practice by noting the clients using the service, the suitability of the program's location, the way the service is delivered, and its effectiveness in meeting its objectives. Where observation is not possible because of issues of confidentiality or impracticality, agency records may be examined to assess client response. Further information can be obtained from the workers providing the service through interviews and by asking them to keep detailed, expanded records in the form of data forms or logbooks for a specified period of time. Information on the success of the service in effectively reaching its target group can also be obtained by some form of community survey. This will allow an analysis of barriers to service use. Client satisfaction surveys will help determine the effectiveness of the services being provided. A combination of some or all of the above methods will provide comprehensive data about the program, which must be analysed to determine whether what is happening in practice is consistent with program guidelines. The final process analysis report should relate to the key questions listed above and make recommendations to improve the actual implementation of the service.

Stages in process analysis

- Observation
- Analysing agency records
- Interviewing workers
- Analysing data sheets or logbooks
- Community survey
- Client satisfaction surveys
- Assessing agency resources
- Making recommendations in a report

Case study—Sexual Assault Service evaluation

In 1992 the regional Sexual Assault Service was evaluated to determine whether the service was achieving its stated objectives and was being conducted in a standard and consistent manner. This evaluation was conducted by external assessors who visited the service and observed the program's implementation. Records were analysed and workers were interviewed to determine their understanding of program guidelines and their perceptions of program implementation.

In examining access to the service, the evaluators noted that the failure to provide sexual assault service information in languages other than English and in an easy-to-understand style may have resulted in a lack of service for victims from a non-English speaking background, for children and for clients with low levels of literacy.

Evaluators noted that the location of the service ensured not only accessibility but also privacy and safety for clients. Operating as an on-call service 24 hours a day and having a solid professional relationship with the police and hospital emergency staff meant that the workers had endeavoured to make the service readily accessible to victims.

In assessing the actual service provided, the evaluators noted that the Sexual Assault Service has been able to deliver the required service by allocating expertise, time and money to developing quality assurance frameworks and through planning and regular evaluation. The service has bi-annual planning days attended by staff; is committed to providing training for staff, including monthly quality assurance meetings; and it regularly conducts client satisfaction surveys. Data collection is in accordance with State guidelines thus adding to the broader research program of the Department. The process analysis section of the program evaluation was largely favourable. Quality checks and balances introduced at State level have ensured a professional level of service at the practice level in this regional service.

Garton, Leslie, Fenton, Joan & Paton, Annette 1992, *Review of Sexual Assault Services: Report on X Sexual Assault Service*, NSW Department of Health, Sydney.

OUTCOME ANALYSIS

An outcome analysis is conducted to determine whether stated objectives have been met (Cheetham et al. 1992, Rossi et al. 1999). Key questions include: How successful is the program? Are clients satisfied? What barriers have prevented optimal outcomes? Is the service targeted effectively? Are the intervention strategies effective? How can the service be improved?

An outcome analysis is important in assessing whether a program is worth continuing. It measures the success or otherwise of the program and, if results are positive, it will allow you to seek ongoing funding, secure in the knowledge that the program is achieving its goals.

How to do an outcome analysis

In order to conduct an outcome analysis you must be very clear about the original goals and objectives of the program. Working from these, you must determine the most appropriate way to measure the outcomes, bearing in mind that this is not always as easy as it sounds. Data may be difficult to assess because of the nature of the program, the sensitivity of the issue or because of a lack of standardised records. An example will illustrate this point.

A women's refuge has as its goal providing crisis accommodation for women and their children who are victims of violence. A relatively easy measure of the success of this program would be to count the numbers of women and children using the service. Examine the trends over a period of time to determine whether the service has been used effectively. Your outcome evaluation may rely on these data only. However, a more analytical evaluation would examine the breakdown of these data by variables such as age, ethnicity, disability and address. This analysis would determine whether the service is adequately targeting older women, women from non-English speak-ing background, women with disabilities and women from more isolated areas. If this analysis demonstrates gaps in the service, then steps should be taken to make it more accessible and to educate the groups that are under-represented. A further stage in your evaluation of this service might be to seek information from police about their work with victims of violence. Are the police aware that some women are reluctant to use the service? If this is the case, what are the barriers?

In research we conducted we discovered that police and refuge workers have a very cooperative working relationship. For example, in one town without a refuge the police drive the victim and her children halfway to the nearest town where they are met by refuge workers from that town. Such arrangements add to the success of a service. In any evaluation you should note the extent of inter-agency cooperation. Are there aspects of program delivery that could be improved through cooperation between agencies?

Further sources of data for an outcome analysis may come from the workers and from the clients themselves. If possible, it is impor-tant to ask the clients what they value about the service and how it could be improved. You should note, however, that Royse (1999) points out that client satisfaction surveys invariably reveal very high levels of satisfaction. The reasons are varied and include the fact that clients very often have little choice of service, have no knowledge of other services with which to compare the services being evaluated, and may be worried about criticising a service they desperately need. It may also be that those who remain with a service are the satisfied ones while the dissatisfied drop out. Given this information, you should treat client satisfaction surveys with some caution.

In the women's refuge example, a further source of data might be local court statistics on the number of protection orders taken out during the period of your evaluation. These will give you an idea of the extent of violence in the area and indicate the percentage of victims using the refuge.

In analysing your data, you should note what the service has achieved, what support has been provided and how successful the service has been in meeting its objectives. Has it produced positive changes for the target population and if so, how great are these changes? You should also note any gaps in service, any groups who are under-represented, any areas where services are lacking, agencies that might benefit from cooperation and whether the service is ade-quate for the demand. Look beyond the obvious statistics and records and ask who might be missing out and why. Further, you should examine the management structure of the service to determine whether information is flowing freely through the system. An inad-equately managed structure will have a detrimental effect on service.

In the area where our research into violence against women was conducted, a domestic violence liaison committee was established. Groups represented on the committee (welfare, health, police and court personnel) realised that women who are victims of violence need support through the daunting court process. None of the agencies had the resources to effectively provide this service. A joint submission for funding to the state government was successful and now a court support service has been established for the region, managed by the inter-agency group. If you discover gaps in service provision, look beyond the agency itself for possible solutions.

How to conduct an outcome analysis

- Be familiar with the objectives
- Analyse service records and statistics
- Interview workers
- Survey clients if appropriate
- Examine the management structure and flow of information
- Determine success in meeting objectives
- Determine gaps in service provision
- Analyse whether inter-agency cooperation should be developed
- Report findings in terms of success in meeting objectives and areas for improvement

---

Case study—Sexual Assault Service evaluation

The Sexual Assault Service aims to provide assistance for sexual assault victims in order to minimise the emotional, social and physical effects of sexual assault. It provides information and practical assistance (medical, legal, social) to victims and endeavours to raise community awareness of sexual assault issues. An outcome analysis would assess how well the service is meeting these commitments. Currently, workers collect data which are passed on to the State health authority for analysis and comparison with other area services. As well, client satisfaction surveys are completed by clients.

An outcome analysis would use this data as the basis for assessment. What groups appear to be under-represented? What do the client surveys indicate about the current program and how could client satisfaction be improved? Interviews with workers will yield rich data about any problems in service delivery and any reasons why the objectives are not being met.

The 1992 evaluation identified a need to disseminate information about the service in languages other than English. It noted the satisfactory level of interagency co-operation and the attention given to quality assurance procedures through the collection of relevant data. The service was commended for noting under-represented target groups and for subsequently developing community education strategies to deal with this. The commitment to provide immediate service to clients has resulted in a 24-hour seven-day-a-week rostering service which has ensured a minimal delay in assessing sexual assault victims. While the report noted that staff are receiving comprehensive orientation training, it did note that this should be extended to the nursing staff in the accident and emergency section of the hospital. One of the few areas of criticism in the report concerns the management structure. Staff were unclear about their responsibilities and consequently, information flow was slow and selective. This problem was compounded by the fact that medical, nursing and counselling staff do not meet together. Consequently, multidisciplinary teamwork was lacking in the service.

These constructive criticisms were detailed in the final report presented to the service.

Garton, Leslie, Fenton, Joan & Paton, Annette 1992, *Review of Sexual Assault Services: Report on X Sexual Assault Service*, NSW Department of Health, Sydney.

COST–BENEFIT ANALYSIS

The final type of program evaluation to be discussed here is cost–benefit analysis, an analysis of the overall benefits of the program relative to the costs of the service. With increasing awareness of accountability issues, this is an important aspect of any program assessment. However, one of the major problems for welfare agencies is to adequately measure the benefits of a program. How does one determine an indication of benefit if one is dealing with the long-term unemployed, for example? It is very difficult to nominate an indicator of service provision that can be measured in monetary terms. How does one give value not only to the immediate service benefit but also to the indirect spinoffs of your intervention for the family or group and for society? As Rossi et al. (1999) note, whose cost and whose benefit are key questions for the evaluator.

Hornick and Burrows (1988, p. 416) note that cost–benefit analysis in social service program delivery can only be used to compare similar services, can be difficult when records are not adequate, can produce different results, and hence have different implications—if costed per case or per client or per hour. They suggest that you only compare agencies that have similar clients and objectives. If the records are inadequate, conduct a time budget survey for a short period of time. When comparing agencies, use the same indicators for each and calculate results in as many ways as possible (per case, per client and per hour of service provision). Remember that a cost–benefit analysis is designed to alert policymakers about the expense of running a program (its efficiency) and its success (its effectiveness) (Royse, 1999).

In selecting indicators of cost–benefit you should be careful to evaluate the effectiveness of the service in terms of both cost and quality. For instance, you might improve the throughput of a skills training program for long-term unemployed by reducing the program from six weeks to four. You are thus able to demonstrate that more people are taking the program for the same cost. However, is the program as effective and is it producing the desired level of training for the clients? Always analyse your cost–benefit data with a careful eye to quality.

How to conduct a cost–benefit analysis

- Use observation to assess effective cost of service delivery
- Compare agency costs and client statistics with other similar agencies
- If records are inadequate conduct a time budget survey
- Use the same indicators for each agency
- Calculate cost per hour, per client and per case

Case study—Sexual Assault Service evaluation

The Sexual Assault Service is one of a number of regional services located around the State delivering a similar service.
A cost–benefit analysis of the service would look at budgetary allocation to the regional service and examine number of clients, rate of service, amount of community education and the staffing profile. This data would then be compared to other regional services to determine whether the service is comparatively cost-effective. If the service appears by comparison to be less cost effective, steps could be taken to introduce measures which have proved successful in other areas.

Garton, Leslie, Fenton, Joan & Paton, Annette, 1992, *Review of Sexual Assault Services: Report on X Sexual Assault Service*, NSW Department of Health, Sydney.

IMPORTANT POINTS ABOUT EVALUATION

Guiding principles

Everitt and Hardiker (1996, chapter 5) caution us to be aware of certain fundamental principles which should guide our work in evaluating practice and programs. They suggest that we must:

- Be aware of the moral debate and the right of all involved to be heard in that debate
- Be sceptical of rational–technical modes of practice which ensure the maintenance of the status quo
- Recognise power, powerlessness and the need for empowerment
- Develop a genuine dialogue between users and those within the organisation
- Be acutely conscious of the fundamental purpose of the organisation and not be diverted into productivity gains which deflect from that purpose
- Encourage openness, criticism and the hearing of complaints both from within and outside the organisation
- Remove the burden of 'otherness' from the less powerful or from clients

Who is involved?

When an evaluation of an agency is conducted, as for any other type of social research, it is important to ascertain who is involved and what is at stake for each party. Many evaluations are commissioned by the funding body, so there may be an assumption that accountability is seriously being questioned. If you are conducting an evaluation, be sure to include all stakeholders from the beginning. As mentioned previously, a steering committee with members drawn from the funding body, the staff, management and, if possible, the clientele will ensure that the evaluation is conducted in such a way that all are informed about the procedure. There is a potential for conflict between the evaluators and the staff because staff may see their positions under threat and their work being scrutinised. If this is the case, they may be inclined to withhold information or be circumspect about the information that is given.

Avoiding conflict

To avoid possible conflict you should state clearly your role in relation to the funding body, clarify the data you require and how this is to be disseminated, and set up an ongoing consultation process with staff. Negotiate with the staff for access to their files and any other data you require and be clear about who owns the final report. At all stages of the evaluation process give brief reports to staff and discuss your interim findings. If changes are called for, decide how this might proceed in consultation with staff.

Internal or external evaluations?

Whether an evaluation is conducted by an internal or external evaluator is a matter for the agency, but the following points should be noted. Evaluations conducted internally within the agency or service have the benefits of reducing costs, of allowing change to be implemented effectively and of allowing staff to 'own' the data. As well, an internal evaluator knows intimately the organisational culture that affects the program's success or failure. The possible drawbacks of internal evaluation include the fact that the evaluation may not be objective, it may brush over problems, and may not have credibility with the funding body. Royse (1999) cautions internal evaluators to draw up a memo with management detailing the purpose of the evaluation, the target audience for the report, the date the report is expected, the way the staff member will be reimbursed in money and/or time to conduct the evaluation, and the budget for the project. External evaluations may also contain bias. Consider, for example, a case where the evaluator is seeking to maintain good relations with the funder of the research in order to secure further contracts.

STAGES IN PLANNING AN EVALUATION

In any evaluation there are four stages which you must go through: planning, collecting the information, analysing the data and reporting your findings.

Planning

During the planning stage, work to develop stakeholder cooperation and set up your steering committee. Several key questions must be addressed during the planning of any evaluation. For example: What is it you wish to evaluate? What and who is the evaluation for? What are the key issues you will be addressing? What type of evaluation are you doing? How will you gather your data? What data do you require and who is able to give it to you? How will you analyse the data and how will it be reported? To whom will the report be distributed and what are the interests of the key stakeholders in this report? What resources are available to you for the evaluation and how much will it cost? Finally, and most importantly, you must work through the ethical issues involved in the evaluation. For instance, is there an ethics committee to whom you must report? How will you ensure client confidentiality? Are you able to examine client records?

Your planning stage allows you to negotiate these issues and to overcome any constraints that may affect your service evaluation.

Data collection

During the data collection phase, decide the ideal ways to gather the data. Appropriate methods include interviewing or surveying key workers, clients and/or target groups, examining records and observing work practices and intervention strategies. It might also include negotiating access to the records of other similar organisations.

A combination of qualitative and quantitative methods may prove the most effective way of gathering the data. Whatever you choose to do, bear in mind what the objectives of your evaluation are and determine the best ways to gather the data that meet these objectives.

Analysing the data

Various methods to analyse your data are discussed in chapters 12, 13 and 14. Your task is to reduce and display your data in an easily interpreted presentation. Bearing in mind your objectives, you will use the data to constructively criticise the program and to make detailed recommendations. As Owen and Rogers (1996) note, you should understand that your evaluation is but one aspect of the information that will influence changes to programs. Others include pressure to maintain the status quo, funding availability, lobby group pressure and changes of government.

Reporting your findings

An integral aspect of your evaluation is the way you produce your findings, how quickly this can be achieved and to whom the information is disseminated. Remember that any research report is politically sensitive and you must ensure that the information is easily accessed by key stakeholders.

SUMMARY

This chapter has outlined the various types of program evaluations that might be conducted by welfare professionals. With economic accountability now being a determining factor of welfare service delivery, it is important that you are able to both conduct your own program reviews and assess the credibility of external reviews conducted for you.

There are five types of program evaluation, which form part of a continuum of appraisal. Needs analysis was discussed in detail in the previous chapter. This chapter has examined evaluability assessment, process analysis, outcome analysis and cost–benefit analysis.

An overall program evaluation may contain all of these stages. You should be aware of each of these aspects of service delivery, because the success or failure of a program may be influenced by any of these.

You should also understand how politically sensitive an evaluation is to key stakeholders and ensure that all are kept informed of the process and outcomes. Being able to understand and conduct evaluations of welfare programs is a critical tool for astute social work practitioners in a climate of increasing accountability.

QUESTIONS

1 What is a program evaluation and why is it necessary?
2 Outline the five types of program evaluation and detail when they would be used.
3 Why would you conduct an evaluability assessment?
4 What is process analysis?
5 How would you conduct an outcome analysis?
6 What measures would you use to determine a cost–benefit analysis?
7 What are the benefits of using an external assessor versus an internal assessor?

EXERCISES

1 Visit a welfare agency and ask whether they have program evaluation reports you might read. Identify the type of evaluation conducted and consider the appropriateness of the methods used and whether the recommendations are well grounded in the data.
2 Interview a worker in a welfare agency about the types of programs and services provided by the agency. Ask about the quality controls built into the programs, and whether the programs are regularly evaluated. Inquire about the type of evaluations that have been conducted, who was involved, what recommendations were made and whether these were acted upon.

FURTHER READING

Cheetham, J. et al. 1992, *Evaluating Social Work Effectiveness*, Open University Press, Buckingham.
Everitt, A. & Hardiker, P. 1996, *Evaluating for Good Practice*, Macmillan, London.
Hornick, J. P. & Burrows, B. 1988, 'Program Evaluation', in *Social Work*

Research and Evaluation, R. M. Grinnell Jr (ed.), 3rd edn, F. E. Peacock Publishers, Itasca, Ill.

Marlow, C. 1998, *Research Methods for Generalist Social Work*, 2nd edn, Brooks/Cole Publishing Company, Pacific Grove.

Owen, J. M. 1993, *Program Evaluation: Forms and Approaches*, Allen & Unwin, Sydney.

Royse, D. 1999, *Research Methods in Social Work*, 3rd edn, Nelson-Hall Publishers, Chicago. Chapter 10.

Shaw, I. & Lishman, J. 1999, *Evaluation and Social Work Practice*, Sage Publications, London.

Sherman, E. & Reid, W. J. (eds) 1994, *Qualitative Research in Social Work*, Columbia University Press, New York.

Wadsworth, Yoland, 1997, *Everyday Evaluation on the Run*, 2nd edn, Allen & Unwin, Sydney.

9   ACTION RESEARCH

What is action research?

Action research is one of the most exciting forms of research evolving in the twenty-first century. For social workers and/or community workers, an understanding of the process of action research is fundamental. Unlike other forms of social inquiry, action research deliberately sets out to create change. As Yoland Wadsworth (1997a) puts it,

> instead of a one-off linear inquiry that 'starts' with questions and 'ends' with answers [action research] is a series of cycles that 'begin' and 'end' with action and incorporate research continuously as feedback to and from action. This is actually not unlike what really happens in the linear research model. But action research is explicit and self-aware . . . (pp. 60–1).

The social psychologist Kurt Lewin (1890–1947) is generally credited with introducing the term 'action research' from about 1944 (Hart & Bond 1995). McTaggart (1997, p. 8) notes, 'We find that the first versions of action research in Western cultures have their roots in community development programs, and though it is seldom acknowledged, in feminist approaches to community activism'. Similarly Reinharz (1992) and Maguire (2001) demonstrate how feminist theorising and practice is a relatively unacknowledged force at the heart of action research.

Modern action research brings together theoretical and practical traditions from many fields—agriculture, social work, education, health, obstetrics, housing and community development, to name just a few (McTaggart 1997). McTaggart argues that this convergence has occurred because it has been demonstrated over and over again that research findings from one context do not necessarily work when applied to new contexts. Instead, 'people must conduct substantive research themselves on the practices that affect their lives' (McTaggart 1997).

The participation of all involved, especially of the researched and the people the research is for (see chapter 1), is thus a key to action research (Wadsworth 1997). To emphasise the importance of participation in and ownership of all stages of the research project by these groups, writers such as McTaggart prefer the term 'participatory action research'.

Action research fits broadly into the tradition of emancipatory research outlined in chapter 1. It includes a whole 'family' of approaches and practices, each grounded in different traditions, philosophies, political commitments and assumptions (Reason & Bradbury 2001). Despite these differences, common themes or elements emerge. Situating action research within the emancipatory or critical tradition, McNiff and Whitehead (2000, p. 201) identify three types of action research worldwide:

The interpretive approach

In this approach, practitioners research their own practice, supported by researchers who may be consultants, academic supervisors or managers. Often this is a form of process management and is conducted around the world.

The critical theoretic approach (or participatory action research)

McNiff and Whitehead (2000) note that this approach is especially visible in Australia, New Zealand and Latin America. The focus is on emancipatory issues and collective action, and on reflection and ownership of the action research process in the struggle against oppression.

Living educational theories

Used most in the UK, USA, Canada, and Ireland, McNiff and Whitehead (2000) report that this approach encourages individuals to clarify the values base of their work.

Social workers find aspects of all three of these approaches useful. They are not mutually exclusive—for example, the action research project studying the role of indigenous social workers in Australia, reported below, combines elements of the first two approaches outlined by McNiff and Whitehead. Whatever the focus, however, we would say that action research always contains two key elements:

1 A focus on action or social change, and
2 Involvement of those who are fundamental to the issue being researched.

An example of a definition from the first type of action research identified by McNiff and Whitehead (2000) is that of Schmuck (1998, p. 29):

> Action research consists of planned, continuous and systematic procedures for reflecting on professional practice and for trying out alternative practices to improve outcomes.

McTaggart (1997, p. 27) offers a more general definition which could apply to all three approaches:

> Action research is the way in which groups of people can organize the conditions under which they can learn from their own experience and make this experience accessible to others.

Finally, Reason and Bradbury (2001) have devised a working definition of action research which aims to include the whole 'family' of different approaches. This definition highlights the importance of action research in the postmodern world as a tool to bring together theory and practice in order to strengthen the values of participatory democracy and work together for a sustainable future:

> action research is a participatory, democratic process concerned with developing practical knowing in the pursuit of worthwhile human purposes, grounded in a participatory worldview which we believe is emerging at this historical moment. It seeks to bring together action and reflection, theory and practice, in participation with others, in the pursuit of practical solutions to issues of pressing concern to people, and more generally the flourishing of individual persons and their communities (p. 1).

WHY DO WE DO ACTION RESEARCH?

Action research is something we undertake individually and in groups when we agree that we want to work together to change things in ourselves, in our organisations and in our social structures (after McTaggart 1997). Similarly, if you want to effect changes as you go, based on rigorous research, and to be part of the research process in partnership with all the people affected, action research is what you will be doing.

Why do action research?

- To work together with people to change ourselves, and the structures around us
- To empower people to become partners in the research process
- To address inequalities
- To solve social problems
- To encourage the democratic process

HOW DOES ACTION RESEARCH DIFFER FROM OTHER FORMS OF RESEARCH?

Action research differs from other types of research in its choice of research problem, its goals, the researcher's role (as facilitator and collaborator rather than as expert) and in the actual process of the research. It may be viewed as more political and is directly applicable to creating improvements in the social system (Doyle 1996, p. 66). Schmuck (1998) has depicted these differences between action research and other research, in relation to data collection, inquiry, problem solving and the role of the researcher, as follows:

Figure 9.1 Two types of research

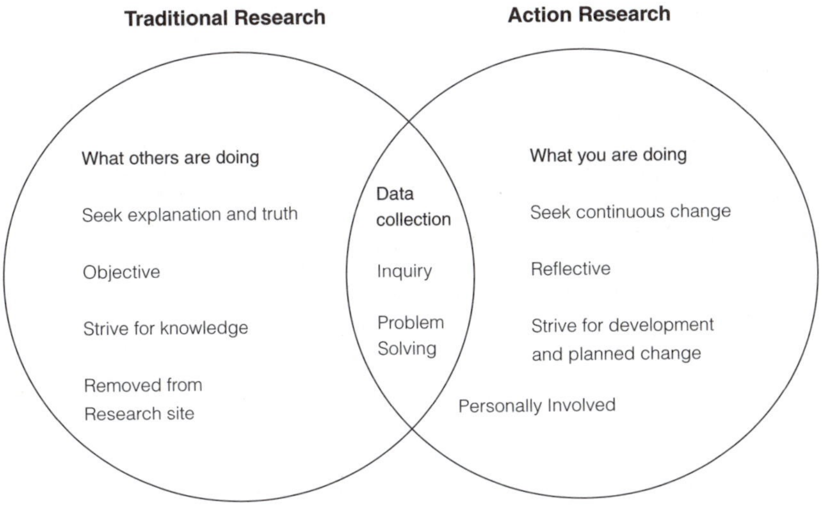

Traditional Research — Action Research

What others are doing / What you are doing

Seek explanation and truth / Data collection / Seek continuous change

Objective / Inquiry / Reflective

Strive for knowledge / Problem Solving / Strive for development and planned change

Removed from Research site / Personally Involved

Source: From *Practical Action Research for Change* by Richard A. Schmuck, © Richard A. Schmuck, 1997. Reprinted by permission of Skylight Professional Development, www.skylightedu.com or (800) 348 4474.

Wadsworth (2001, p. 431) paints a vivid picture of the differences between action research and other research in a table comparing the standpoints of 'the researcher' and 'the facilitator' which is reproduced here as Table 9.1

Table 9.1   A comparison of standpoints—'The Researcher' and the 'The Facilitator'

The researcher	The facilitator of research
The inquiry is the researcher's inquiry.	The inquiry is more or less the participants' inquiry.
The stakeholders are the researcher's subjects, or they are recipients of the researcher's final report.	The stakeholders are participants and co-researchers with the facilitator.
The researcher conducts a usually one-off, time-limited inquiry, implementing a research plan established and agreed at the outset.	The facilitator assists an iterative, emergent inquiry that might be more or less continuous and responsive. Often longer-term, over time.
The researcher (and/or their assistant/s) selects the methods and the questions, asks the questions, interprets and analyses the data, draws conclusions, makes recommendations and writes up the report.	The facilitator involves and works with the co-researchers to choose the methods and questions to be asked of (and possibly by) the co-researcher, and circulates the responses among them; together they interpret, analyse and draw conclusions and decide on new actions, and then experiment with these, self-monitoring them, and so on.
The researcher sees disparities of power as irrelevant, or accepts them as inevitable, works around or avoids them as much as possible.	Disparities of power require the facilitator to design strategies so that all people may both speak and be heard accurately.
The researcher remains at arms' length from each stakeholder, examining the operation of the variables 'through a microscope'.	The facilitator enters into an engaged, intersubjective process with the participants, and together hold up mirrors and magnifying glasses to themselves and each other.
Worst possible results are 'getting it wrong' and being rejected as 'academic' or vilified as 'subjective' or 'political' (or worse, you don't ever know the impact); or you leave behind simmering resentment from those who never felt heard.	Worst possible results are that self-understandings are still not achieved and the group or organization is left with its status quo practices and conflicts. (Facilitator vilified as not having come up with 'the answers'!)
Best possible results are you get it right and are lauded as 'objective'!, although it may either not be different from what was thought, expected or planned at the outset, or it may have been used to introduce changes wanted only by one or some parties (who had the power to make them).	Best possible results are new insights are gained by all the relevant players and are more or less quickly applied in practice without need for executive direction. (But it never gets written up!) Over a sequence of cycles, more and more desirable changes are a result of the inquiry.

Source: Reproduced from Wadsworth (2001, p. 431) in Reason and Bradbury (eds), *Handbook of Action Research*, 2001, by permission of Sage Publishing Ltd.

HOW DO WE DO ACTION RESEARCH?

Traditionally, action research has been seen as a spiral of self-reflective cycles of the following activities (Carr & Kemmis 1983, Wadsworth 1991, McTaggart 1997, Reason & Bradbury 2001):

- Planning
- Acting (implementing or making changes)
- Observing (systematically)
- Reflecting

Schmuck (1998) has identified two ways of following this cycle, which he calls proactive and responsive action research. You can see from his summary, reproduced here as Table 9.2, that you can begin either with a new practice that you then evaluate, or by collecting data and then trying a new practice, depending on the situation.

Table 9.2   Ways of following the action research cycle

Proactive action research	Responsive action research
1. Try a new practice	1. Collect data to diagnose situation
2. Incorporate hopes and concerns	2. Analyse the data
3. Collect data regularly	3. Distribute data and announce changes
4. Check what data means	4. Try a new practice
5. Reflect on alternative strategies	5. Check others' reactions
6. Try another new practice	6. Collect data

Source: Schmuck (1998).

In practice, action research can begin at any point in the cycle. You might get some reactions about an issue or a practice that inspires you to begin a piece of action research. Or you might wish to make a change of some kind and systematically evaluate its impact. However you begin, the elements of working together with the people affected by the outcomes of the research and/or those involved in the practices you are investigating, reflecting with them about the process each step of the way, and having some kind of action or change at the heart of the research, are what sets action research apart from other methods.

Note the warning of Eden and Huxham, quoted in Hart and Bond (1995), that 'one way of excusing sloppy research is by labelling it "action research"'. Good action research is as rigorous as any other method, and leaves a clear trail as to how it was carried out so that others may learn from its successes and failures.

There is no one method of going about doing action research. This makes the issues in the other chapters of this book—theory, politics, values, choice of method, clarity in formulating and asking questions—all-important if you want to undertake effective action research. Instead of an identified method, there are several principles

163

or suggestions from other action researchers that you could incorporate into your practice, listed in Table 9.3

Table 9.3.   Some principles of action research

- Involve the people in the research process as co-researchers in all decisions—about content and method—in the reflection phases
- Get started quickly
- Start small—do it yourself and gain momentum
- Be explicit about collecting data
- Seek out contradictions
- Be explicit about power relations
- Engage with the politics
- Ensure the validity of the research by moving between reflection and action several times in your inquiry cycles

Source: Adapted from Heron & Reason (2001), McTaggart (1997) and Wadsworth (1997).

Heron and Reason (2001, pp 180–1) identify four phases of the action research cycle for cooperative inquiry groups—that is, groups of people with similar concerns who agree to work together to understand and change their world and/or themselves:

1 Co-researchers meet and agree on the focus of the inquiry and the methods they will use to collect data.
2 Co-researchers become co-subjects—they engage in the actions they have agreed to and observe and record the process and outcome of their own and each other's experiences.
3 Co-subjects become fully immersed in and engaged with their action and experience.
4 Co-researchers re-assemble to share their practical and experiential data and to consider their original ideas in the light of it.

As a result the co-researchers may develop their original ideas or test new ones during the next inquiry cycle. Heron and Reason (2001) recommend repeat cycling through these four phases to enhance the validity of the findings. Cycles may be long or short—they report that six to ten cycles may take place over a short workshop, or over a year or more, depending on the nature of the inquiry.

We conclude our review of action research with a case study from Australia.

Case study—listening to the stories of Australian indigenous social workers: a report of a collaborative research partnership

Over an 18-month period during 2000–01, a collaborative research project was undertaken to explore the nature of

164

Australian indigenous social work practice. The research was initially conducted by a non-indigenous social work practitioner and following the pilot interview evolved into co-research involving this indigenous practitioner and later, the other participants. The aims of the research were to identify how indigenous social work practitioners reconcile their indigenous identity with their social work roles; balance their cultural knowledge and practices alongside a social work discourse that reflects the dominant culture and construct their personal and professional boundaries.

An initial number of indigenous social workers were invited to participate in the research. They were asked to identify others who might be interested in being interviewed. Each participant was sent a transcript of their interview and encouraged to change any aspect of the data. Once the interviews were completed the researchers then undertook a joint thematic analysis of the data. Participants were informed of the involvement of the co-researcher. They were invited to collaborate in the research process. The researchers met with members of the community and participants to discuss the research and to gain feedback at regular intervals.

The six indigenous social workers who participated in this study come from Queensland, New South Wales, Northern Territory, ACT and Western Australia. They are qualified social workers with two to six years' practice experience ranging from: child protection, family support, income support, child and adolescent mental health, juvenile justice, social policy, research and teaching. The participants work in both indigenous specific and mainstream positions, exposing them to practice with indigenous and non-indigenous clients and communities. They are aged in their thirties and forties. Two men and four women were interviewed.

Participants expressed their excitement that the research was being conducted in a collaborative culturally appropriate way. It was an opportunity for them to be truthful about "the lifting of the secret". Additionally the research was deemed timely and necessary to challenge the value system and theories which inform Australian social work practice.

The results of the research reveal some of the tensions of being an indigenous social work student. Some areas covered were: being taught indigenous subjects by non-indigenous lecturers and the isolation of being one of the few students from a culturally diverse background and often the only indigenous person.

Different features of indigenous social work practice were

also explored. These included investigating the effect of personal experiences in indigenous communities and the impact this has on being an indigenous social worker. Notions of obligation, kinship ties and identity contribute to the complexity indigenous social workers experience in their professional lives. These factors conflict with the dominant social work discourse on personal and professional boundaries.

There have been a number of outcomes in the research process. These include: an opportunity for both researchers to learn from each other in terms of cultural knowledge and research theory; the participants being given the opportunity to explore their cultural, personal and professional identities and their fit with social work, the ability to increase indigenous networks and the opportunity to challenge the social work profession to incorporate indigenous values within theory, practice and self.

Bennett, B. & Zubrzycki, J. (2001) 'Indigenous Social Workers: Putting stories into practice'. Conference paper, AASW National Conference, Melbourne.

SUMMARY

Action research is characterised by its commitment to action and by the incorporation of stakeholders as co-researchers and co-subjects in the research process. The action research process is often viewed as a spiral of planning, observation, reflection and action moving into a new planning phase. Several cycles through these phases is recommended to increase the validity of the study. Action research does not end with a report listing recommendations, it consciously goes on to ensure the implementation of the actions and a renewed study and evaluation of the results as part of the 'inquiry cycle' (Heron & Reason 2001).

Action research is especially important for social workers because of its symbiotic relationship with practice and theory, reflection and action. Action researchers are concerned to address inequities and seek to change the social system as well as themselves and their own practice as part of the research process.

The methods used in action research may be any from the conventional tool kit of social science research. The researchers must, however, consciously remove themselves from the role of expert and become an involved facilitator, colleague or co-researcher and co-subject, empowering others to work with them for change.

QUESTIONS

1 What is action research?
2 How does it differ from other forms of research?
3 List the three main types of action research. When would it be appropriate to conduct these?
4 What are the key principles in action research?
5 What stages do action researchers cycle through during the process of action research?
6 What are the most appropriate methods for action research?
7 Why is action research important for social workers?

EXERCISES

1 Define a problem in your organisation or institution which impacts adversely on the way you work. It might be access to a telephone service or a staff or student canteen policy. Outline how you might conduct a piece of action research that might lead to changes in the policy.
2 Imagine you are a worker in a nursing home. You are concerned about the overmedicalisation of patients. How might you conduct action research to effect change?

FURTHER READING

Hart, E. & Bond, M. 1995, *Action Research for Health and Social Care: A Guide to Practice*, Open University Press, Buckingham.
McNiff, J. accompanied by Jack Whitehead, 2000, *Action Research in Organisations*, Routledge, London.
McTaggart, R. (ed.) 1997, *Participatory Action Research; International Contexts and Consequences*, State University of New York Press, New York.
Reason, P.& Bradbury, H. 2001, *Handbook of Action Research Participative Inquiry and Practice*, Sage, London. This book has many useful chapters about action research, with examples from many prominent action researchers from around the world. Chapters referred to include: Heron, J. & Reason, P. 'The Practice of Co-operative Inquiry: Research "with" rather than "on" People' (pp.179–88); Reason, P. & Bradbury, H. 'Introduction: Inquiry and Participation in Search of a World Worthy of Human Aspiration' (pp. 1–14); Wadsworth, Y. 'The Mirror, the Magnifying Glass, the Compass and the Map: Facilitating Participatory Action Research' (pp. 420–32).

Schmuck, R. A. 1998, *Practical Action Research for Change*, Hawker & Brownlow, Australia.
Wadsworth, Y. 1997, *Do It Yourself Social Research*, 2nd edn, Allen & Unwin, Sydney.

10 BEST PRACTICE EVALUATION

While in previous chapters we have discussed methodologies and methods suitable for social workers undertaking research and evaluation projects, in this chapter we turn to a discussion of ways in which we can use this knowledge and these skills to evaluate our own practice. Effectively we are considering ways of turning the research spotlight on ourselves and the way we operate in the workplace. By contrast with research, practice evaluation is not so much about creating new knowledge as it is about assessing whether desired outcomes have been achieved (Dangel 1994). Are the processes we use and the outcomes we achieve effective, efficient and competent? Is our practice based on a well-grounded evaluative process? Are we achieving best practice standards? In plain English, are we doing a good job?

To date, our discussion has located research activities as projects undertaken as part of the social work professional role. A more fundamental issue now emerging for many professionals is how well they are performing in this social work role. You may be aware of the move towards evidence-based practice in social work, and the impetus to develop an 'evidence-based culture' in social work. In Great Britain, centres such as the Centre for Evidence-Based Social Services (CEBSS) and international organisations such as the Cochrane Collaboration encourage practitioners to use the results of research in their practice, to become informed consumers of research, and to undertake research as part of good professional practice. In

England at CEBSS, Professor Brian Sheldon and his colleagues have formed partnerships between researchers and the departments of health and social services throughout the south and southwest of England to encourage the growth of this research–practice culture. Visit the publications page of the Centre's website <http://www.ex.ac.uk/cebss/pages/publications.html> for an idea of the range of activities of this organisation. In Australia, the Australian Association of Social Workers has established an interest group in evidence-based practice and maintains a website page which provides updates on developments <http://www.aasw.asn.au/news/research.html>.

Just what constitutes evidence-based practice is a matter of debate—particularly the place of qualitative research and whether, as some claim, randomised control trials (RCTs) are the 'ultimate' in evaluating social work practice effectiveness (see for example, Sheldon and Macdonald's (1999), located on the CEBSS website listed above). This chapter not only provides you with a range of ideas for evaluating your own practice, but also offers several entry points into the debate about best practice and evidence-based practice. This debate is becoming one of the hot topics for social work in the twenty-first century.

In the previous chapter we saw how one type of action research is devoted to workers evaluating their own practice. This chapter turns us inward, suggesting additional ways to reflect on our own practice and methods we might use to evaluate our work. Such a task requires us to do more than outline a series of methods. It also calls on us to reflect on the social work profession, on its place in a postmodern world, on our values and our role in a rapidly changing political and ideological landscape, and to reflect on best practice standards and strategies to achieve those standards. These are big issues and it is quite beyond the scope of this chapter to explore them fully. Nevertheless, it is important that we address them briefly if we are to reflect on our practice and competently self-evaluate.

SOCIAL WORK PRACTICE IN THE TWENTY-FIRST CENTURY

Like most professions in the postmodern era, social work has lost its sense of certainty and its faith in rationality. The acceptability of a body of knowledge and the role of the professional as expert have both been called into question. As Fook (2000) notes, social workers' claims to legitimacy based on their knowledge base, and the grand narratives used to explain the social world, are breaking down. Rossiter (2000) argues that until now an uncritical acceptance by social workers of a social work knowledge base as an acceptable explanation of human behaviour and of social work interventions as effective has legitimated social work status and expertise. Those who operate outside the norms of expected human behaviour become marginalised and are the targets of social work intervention. Social workers are thus part of the power relations operating in society to enforce certain mores and values, and their interventions may result in some groups being labelled, targeted and disempowered. Rossiter (2000) argues that the power of social workers to construct situations as social problems creates the situation where they are complicit in inequitable relations. They may, in fact, be maintaining structural inequalities (Fook 2000). If this is the case, then we need to seriously reflect on our roles before we can evaluate how competently we practise.

Before we can do this we should first address such questions as: What are the problems we are dealing with? Whose reality are we operating under? What are the optimal outcomes we are working towards? Who is the client? Do we see the client as the expert in her/his own situation? Where are we focusing our actions? Are we aware of the power relations operating in the situation? Are we marginalising people by labelling them only because they are operating outside a currently acceptable norm? Does our language and terminology disempower clients? Do we pathologise difference and explain deviance by a concentration on individual pathology?

These are big questions that require us to be critically aware of the frameworks that bind our practice before we can evaluate how well we practise. We do not intend to engage the reader in a philosophical and ethical debate but we would urge social workers to engage in a constant process of self-reflection. Building on the discussion in chapter 1, we urge you to consider the following issues.

THEORETICAL AND IDEOLOGICAL POSITION

The practice of social workers is necessarily embedded in a theoretical and ideological framework. Each practitioner holds a theoretical position with which they are most comfortable and through which they interpret the social world around them—it may be feminist, social constructivist, postmodern, neo-Marxist or any one of a number of others. Our ideological position also shapes what we determine to be an ideal social world. This may be conservative, radical, neo-liberal or any one of a variety of positions through which we gauge the way we operate in the world and what we view as an ideal world. The way that we interpret and view the world frames as much as anything the way we approach practice, the methods we use and the outcomes we are seeking.

In evaluating our practice we must be able to articulate, as well as defend, the theoretical and ideological framework/s guiding our practice so that we can self-consciously reflect on our effectiveness. At the same time we need to be aware of the methods we use to achieve our desired outcomes. Most workers have a preferred practice method or methods, be it narrative, systemic, psychoanalytic, etc. Our reflection on practice must allow us to interrogate the methods and styles that we use and to be genuinely evaluative of our approach. This self-conscious understanding of our position and practice methods is the first step in undertaking practice evaluation.

PERFORMANCE CRITERIA

When assessing practice performance, carefully defined performance criteria are essential to best practice. Determining such criteria is not as easy as it may sound, as we must first determine the criteria by which we are judging ourselves, our services and practices. For example, when assessing our practice we may be more concerned about optimal client outcomes, client satisfaction and/or a reduction in recidivism. If we are concentrating on the services we provide, we may be more concerned to demonstrate that our service is effective for clients, that our response times are minimal or that we have used our resources effectively and so are providing a cost-efficient service. You should note that the desired outcomes, and hence performance criteria, will differ depending on the practice situation you are evaluating and the theoretical/ideological position in which you are based.

Equally perplexing is the dilemma of accountability in practice. We should of course be accountable for our actions, but accountable to whom? Is our main responsibility to our agency hierarchy, our clients, our colleagues, policy makers or other professionals? You will note that each of these groups will require different measures of practice effectiveness—the agency hierarchy that the service is being delivered professionally and cost effectively; the clients that their situations are improved; our colleagues that we are acting according to our professional codes, and policy makers that we are reinforcing existing policy guidelines.

Another dilemma we face when assessing practice is whether to collect evidence that is quantitative and therefore measurable providing objective evidence against established criteria. On the other hand, qualitative evidence may be more subjective but provide a rich source of evidence of effective practice. Perhaps the most effective response is to gather a wide variety of data that gives a comprehensive picture and meets the needs of a variety of audiences.

You can see from this discussion that it is important that we carefully define what the criteria against which we wish to measure ourselves may be, who are the key stakeholders, and how we might most effectively measure performance. In relation to practice effectiveness these measurements should be conceptualised through a process of self reflection on practice in a political and ideological context.

Issues influencing practice evaluation

- Theoretical position
- Ideological position
- Preferred methods
- Desired outcomes
- Stakeholder groups
- Accountability measures for different stakeholders
- Type of qualitative and quantitative evidence needed to test outcome and accountability measures

---

THE REFLECTIVE PRACTITIONER

Fook (1996, 2000) urges us to be self-reflective when attending to practice parameters. She argues that the reflective approach rejects the scientific, positivist and rational approaches in favour of more emancipatory and participatory approaches. A self-reflective practitioner will acknowledge the power differentials inherent in practice, will note the contextual issues and will view the client not as some marginalised 'other' but as the expert in their own situation and as a collaborator in determining optimal outcomes. A self-reflective practitioner will question their own role in maintaining marginality, their claim to professional expertise and their collusion in framing what is normal behaviour. A self-reflective practitioner will analyse the implications of policy for creating unequal power relations and challenge constructions of language that disempower.

A short example may assist in our understanding of the reflective process. The discourse and language surrounding mothers has changed in recent times in response to a conservative leaning in Western society. The very label used to describe women who raise children on their own, 'single mothers', creates a situation of inequality. There is no similar popular terminology for mothers in a marital relationship such as 'married mothers'. Through language and discourse single motherhood is problematised. Policy relating to mothers raising children alone has been directed towards increasing the incentives for women to participate socially and economically in society (Reference Group on Welfare Reform 2000). Again, there is no such urgency for 'married mothers' and no expectation that a workplace commitment, although desirable, is expected. Discourse and language and the resultant power relations create a view that certain groups

173

acting outside societal norms are a social problem to be dealt with through social policy. Social workers are used as part of the apparatus of power relations that are assigned to address these 'problems'. We must be able to critically reflect on language and discourse and resulting policy if we are to be an able reflective practitioner.

Bronson (1994) notes that a practitioner who is good at self-evaluation will constantly monitor their practice, will think critically about their own biases, will use their failures to improve their practice, will use evaluation techniques to determine whether to change their interventions and will use the knowledge gained through evaluation to assist the development of the profession. We would add that clients should be included in any self-evaluation design.

Social workers need to respond to client situations in a self-consciously self-reflective way, questioning the way discourse shapes and directs policy and empowers some and disempowers others. In working to become reflective practitioners we should question the very nature of our practice, how we define social problems, what power relations are operating and the language and discourse of social work. Only then can we determine what are the desirable outcomes. Ideally this is done in consultation with the experts—the clients themselves.

A reflective practitioner

- Is aware of the assumptions and biases underlying different evaluation methodologies
- Views the client as expert
- Acknowledges power differentials
- Self-consciously questions their own role
- Notes conceptual issues
- Considers context
- Analyses the implications of policy
- Challenges the construction of language and discourse

This lengthy introduction has been essential to an understanding of best practice evaluation. We cannot evaluate our performance if we do not question our knowledge, values, status, power and discourse, and what our proposed outcomes might be.

GUIDELINES FOR CONDUCTING EVALUATION RESEARCH

There are a number of methods available for assessing practice, some of which are more effective than others. These range across the spectrum of methods from the experimental design to qualitative models of assessment. We have taken the position that we should present a variety of methods, allowing the reader to come to their own conclusion about the effectiveness of each. We would argue that some methods are inadequate when used in isolation and some have questionable validity. However, if used in combination and in accordance with the guidelines outlined below there is some value in all.

First we would urge that any method adopted be client centred. Ensure that clients agree on outcomes, on what is being measured, are engaged in design, agree on the goals and see the research as worthwhile. Ensure that performance criteria are developed in response to client-established targets. We would also urge that any method be used in a self-reflective way. Be aware of contextual issues and power relations and, finally, use a combination of methods. If these guidelines are followed then methods can be adapted, used in combination, and tailored to meet the needs of the context and practice issue.

Guidelines for conducting evaluation research

- Ensure that methods are client centred
- Engage clients in the design of the research where appropriate
- Ensure that performance criteria are developed around client-defined outcomes
- Be a reflective practitioner
- Use a combination of methods

BEST PRACTICE EVALUATION METHODS

During the latter part of the twentieth century the use of experimental methods gained popularity in response to the dominance of the scientific, rational model of empirical design. Many social work research texts outline practice evaluation techniques that are grounded in a scientific, rational approach. In particular the use of experimental methods using strict scientific design came to be seen as the optimal design model. This approach relies on certain conditions and objective measurement to determine whether practice is effective. Basing practice decisions on measurable outcomes has led practitioners to seek quantitative indicators of success and could even influence the types of outcomes or goals which are acceptable. As a result there has been growing criticism of the scientific, rational approach as an adequate way of assessing practice performance. Bronson (1994) provides the following critique of the over-reliance on the scientific rational method:

- There are conflicting objectives between scientific research and practice.
- Methods used to assess the causal links between interventions and outcomes may interfere with service delivery.
- Methods such as single-system design are inapplicable to many types of practice—for example, short-term and crisis situations.
- There are often practical difficulties associated with collecting data.
- Many practitioners undertaking this type of research lack the necessary research skills to complete the process successfully.
- There are problems with replicability.

In this section we will outline some common quantitative methods. Given our criticism of the scientific approach as a useful way of evaluating practice we would urge caution. However, if used in conjunction with our guidelines for conducting such reviews they have some value, particularly if used in combination with other methods.

Quantitative methods

Experimental design

Before describing the various quantitative methods of practice-based evaluation, we introduce the principles of experimental design. In social work, experimental design is not often appropriate or possible. However, the quantitative methods that we can use are derived from this design, so it is important to understand it and the various compromises that have to be made when we use other quantitative methods.

Experimental design involving control groups has been used in the social sciences (beginning with psychology and education) since 1901, when Thorndike conducted some large-scale experiments to demonstrate that teaching Latin and shopwork had similar effects on increasing intelligence. Among other things, he used these results to argue that universities should not exclude potential students on the grounds that they had studied shopwork rather than Latin (Kerlinger 1973). Controlled experimentation without control groups goes back much further however, with reports of Pascal using it as early as 1648 (Kerlinger 1973).

Experimental design aims to establish causality; that is, to establish that changes in the independent variable X cause changes in the dependent variable Y. The main elements of experimental design are:

- Random assignment of subjects to control or experimental groups
- Manipulation of the independent variable
- Observation of the results on the dependent variable

The simplest experimental design can be depicted thus:

$$R \frac{X \quad Y}{X_1 \quad Y}$$

In this diagram, R indicates that subjects (usually clients) are *randomly* assigned to two groups—the experimental group (top line) and the control group (bottom line). The independent variable X is manipulated in the experimental group (that is, the experimental group undergoes some intervention) but not in the control group. With large enough groups, random allocation to both groups means that there are equal chances that other factors (interfering variables) will affect both groups (that is, theoretically, all possible independent variables are controlled). Therefore, any change in the experimental group compared to the control group (measured on the dependent variable Y) can be attributed to changes in the independent variable X.

For example, say we randomly select two groups of twenty six-month-old babies. We administer a controlled crying program to one group for one week at night and do nothing with the other group. At the end of the week we measure how long the babies in both groups are sleeping at night. If the babies in the group with the program are sleeping through the night and babies in the other group are not, we could attribute this difference to the controlled crying program. We could say that the controlled crying program causes babies to sleep through the night.

Mostly, however, we cannot randomly assign subjects from a defined population to experimental and control groups. Usually we have non-random assignment of subjects, in that our clients are selected on the basis of eligibility and need for a service, rather than random allocation. This means that technically we cannot generalise the results of our experiments beyond the sample of clients whose outcomes we are evaluating.

One way of improving generalisability, if we cannot randomly assign subjects to experimental and control groups, is to replicate studies at different times and/or at different places or with different subjects. If the relationship holds up in different conditions, we can be fairly certain that a causal relationship exists.

Another 'compromise' human services workers may have to make is that it may not be ethical to use control groups; that is, to have a group of people who do not receive a service. (In some situations people may volunteer to do this, but normally social workers are dealing with people who have approached their organisation because they want a service. In any case, if people volunteer to be controls, randomisation is again lost.) In these situations, social workers may use the clients themselves as a type of control—observing changes in the clients before and after intervention.

The following examples of quantitative evaluation designs

illustrate how compromises on the classic experimental design are made. Note that it is because these compromises are made that we cannot make claims generalising our findings outside our cases, without strong theoretical or other arguments for doing so. Some writers refer to these designs as quasi-experimental designs.

The single-system design

Adopted for social work evaluation, the single-system or single-subject design gained extraordinary popularity in the United States and became part of the curriculum in schools of social work. The single-system design focuses on a single, observable target behaviour such as binge eating, bullying, or school avoidance behaviour. It takes as the objective measurement of success of the intervention a reduction in the observable problem behaviour. Repeated measurements of the pattern of problem behaviour (the dependent variable) over time are graphed to indicate success or otherwise of the treatment intervention (the independent variable). Before treatment is commenced several measures of the problem behaviour are taken to establish the *baseline* measure.

To illustrate this method, consider the example of Susan, a ten-year-old girl, suffering school phobia. When Susan presents for treatment she has a pattern of school absence averaging three days per week. Her mother notes that on these days Susan suffers nausea and crying in the morning sufficient for her mother to keep her home from school. Before the social worker begins her treatment she asks Susan's mother to keep a diary for two weeks noting the ongoing pattern of behaviour. This data provides the baseline data against which treatment outcomes will be measured. The diary suggests that on three mornings in the first week and four in the second, Susan is unable to go to school. Once treatment commences, the social worker tracks changes in Susan's school phobic reactions and graphs the number of times the child is attending school. The following graph in Figure 10.1 illustrates the pattern of behaviour. Note that weeks one and two are the baseline period.

Figure 10.1 Susan's treatment phase

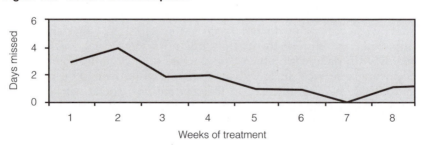

The graph illustrates that the treatment period represents a marked improvement on the baseline data. This would suggest that the treatment given by the worker has been successful. Royse (1999) suggests that when using this method of evaluation the identified target behaviour should come from the client, and that the behaviour chosen should be one giving the most concern to the client. Royse also notes that the worker should avoid this method when problems are difficult to measure.

You should note that this type of design is called an 'AB design'. That is, the A period represents the baseline and the B the treatment period. There are variations on this design, including the 'ABA design' where A is the baseline, B the treatment period and the second A represents a baseline reading taken some time after treatment. Using the example of Susan and her absence from school, an ABA design would be represented by a baseline period A, followed by a treatment period B as illustrated in Figure 10.1, followed by a further measurement period some time after treatment has ceased to determine whether there had been a period of sustained improvement in Susan's school phobia.

'ABAB design' is another variation of the single-system design and includes a baseline period represented by A, a treatment period B, another baseline period A some time after treatment ends, and B a new period of treatment. 'ABC design' represents a period of baseline assessment (A), with B being the treatment period and C a period of a different type of treatment. 'ABCD design' represents a baseline period A and three types of treatment.

Single-system designs are useful ways of assessing whether one or another type of treatment is effective with a particular client, whether the client's problem behaviour returns over time and whether the intervention used by the worker is effective. They have been popular because of the simple design, and because they do not require detailed knowledge of statistics.

There are, however, serious limitations with single-system designs. First, the choice of behaviour focused on and the best way to measure changes represent quite serious problems. What is being measured and is it an adequate representation of the problem? Who is measuring the behaviour? If it is the client or a member of their family, are we able to assess the accuracy of the information? Are they reporting socially desirable outcomes rather than what is really happening because that is what they feel is expected?

In addition, the different phases should be of equal length to allow adequate comparison. This may be difficult to achieve in practice and may also result in periods of non-treatment that may present some risk to the client. It may be that treatment should start immediately, thus eliminating the period of baseline comparison and rendering the quasi-experimental design inappropriate.

Additionally, the results may be ambiguous. There may also be limited or no controlling for intervening variables. Taking Susan's case, there may be other variables influencing her behaviour. For example, the attention she receives during the treatment phase rather than the treatment itself may be causing the improvement, or it may be that a difficult classmate has left the school, thus making her school phobia less extreme. With a limited focus on the behaviour under study and a lack of control of intervening variables, it is difficult to establish whether the social work intervention is the cause of the behaviour change.

Additionally, single-system designs usually operate with a sample of one making generalisation of the findings limited. It is difficult to draw conclusions about how the treatment may affect other clients, or how effective it may be in another setting. Finally, as Rubin and Babbie (2001) note, it is almost impossible to capture the complexity of human relationships and interventions by experimental means.

Despite the criticisms of single-system designs we have presented them here as a tool that may be used *in conjunction with* other methods. In some situations there will be merit in assessing problem behaviours using a single-system design, but always with supporting methods such as in-depth interviews and observation studies to give added strength to the findings.

Client satisfaction surveys

Another quantitative technique that may be used to assess your practice performance is a client satisfaction survey. Client satisfaction surveys are often used to assess the level of client support for programs and program designs. Using them to assess your own practice is a simple extension of the logic of engaging clients in social work practice. Questions could be included to assess the level of satisfaction with your assessment processes, your intervention strategies, the outcomes of treatment, your interpersonal style, your methods, etc. Additional questions could allow the client to nominate things they found helpful and things they found unhelpful. Note the caution you should exercise with regard to the results of client satisfaction surveys (which are often very positive) which we discussed in the last chapter.

File searches

Another useful quantitative method is an analysis of your client files to establish consistency of your style and treatment and the pattern of client outcomes. You may like to assess, for example, the number of client sessions, the consistency of treatment procedures, the type of interventions used, whether clients continue with treatment and any other quantitative variables listed in the files that allow you to assess your practice.

Resource assessment

The cost effectiveness of your practice is another useful parameter of practice effectiveness. You might consider assessing the amount of resources allocated on a client-by-client basis. This might be done by costing your time and the resources consumed to give an indication of whether some treatment procedures are more cost effective than others. In assessing the cost effectiveness of your practice you should also balance the dollar value with a qualitative assessment of the success of the intervention. It may be more cost effective to see a client four times, but client outcomes may be markedly better after six sessions. It is important that cost efficiency does not become the sole determinant of practice methods.

Qualitative methods

Semi-structured interviews

One of the most effective ways of assessing your practice is to conduct semi-structured interviews with clients and colleagues seeking feedback on your practice methods and the effectiveness of your interventions. Qualitative interviews allow those interviewed to reflect on the issues raised and to give reflective feedback on your performance. This method is also empowering for clients in that it allows them to give feedback on their experience of treatment. In some circumstances you may ask another worker or person to conduct the interviews, so that clients can say what they think without being identified by you.

Focus groups

Another useful method is to conduct focus group discussions with groups of clients with whom you may have dealt individually or in group sessions. A focus group to discuss your practice effectiveness is a good way to allow clients to reflect on and discuss their experiences (see chapters 6 and 7).

Supervision

One method of evaluating practice used by many social workers is structured supervision sessions with an experienced senior social worker. These regular sessions are used to reflect on practice and on cases, on methods and on outcomes, and to provide some benchmarking of practice standards. Many agencies provide avenues for professional supervision of staff. Regular supervision sessions are encouraged as examples of best practice.

Observation and reflecting teams

In clinical settings, supervision involving direct observation of practice, using either one-way mirrors or videos, or with the supervisor sitting in on the interview, is common practice. Some agencies use reflecting teams of colleagues and others for this purpose. Clients can also be involved, either reflecting on the process (or the supervisor's comments) as part of the evaluation, or commenting on videos of sessions in retrospect.

If the observations are recorded systematically and written up, you have a good best practice tool available using existing organisational processes and requiring only minor additional resources (the time to write up the feedback systematically). Of course, we recommend that these evaluation methods be conducted in the spirit of constructive criticism—otherwise you will become reluctant to subject your work to such intimate appraisal. It may also be useful to seek permission to observe others in their practice to allow you to view and learn from their work. (In organisations using peer reflecting teams, this will automatically be part of the structure of your work.)

File searches

Client files can also be assessed qualitatively. It is useful to provide qualitative comments in your files that give a summation of each case. These memos can then be used to assess your interventions across a range of clients and intervention strategies. Files can also be assessed for the type of language used to report cases, the theoretical and ideological position displayed, the effectiveness of the outcomes and the mode of interaction with the client.

BEST PRACTICE STRATEGIES

Your motivation in evaluating your own practice and the effectiveness of your service should be to use the information to continually improve your practice. You should be constantly working to become a leading professional in your field and to provide the best service you can possibly achieve. Reviewing and monitoring your progress should be a constant part of your practice. In this section we take you further and outline some of the uses of the evaluation results.

Develop quality standards

We suggest that you work towards providing a transparent set of standards for your practice and service that allows workers, clients, funders and other interested parties to be clear on what it is you are providing. This set of standards will include the type of service being provided, the amount of time for each client, the type of intervention procedure, the resources available, etc. A standards document can be developed in consultation with clients and staff and be reviewed annually. This standards document, which should include details of any complaints mechanism established in the agency, can then be presented to each client. Reference to your professional association's code of ethics should also be included.

Develop a client charter

A client charter should also be developed in consultation with client group representatives, outlining the standards clients should expect, the level of service, acceptable waiting periods, length of intervention, associated costs, resource allocation and any other relevant aspect of the service and of your practice. Consultation procedures and complaints mechanisms as above should also be spelt out.

Consult and empower

Where possible clients should be regularly consulted about practice strategies and your practice effectiveness. They should also be included on any organisational body relating to the service.

Provide information

Information about the service and your practice procedures should be readily available to service users and to other interested stakeholders. Information should be kept up to date and be accessible. This may be done through pamphlets, the Internet, service advice, annual reports, newspaper reports or other means. The information should be accessible to a culturally diverse population and to isolated groups.

Develop client satisfaction monitoring processes

Client satisfaction surveys, interviews and/or focus groups should be developed as standard and regular procedures for assessing practice. These should be conducted and reported on at regular intervals and results made available to service users and other interested parties. Surveys can be included with service documentation or be available in the service location. It is also desirable to allow clients to anonymously report on their experiences, so a collection box within the organisation should be provided.

Regularly review the complaints policy

Establish a transparent, accessible and unbiased complaints mechanism that allows service users to report on service experiences. This may include a panel of professionals and client representatives from outside the service. Widely disseminate the information about your complaints mechanism and regularly review its composition, its effectiveness and channels of communication.

Assess accessibility

Regularly assess your client profile to determine whether any sections of the community are denied access. Are there limited provisions for non-English speaking clients? Is information provided in several languages? Is your office wheelchair accessible? Is it in an area where clients are guaranteed privacy should they enter the building? Are the hours of operation suitable for potential clients? Are there strategies that should be developed to increase accessibility?

SUMMARY

In this chapter we have presented ideas to assist you to successfully evaluate your practice and to use the results of such evaluations to improve your practice. Your practice is critically affected by your own view of the world (your theoretical and ideological position), your professional and practice standards and methods, the context of practice, your desired outcomes and the relevant stakeholder groups (clients, professionals, agency personnel, the funding body, etc). If you are to effectively evaluate your practice you must be able to critically reflect on your own position and practice standards. We suggest you follow our guidelines to allow you to become a reflective practitioner able to critically self-evaluate.

We have presented a variety of quantitative and qualitative methods that can be used in combination to provide effective evaluation of your practice. We suggest that you use the information gained from self-evaluation to improve your practice. With this in mind we have outlined strategies that allow you to work towards best practice standards. These include developing transparent standards, providing accessible information, consulting with clients and others and regularly evaluating your performance and the service you provide. Of course, you should also actively seek out the results of relevant research done by others and consciously and critically incorporate the findings into your practice. By attending to these strategies you will be actively working towards best practice and establishing the foundations for a well rounded evidence-based culture in your work.

QUESTIONS

1 What factors influence social work practice effectiveness?
2 What is a reflective practitioner?

3 What important points should you note when evaluating practice?
4 Outline some of the criticisms of the scientific approach in relation to social work practice evaluation.
5 Note three quantitative and three qualitative methods you could use to evaluate practice.
6 Outline three best practice strategies.

EXERCISES

1 Visit a social service agency and seek information on services provided. Examine the literature you receive to determine whether quality standards, monitoring processes and a complaints mechanism have been outlined. Discuss the best practice strategies in relation to this organisation.
2 Go to a local health agency. Assess whether their information is provided in an accessible way for a culturally diverse population. Note whether the service is physically accessible for all clients and whether operating hours are accessible.
3 Pair up with a colleague or another student in class. Seek feedback on how well you perform in your role as a student/professional. Give similar feedback to your partner. What criteria did you each use to assess performance?

FURTHER READING

Practice evaluation is a relatively new area and traditional references are hard to find. However, there is a great deal of material on practice evaluation emerging on the Web. You should spend some time searching on the Internet, beginning with the sites suggested at the beginning of this chapter.

11 OTHER METHODS

In previous chapters we have addressed the most common types of social work methods you may use in your role as a researcher. This chapter will outline some further methods that will be very useful for you to have in your research tool kit. When you are conducting a piece of research, it is important to use the most appropriate method to gather the data you need. Often your choice will be circumscribed by the amount of funds available to you as well as by other resources such as time, help from other staff, access to computer equipment and access to the data source. Your choice of method is made on the basis of a careful weighing up of all options. Study the methods in this chapter carefully and reflect on their usefulness to you. They may allow you to be more creative and in some cases, as with secondary analysis, may save you valuable time and resources.

SECONDARY ANALYSIS

Secondary analysis is the process of using data which has already been collected for some other purpose to provide answers to your research question. As a practitioner, you will be aware of the types of data available in a practice setting. For example, imagine that you are working in a community health centre attached to a large hospital. You will have around you client files of your own and other workers,

detailed hospital records and, presumably, historical records. Whether
you have access to all of these records is debatable. If you wish to
conduct research on files and records to which you have no access,
you must submit a proposal to the hospital ethics committee detailing
why you need access and to what purpose the data will be put. The
main point to note is that in most agency settings, there is much
existing material that may be the source of rich research data.

Of course, there are public domain sources as well and no doubt
you are familiar with many. These would include the national census
data, material produced by federal, state and local government
authorities and reports published by non-government welfare agencies. This type of material is increasingly available in on-line formats
and will be useful for any study undertaken, even at local level. For
example, suppose that you wish to study non-English speaking background (NESB) people and their access to your community health
centre. It would be useful to know, first, what is the ethnic breakdown
of your local area, a factor that is readily obtained from census
material. When studying the census data (which will be available
through your local library) note also the proportions of different
ethnic groups. Imagine that the ethnic population of your area is
30 per cent and (to simplify) that one-third of these are from Asian
countries and two-thirds from southern European areas. Now examine the records kept at your community centre. If less than 30 per
cent of those using the service are from non-English speaking background, then you have a problem. If, for example, only 2 per cent of
clients are Asian immigrants and 5 per cent are southern Europeans,
you have a serious problem. What you should note from this example
is that you have conducted a research project without having gathered any original data!

TYPES OF RESEARCH USING SECONDARY ANALYSIS

It is important to note that you are able to use secondary analysis to
conduct an exploratory study, a descriptive study or even an explanatory study. Exploratory studies are about exploring the possibilities
and generating ideas for further research. You may, for example,
explore your records to assess client composition. This exploration
may reveal that women make up more than 50 per cent of the
agency's client load and that these are clustered in the 25–45 age
bracket. This exploratory study may generate a hypothesis that males
are less likely to seek help. Remember, this has not been *proven* by
your exploration. You would need to conduct a further study to *test*
such a hypothesis. Exploratory studies are good ways of generating
hypotheses in research areas where you have some interest.

Secondary analysis is an excellent source of descriptive material in that records may be assessed to provide a descriptive profile of the client source. Similarly, secondary analysis can provide explanatory material which supports a hypothesis concerning causal links between variables.

Secondary analysis

Secondary analysis is:
- The process of using data which has already been collected for some other purpose to provide answers to your research question

Secondary analysis can be used for:
- Exploratory studies
- Descriptive studies
- Explanatory studies

Sources of secondary data:
- Agency records
- Client files
- Census records
- Other public domain material
- Data collected for other research

PROBLEMS WITH SECONDARY ANALYSIS

While secondary analysis is an excellent way of conducting research, you should be aware of some serious pitfalls associated with this type of data. First, think back to the examination of the NESB composition of the community health centre's clients. If your centre is in an area which has a high transient population you may be using an unreliable source of data. Because censuses are conducted only once every five years (ten years in some countries), and it takes up to two years for the data to be analysed and disseminated to the public, you may be using material that is dated and no longer relevant to your area. Be aware that the data you use for secondary analysis may be seriously out of date!

Further, you must also be aware that the original data you are using for secondary analysis was conducted for a particular purpose. It may be that this purpose undermines its validity. For example, in research conducted on Australian farm women, Margaret Alston discovered that historical census material would indicate that no women worked in agriculture or mining in the nineteenth century. This was perplexing, as she knew from other historical records such as diaries and newspapers that women were working in these areas. All was

188

revealed when she discovered through further sources, including parliamentary records, that a decision was made in the 1890s to discard the records of women in these fields because politicians of the time wished to present a face to the world that showed Australia was a *developed* nation. The idea of women working in the fields would have destroyed this image! Consequently, historical records do not record this information and do not give an accurate picture of the work of women (Alston 1995). If you are unaware of the context in which the data is recorded you may accept records with serious errors as true recordings. Be aware that secondary analysis data must be seen in *context*.

You should also note that records may be unreliable because people may record what they think *should* be recorded, not necessarily what *is*. In her investigation of farm women, Margaret Alston realised that many men who filled out census records under-reported the farm contributions of their wives. This appeared, in most cases, to be an unconscious factor shaped by their limited definition of farm work. Women took farm work to be a broader range of activities including bookwork, travelling to buy parts and supplies, providing meals for staff, etc. Be conscious of the fact that those who contributed the original data may hold a different interpretation of reality to that which you may hold!

You should also remember that data may be inconsistent because of problems with the original recording. If you are using agency records, for example, different staff may record similar cases in a different way, they may also be under pressure as a result of overwork and lack of time and therefore inconsistently record their own cases. Be aware that recording may be inconsistent!

Additionally, you should note that some records may be missing or may have been destroyed and that, consequently, you might not have a reliable source of data. For all these reasons you should carefully assess the source of your data and consider how reliable and valid it is. Relying on flawed data will ensure that your results are also flawed. A useful way to get around this problem may be to use other sources of data as well to ensure that your results are valid.

Problems with secondary analysis

- Data may be dated
- Data must be seen in the context of the time in which it was recorded
- Data may present a sanitised version because of different interpretations
- Data may be inconsistently recorded
- Some data may be missing

USING THE INTERNET IN SOCIAL WORK RESEARCH

Before leaving the topic of secondary sources, we must mention the use of the Internet as a valuable resource for doing social research. The recent explosion in information and technology through the development of the Internet has led to a treasure trove of new resources for social researchers. A major challenge, however, is learning to navigate your way through this treasure trove and working out what is valuable and what is not.

All the problems we have discussed in relation to using secondary sources apply to using data from the World Wide Web. An important skill for every researcher these days is to be a critical consumer and navigator of the Web. The Internet itself provides excellent resources in how to evaluate information on the Web. Many university libraries also have on-line tutorials in evaluating Web-based material on their home pages.

While the Internet is increasingly being used as a medium for social research, with on-line surveys becoming more popular, be wary of using results from such research, or this medium as a research tool, too freely. Remember that only people with access to the Internet at home or work will be likely to respond to such surveys. The focus of social work research is usually aimed at people who are disadvantaged and who therefore, at least for the near future, will probably be excluded from participating in Internet studies.

On the other hand, libraries are increasingly providing free on-line full text versions of journal articles and research reports as well as abstracts of the contents of journal articles. Their catalogues and databases are often available to you through your home computer and offer a marvellous resource that was unthinkable only a few years ago.

Another valuable use of the Internet is as a source of types of questions, questionnaires, data sets and codebooks that are related to the topic in which you are interested. There are also sites which offer help in just about every aspect of doing research. De Vaus provides an excellent guide to using the Internet, both in learning how to do surveys and in conducting them, in the fifth edition of his book *Surveys in Social Research* (2002). As part of the resources for this book, he maintains a Website of all the links listed in it as well as new and updated ones. You can go to this website and click on any of the links to explore a variety of sites on how to do research as well as sites of valuable resources for researchers. The address is <www.social-research.org>.

Using the Internet in social research

- Learn to critically evaluate Web-based material

190

- Be aware of the limitations of using the Internet as a primary research tool in social work research (e.g. for surveys)
- Take full advantage of the Internet's rich resources in teaching how to undertake research
- Learn to access the array of resources reporting existing research, including databases and library catalogues, questionnaires and databanks of questions, datasets and tools for interrogating them

CONTENT ANALYSIS

Another research method which is very useful is content analysis, the analysis of some form of communication—written, audio or visual—for trends or patterns and to analyse the style and techniques used. Like secondary analysis, content analysis examines existing material and does not necessarily require the researcher to collect original data. Content analysis is useful for examining not only what is included and how it is presented but also what is excluded. For example, content analysis of women's magazines from the 1950s would provide an interesting idea of the issues which were seen to be relevant for women at the time. While there may be much on household tips, dressmaking and cooking tips, there would, perhaps, be few articles on juggling work and family, coping with stress or dealing with sexual harassment in the workplace. Consequently, when conducting a content analysis study be very conscious of what is not there as well as what is, and analyse what the message means for the recipient. It may be interesting for us, as social workers, to conduct a comparative content analysis of historical social work records with more modern records. Such a study would tell us much about the types of interventions used or the methods of assessment as well as about the way records were kept!

Content analysis

Content analysis is:
- The analysis of some form of communication for trends or patterns

How to conduct a content analysis

When conducting a content analysis study bear in mind that you may be interested not only in a quantitative analysis of the material, but also in a qualitative assessment of the way the material is presented, its style and the values represented. A content analysis study should include a series of well-planned steps. First, you must isolate your sample. If you are studying social work records in your agency, you might decide to compare a sample of records from the first year of operation with a sample from the current year. You note that the social work service began in 1968. You therefore choose to sample all records from February–June 1968 and compare the material with that from February–June 2002. Bear in mind that the time frame is arbitrary and depends largely on the amount of material available. In a large agency a week of records may be as much as you can handle! Alternatively, you may choose a random sample of records, a systematic sample, or some other form of sampling method which may be appropriate. Refer to chapter 5 for types of sampling methods.

Your next step is to decide on the categories to be employed in your analysis. This might be based on the type of content of the documents you are studying or on certain values expressed in the material. Whatever the categories you choose, they should be exhaustive and mutually exclusive. With the social work records study, you might choose to divide records into categories associated with assessment procedures and intervention strategies. Alternatively, you may be more interested in the values expressed in the reports, or some other form of categorisation.

The third step is to determine what it is you wish to measure. This may be based on the number of times a word or a theme appears, or on the amount of space or time given to a certain category. Finally, you must determine how you will record your analysis—in a database, in a frequency table or in some other systematic way.

Once your data is collected you must carefully analyse the material to determine what conclusions you should draw. For example, your social work records study may have revealed that the historical records indicate that methods of assessment and intervention were very conservative and that the thrust of the intervention strategy was to change the client. Modern records may reveal more diverse types of interventions and a more critical evaluation of the social system. Of course, they may reveal nothing of the sort! What such a study will do, however, is provide a very interesting comparative analysis.

Conducting a content analysis

- Determine your sample
- Decide on categories to be employed
- Determine what it is you are measuring
- Decide on the recording technique
- Analyse data
- Draw conclusions

Case study—an analysis of sports reporting in rural media

In 1996 Margaret Alston conducted an analysis of media representations of women's sport in rural New South Wales. The study was funded by the NSW Department for Women and its aim was to determine whether media bias existed in sports representation. Three rural areas of differing sizes were selected for the study. All media—newspapers, radio and television—were investigated. Alston was concerned to gain a comprehensive picture of both winter and summer sports coverage and to look at quantitative as well as qualitative measures of presentation.

Because of the amount of media material Alston decided to sample one month of newspapers in winter and one in summer and two weeks of radio and television in both summer and winter. The quantitative categories selected were female only, male only, mixed sport, horses and dogs. Alston determined that this would be measured in the newspapers by the number of articles and the space in square centimetres and by the number and size of photographs. For radio and television the same categories were used and these were measured in seconds of air time devoted to each category. The qualitative measures were the style of language used and (for the newspapers) whether photographs were active or passive shots (that is, were those photographed actively engaged in sport or posed for the camera).

A database was set up on computer, which allowed the research assistant to enter extraordinary amounts of data. For example, there were over 4500 entries for newspapers alone. Once entered in the database the program allowed data to be manipulated, counted and analysed very easily and efficiently.

Not surprisingly the data revealed that media bias in sports reporting was widespread and overwhelming. Newspaper coverage of women's sport was only 5 per cent of total sports coverage, while for television it was 13 per cent and for radio 7 per cent. Female sport received far less coverage than horses and only slightly more than dogs. Qualitative analysis revealed that the language used to report male sport was often aggressive with terms such as 'battle' and 'strong' common, while female sports stories were often colourless and banal. Female sports photographs were also much more likely to be posed while male photographs were more often action shots. By using content analysis, this study was able to reveal the full extent of media bias against women's sport and the nature of the forms of bias. Subsidiary methods such as interviews with sports administrators and female athletes demonstrated the full implications of this bias such as a resulting lack of sponsorship, a lack of priority given to talent development opportunities for girls, less motivation to succeed and a dearth of female role models in sport.

Alston, Margaret 1996, *Goals for Women: Improving Media Representation of Women's Sport*, Centre for Rural Social Research, Charles Sturt University, Wagga Wagga, NSW.

OBSERVATIONS

A particularly important method for social workers is observation. Observation allows us to overcome some of the limitation inherent in other methods. For instance, a survey of school children may reveal that none admit to being schoolyard bullies. While this may be true, it may also be that respondents do not admit to being bullies because it is not socially desirable behaviour. A study using observation techniques, with the researcher spending time in the playground observing the behaviour of children, may reveal quite different information.

Observation, quite simply, is the process of *observing* behaviour. It may be structured or unstructured and it may involve the researcher being a participant or a non-participant in the behaviour being observed.

Observation

- Structured
- Unstructured
- Participant
- Non-participant

Structured observation

Structured observation is a method of systematically observing certain pre-defined behaviours and using a predetermined set of observation categories. These observations may be noted by the research participant themselves (for example, a client suffering depression may keep a diary of the number of times they are distressed) or by the researcher. Taking the schoolyard example, a researcher may observe the playground activities and note each time unnecessary physical and verbal force is used.

Structured observation is employed in quantitative studies where precise and quantifiable measurements are sought. In such cases the problem is carefully defined, the observation site is determined, and the observation categories clearly developed. Those categories may include actions, attitudes, modes of speech or any other element which is a key factor in the research study. Because of the nature of the research design, structured observation studies are chiefly used in explanatory research.

Structured observation

- Quantitative
- Carefully planned
- Behaviour type observed and carefully defined
- Categories developed
- Time period determined
- Observation study completed
- Used mainly in explanatory research

Unstructured observation

Unstructured observation is a more qualitative method because there is no careful definition of the behaviour to be studied. The researcher observes behaviour and events in an endeavour to *explore* the situation under investigation. There is no careful plan and no organised categories of observation units. An example of an unstructured observation study may be one where the observer spends time in an institutional setting (for example, a nursing home) observing the way the organisation operates, the interactions between staff and residents and other elements of the institution. The researcher may have no stated research objective other than to observe the effect of institutional life on residents. After a while the observer may note patterns of behaviour or operation which affect the health and wellbeing of residents. This may be medication regimes, policies relating to the time residents are woken each morning, the way meals are delivered or other factors. Unstructured observation allows the researcher to 'soak up' the environment and to make observations which are free from any preconceptions about the situation. In a study using unstructured observation, the researcher may record incidents, impressions, dialogue and other important points about the research situation. Because of the research design, unstructured observation is more likely to be used in exploratory or descriptive studies.

Unstructured observation

- Qualitative
- Flexible research plan
- No preconceived ideas about what behaviour is to be observed
- Categories developed during the study
- Time period determined
- Observation study completed
- Used mainly in exploratory or descriptive research

Participant observation

The extent of the involvement of the researcher in the study situation must be assessed before research begins in an observation study. The researcher may choose to be a participant observer in the study or be a non-participant observer.

A *participant observer* becomes a part of the research situation. They participate in all activities and interact with the researched. There are serious ethical dilemmas which must be considered before undertaking such a study. Some of the more famous participant observation studies (such as Whyte's [1955] study of street-corner gangs) collected rich data because they *did not* disclose to the observed that behaviour was being researched. Nowadays, such studies are viewed as ethically untenable and we are no longer able to conduct such research. Participant observers must note that disclosing their research activities will necessarily influence the behaviour being observed. Subjects will be less likely to disclose sensitive and critical information and they may be inclined to change their behaviour to conform to what is seen as socially desirable.

The participant observer must decide what data to record, how they will do this given that they are participating in the situation, and how this data is to be analysed. Participant observation studies may be quantitative or qualitative depending on the research objectives. Such a study may be useful if you are evaluating the effects of a new social work program. You may choose to become a participant in the program to assess the issues from a client's perspective. By contrast, a non-participant study is one where the researcher is not participating in the behaviour or situation being examined.

Participant observation

- Researcher is part of the study situation
- Ethical considerations require disclosure
- Must assess effect on research situation of disclosure

- May be quantitative or qualitative
- Must decide what is to be recorded
- Time period determined
- Note that presence of participant observer may influence the behaviour being studied
- Observation study completed

RESEARCH DESIGN IN OBSERVATION STUDIES

As with any piece of research, you should give careful thought to your research plan, noting that this will depend on whether you choose to use a quantitative or qualitative research framework and on whether you are a participant or a non-participant. Give some attention to defining your research problem. Determine the level of your participation and whether your observation will be structured or unstructured. Decide on the sample, bearing in mind that it will include the observation site or event, the people to be observed and the duration of the observation period. Before you begin your study you must decide how you will gain entry to the situation. It may be very difficult to become a participant observer in certain closed situations such as an institutional setting. Finally, you must decide how the data are to be analysed and reported.

While observation studies provide valuable information that may be unavailable through other means, you should note the limitations of these methods. By definition they are time consuming and cannot be used for large groups or for different time periods. Further, findings may be influenced by the participation or presence of the researcher and there is no guarantee that the data are valid. Nevertheless, observation studies are useful in providing information about behaviour in a natural setting and allow the researcher to observe and record a wide range of information.

Research design in observation studies

- Define the problem
- Choose sample including site, event, people to be observed and the time frame
- Determine level of researcher participation
- Determine whether observation is structured or unstructured
- Decide what is to be recorded
- Analyse and report results
- Note advantages and limitations of the method

CASE STUDIES

Case study research is research focused on a single case, issue, group, organisation or event. It is quite different to the single system design discussed in the previous chapter. In contrast to other methods, case study research does not seek patterns of behaviour by comparative analysis of a number of subjects. Rather, it examines one case, usually defined as a typical case, in order to fully investigate and thoroughly analyse the details which may be lost in a larger study. Case study research is particularly important in social work settings because it allows a typical case, client, event, group or other phenomenon to be studied in order to reveal information which will aid the analysis of, and afford insights into, the wider target group. The information will assist in the development of an appropriate intervention strategy.

Imagine that one of your clients is a carer of an HIV/AIDS patient. This may be a new and increasingly significant group which you know little about. By investigating the situation, tensions and pressures placed on your client, your case study research will give you a great deal of information about the wider population of carers of HIV/AIDS patients.

Single-case research is also useful when you wish to study a particular group (for example, you may have established a group of sexual assault survivors), an organisation (such as a branch office), or an event (such as a social action campaign). Such single-case studies will yield rich data about the wider population or social system and, as such, this type of research should not be dismissed as insignificant research.

Case studies may be used in quantitative research as a means of clarifying the research hypothesis and as a form of pretest. In qualitative studies, case study research is an important exploratory method. Feminist researchers view case study research as a very important way of exploring the experiences of different groups of women in different situations and cultures. As Reinharz (1992) states:

> The case study is a tool of feminist research that is used to document history and generate theory. It defies the social science convention of seeking generalisations by looking instead for specificity, exceptions and completeness. Some feminist researchers have found that social science's emphasis on generalisations have obscured phenomena important to particular groups, including women. These case studies are essential for putting women on the map of social life (p. 174).

When conducting a case study, you need to determine what it is you wish to investigate, what particular characteristics of the case study are important, and what it is you wish to achieve. Choose your case carefully, as it must represent a typical or special example, and decide how the data will be gathered and analysed. Finally, give some thought to the reporting of the case and how best to disseminate your insights and discoveries.

The advantages of case study research include the fact that data are often readily available, that it allows an examination of complex situations which may render other methods unsuitable, and that it may require less resourcing. The limitations include a lack of quantification and a lack of ability to generalise.

Case study

- Studies a single case, group, organisation or event
- Does not seek generalisations or comparisons
- May be used in qualitative or quantitative research
- Particularly important in feminist research
- A case study design includes an outline of the problem, how the case will be chosen (sampling), data collection and analysis techniques and the way the study will be reported

---

SUMMARY

This chapter has presented a range of methods which will be useful for social work researchers. Methods presented here include secondary analysis, content analysis, observation and case study research. We have also discussed some critical points about using the Internet in social work research. Each of these methods has its own particular advantages and limitations. The method you choose will ultimately be determined by the type of data you are seeking, the resources at your disposal (including time), your access to the situation and the nature of the research subjects. By balancing these factors you must determine what is the most appropriate method to address your research problem.

Remember that with any piece of research you should consider the value of triangulation—using more than one method to provide comprehensive data. Each of the methods described in this chapter, while important in their own right, can be used in conjunction with other methods to increase the validity and reliability of the data and to add weight to the conclusions drawn from the study.

QUESTIONS

1 What is secondary analysis?
2 What sources of data are available for secondary analysis in a social work setting?

3 What are the advantages and limitations of secondary analysis?
4 List some of the ways the Internet can be used in social work research. What cautions apply?
5 What is content analysis?
6 How would you conduct a content analysis study?
7 Outline the different types of observation studies.
8 What are the advantages and limitations of observation studies?
9 Why is case study research important?
10 What are the advantages and limitations of case study research?
11 How would you undertake a piece of case study research in your work or study setting?

EXERCISES

1 Go to the library and study the census records for your area. List the ethnic and age breakdown of your community and the five dominant occupations for men and women. What have you learned about your community and what do you think might be its welfare service needs?
2 Examine the front page of your local newspaper for a one-week period. How many stories featured women and how many featured men? What does your analysis suggest?
3 Spend some time in the waiting room of the accident and emergency section of your local hospital conducting an unstructured observation study. What have you learned?
4 Spend time with a work colleague or fellow student assessing how they balance their work/study activities with their family life. What does your case study tell you about the issues facing workers/students in your organisation?
5 Visit the Website <www.social-research.org>. Explore some of the links, including the one for evaluating information found on the Internet.

FURTHER READING

Babbie, E. 2001, *The Practice of Social Research*, 9th edn, Wadsworth, Belmont, USA. Chapter 11, 'Unobtrusive Research'.
Berg, B. L. 1995, *Qualitative Methods for the Social Sciences*, Allyn & Bacon, Boston. Chapter 7, 'Unobtrusive Methods in Research'; chapter 9, 'An Introduction to Content Analysis'.
de Vaus, D. A. 2002, *Surveys in Social Research*, 5th edn, Allen & Unwin, Sydney. Chapter 3 has an excellent guide to using the Internet to review existing information and research. Throughout the book

there are 'Web-pointers' summarising links to the Internet for assistance with nearly every aspect of conducting social research.

Grinnell, R. M. Jr (ed.) 1993, *Social Work Research and Evaluation*, 3rd edn, Peacock Publishers, Itasca, Ill. Chapter 12, 'Structured Observation'; chapter 14, 'Secondary Analysis'; chapter 15, 'Content Analysis'.

Kidder, L. H. & Judd, C. M. 1986, *Research Methods in Social Relations*, CBS Publishing Japan Ltd. Chapter 12, 'Observational and Archival Research'.

Mark, R. 1996, *Research Made Simple: A Handbook for Social Workers*, Sage, Thousand Oaks, CA. Chapter 9 examines observation.

Reinharz, S. 1992, *Feminist Methods in Social Research*, Oxford University Press, New York. Chapter 8, 'Feminist Content Analysis'; chapter 9, 'Feminist Case Studies'.

Royse, D. 1999, *Research Methods in Social Work*, 3rd edn, Nelson-Hall, Chicago, Chapter 8, 'Unobtrusive Approaches to Data Collection— Secondary Data and Content Analysis'.

Rubin, A. & B. Earl, 2001, *Research Methods for Social Work*, 4th edn, Wadsworth, USA. Chapter 14, 'Unobtrusive Research: Quantitative and Qualitative Methods'.

Sarantakos, S. 1998, *Social Research* 2nd edn, Macmillan, Melbourne. Chapter 8, 'Case Studies'; chapter 9, 'Observation'; chapter 12, 'Indirect Methods of Data Collection'.

Sherman, E. & Reid, W. J. (eds) 1994, *Qualitative Research in Social Work*, Columbia University Press, New York.

12 PRODUCING RESULTS: QUALITATIVE RESEARCH

In this and the following two chapters, we discuss how to analyse the information you gather (data), in order to address the questions which generated your research project. In this chapter we introduce the key aspects of analysing data from qualitative studies. Chapters 13 and 14 discuss data analysis for quantitative research.

Traditionally, the thought of data analysis has struck terror into the hearts of many research students in the social sciences, with visions of having to calculate statistics from difficult mathematical equations. However, this first chapter on qualitative data analysis deals with analysis which traditionally does not rely on mathematics at all. Even in quantitative analysis, nightmares about mathematics are now a thing of the past. Computers make calculations the easy part of research. In these chapters we discuss the basic principles of organising your data so that computers can perform the statistics you need. We also introduce you to some of the basic principles of data analysis as a preparation for the procedures that you will need to learn for your own specific research. The aim is to demonstrate the links between research questions, design and data analysis, and to provide a framework for thinking through fundamental approaches to data analysis as you plan a research project. Remember that the goal of research is to find answers to research questions and to develop theory. Whether we do this through qualitative or quantitative means or a combination of methods depends on what are the most comprehensive ways of addressing the research question. You should therefore familiarise yourself with both methodologies and think creatively about their uses in undertaking your own research.

In this first chapter about qualitative data analysis, we discuss how qualitative researchers deal with the data they collect, and the careful processes that are undertaken to analyse this data. For simplicity we will explore the main principles of qualitative analysis using illustrations from one approach only: Strauss and Corbin's (1998) grounded theory approach to qualitative data analysis, a method based on Strauss and Glaser's work (see, for example Glaser 1978, 1992; Glaser and Strauss 1967, and Strauss 1990). This approach has been chosen because Strauss and Corbin give a clear explanation of what qualitative researchers actually do with their data, and because Strauss has developed useful guidelines for each stage of data analysis. This approach encompasses many of the principles of data analysis used in other types of qualitative research, although the emphases are different, and so serves as a useful introduction to qualitative analysis generally (Reissman 1994, Sarantakos 1998). The chapter concludes with a detailed example of qualitative analysis which illustrates the usefulness of the computer program *Ethnograph*.

DIFFERENCES BETWEEN QUALITATIVE AND QUANTITATIVE ANALYSIS

Qualitative data analysis is different from quantitative analysis in several fundamental ways. First, as noted above, it does not rely on mathematics or numbers in the same way as quantitative analysis. Sometimes qualitative researchers count numbers of themes, or the numbers of people for whom certain themes apply, and sometimes they use computer packages in a similar way to quantitative researchers for certain aspects of their work. They may also describe their sample using quantitative terms (for example, 56 women and 24 men, five under 40 and ten who are 40 or over). In the main, however, qualitative researchers analyse their data using logic and theoretical and methodological principles, rather than applying statistical formulae or quantification.

Thus, qualitative data analysis is about interpretation rather than mathematics. It is about finding the meanings that people ascribe to their experiences. Strauss and Corbin (1998) describe qualitative analysis as using the same kinds of problem solving and other common modes of thinking that occur in everyday life, except at a more self-conscious and scientifically rigorous level than usually occurs. As they do not emphasise figures or calculations, qualitative researchers mainly use text and explanation to present their data, instead of the charts and graphs that are typical of quantitative research results.

Second, there is not the same agreement on how to perform data analysis as exists in quantitative approaches (Reissman 1994, Sherman & Reid 1994, Berg 1995, Tutty et al. 1996, Strauss & Corbin 1998). Whereas quantitative researchers have well-documented, structured rules and procedures for data analysis (see chapter 13), the procedures used by qualitative researchers are not as explicit and are more subjective. In fact, qualitative researchers argue that it is one of the strengths of qualitative research that it does *not* have a set of rules for data analysis. For example, Strauss and Corbin (1998) maintain that standardised sets of rules would only stifle and constrain qualitative researchers in their efforts to develop new theories. They point out that qualitative researchers work in such different contexts, with different aims, methods, gifts and talents, that it is impossible as well as undesirable to have strict rules of data analysis. They stress that their method of qualitative data analysis is meant to provide a guideline or framework only, rather than a set of rules such as quantitative researchers would provide, and that researchers should view qualitative analysis as an art as well as a science.

A third major difference between qualitative and quantitative data analysis is that qualitative data analysis usually occurs simultaneously with the data collection phase, in a continuous, cyclical process. As Tutty et al. (1996, p. 115) suggest, 'you must be flexible and move back and forth between and among the steps and tasks to produce rich and meaningful findings'. Padgett (1998) and Strauss and Corbin (1998) refer to the process of moving from inductive analysis to deductive and back to inductive, with Padgett describing it as 'constant comparative analysis'. Indeed, Strauss and Corbin (1998) emphasise that data analysis can begin with the first interview or piece of evidence that is gathered, a process which encourages the researcher to think analytically rather than descriptively, and so move on to theorising without becoming lost in a mass of complex data. In quantitative analysis, by contrast, the data collection phase occurs first, and data analysis only begins when the last interview or questionnaire has been coded and entered into the computer.

A fourth difference between qualitative and quantitative research, already alluded to, is that qualitative researchers may use a variety of methods as the study progresses. For example, a qualitative researcher may use information that is analysed from documents, as well as interviews that evolve as the researcher obtains more insights into the issue being researched. The researcher may also hold small group meetings to clarify the emerging issues. In this way the researcher builds up the data, creating a rich understanding of the study area. Whether such different methods are used will depend on the context of the study, the relevance of various sources as they are discovered and the hypotheses that evolve.

If a particular study does not yield useful information as planned, there is little the quantitative researcher can do but report the results as they occur, whereas in qualitative research the researcher is free to pursue alternative directions and use different methods of analysis according to their usefulness. As we have noted, this variety of methods makes standardised techniques for qualitative data analysis difficult. But we are able to give guidelines about the process. What is rigorous in qualitative data analysis, however, is the approach to thinking analytically and creatively about complex social phenomena. Essentially there is no substitute for experience where qualitative data analysis is concerned.

These differences between qualitative and quantitative data analysis mean that they have different *strengths* and *weaknesses*. This was alluded to in our earlier discussion of reliability and validity (chapter 3), in which it was noted that qualitative research prides itself on its validity, but that criticisms have been levelled in regard to its reliability (or consistency or ability to be replicated). In contrast, the findings of some quantitative studies have been criticised as not being valid in the real world, or for simplifying complex issues to the point where they are not relevant. The strengths of quantitative studies include that they are relatively easy to replicate (that is, their reliability is easy to establish) and that they generally involve sophisticated comparisons of variables. Qualitative studies, on the other hand, because they often study a single situation in depth, have a corresponding weakness in their ability to compare variables in different conditions or to make claims about causality. However, because qualitative studies take into account the context in which the research is conducted and researchers have the flexibility to check and re-check their findings in the field (since data analysis occurs simultaneously with data collection), they claim validity.

Four differences between qualitative and quantitative data analysis

- Qualitative analysis relies on interpretation and logic whereas quantitative analysis relies on statistics (qualitative researchers present their analyses using text and argument, whereas quantitative researchers use graphs and tables)
- Qualitative analysis has no set rules but rather guidelines, whereas quantitative analysis follows agreed upon standardised procedures and rules
- Qualitative analysis occurs simultaneously with data collection whereas quantitative analysis occurs only after data collection is finished
- Qualitative analysis may vary methods depending on the situation, whereas methods of quantitative analysis are determined in advance as part of the study design

THE PROCESS OF QUALITATIVE DATA ANALYSIS

Before outlining Strauss and Corbin's 'grounded theory' approach to qualitative data analysis in detail, we will discuss the general assumptions behind, and steps involved in, the process of data analysis that all researchers from qualitative perspectives follow in some form. This may seem slightly contradictory, having just asserted that qualitative researchers do not follow standardised rules of data analysis. Nonetheless, despite there being no agreement on specific rules of analysis, there is agreement on the processes that qualitative researchers undertake to analyse their data, even if these are expressed in different ways by different researchers.

Several assumptions underlie most processes of qualitative data analysis. First, remember from earlier chapters that qualitative researchers are interested in the complexities of social reality. Their methods of data analysis, therefore, attempt to capture the meanings and relationships involved in these complexities.

Another assumption often made is that the experiences of both the researcher and the researched can be taken into account when collecting and analysing the data. Strauss and Corbin (1998, p. 13) describe analysis as 'the interplay between researchers and data'. For example, in the study on postnatal depression described in chapter 3, the researchers consulted the participants about the questions to be asked and reported back their initial results for discussion and analysis. In chapter 1 we discussed how qualitative researchers often see themselves and their experiences as an important part of the research process, because they reject notions of objectivity. Instead of being separate from the research process, qualitative researchers may analyse their own interactions with the issues and/or people they are researching as a critical part of the analysis. Strauss (1990) terms the use of the researcher's own experience and skills 'experiential data' or data 'in the head' drawn from the researcher's personal, research and literature-reading experiences. He argues that explicitly 'mining' this source of data leads to much better theory building, which is the ultimate task of qualitative researchers. However Strauss and Corbin (1998) warn that experience should not be used as primary data but rather as something to be drawn on in sensitising the researcher to nuances of their data.

In earlier chapters we described the process of qualitative research as being 'inductive'. By this we meant that the hypotheses and theory coming from the research are generated from the data itself (in the cyclical process described above), and are thus 'grounded' in the data that the researcher has gathered. In chapter 2 the analogy of a climbing pyramid was used to describe how qualitative researchers begin at the bottom rungs, the broadest base of the pyramid, before they gradually climb up to higher levels of abstraction. This is the opposite to quantitative researchers, who begin at the top of the pyramid, with concepts, dimensions, indicators, variables and hypotheses worked out before the data are collected.

de Vaus (2002), a quantitative researcher, Strauss and Corbin (1998) and Padgett (1998) qualitative researchers, all make the following important point about inductive and deductive activities in the research process: all researchers are involved in both inductive and deductive thinking in a cyclical manner. The difference between qualitative and quantitative research is the starting point of the process.

Sarantakos (1998) identifies three general stages in qualitative data analysis, which describe what is going on during induction, deduction and verification. Again, it is emphasised that these stages occur cyclically. The first stage Sarantakos (1998) terms *data reduction*. This is the stage where data are coded, summarised and categorised in order to identify important aspects of the issue being researched. Data reduction also helps the researcher decide what further data to collect, how and who to sample next, what methods of analysis to use and, finally, to arrive at conclusions. All these activities involve induction, and sometimes deduction as well. The important goal of data reduction is to identify the main themes emerging from the research by categorising the information as it is collected. In some forms of qualitative research, data collection, data reduction and data analysis are almost indistinguishable (Sarantakos 1998).

The second stage of qualitative data analysis according to Sarantakos (1998) is *data organisation*. This is the process of assembling the information around certain themes and points, and presenting the results, usually in text. The third phase is *interpretation*. This involves identifying patterns, trends and explanations which lead to conclusions which can be tested through more data collection, reduction, organisation and interpretation. Further data collection, reduction, organisation and interpretation occur until the categories or themes that are being researched are 'saturated'; that is, there are no more new insights or information being generated.

Aspects of qualitative data analysis

- Qualitative data analysis aims to capture the richness and complexity of lived experience
- Qualitative data analysis includes the experiences of the researcher, both before and during the research (experiential data)
- Qualitative data analysis consists of three general stages which follow one another in a continuous cycle: *data reduction, data organisation* and *interpretation*

QUALITATIVE DATA ANALYSIS: THE GROUNDED THEORY APPROACH

Strauss and Glaser first published their book *Discovery of Grounded Theory* in 1967 (Glaser & Strauss 1967). In this section we summarise Strauss and Corbin's (1998) version of the grounded theory approach to data analysis to illustrate the rigorous thinking that goes into analysing qualitative data and the processes involved in transforming this data into 'grounded theory'. You will see that Strauss and Corbin's approach involves the three activities (data reduction, organisation and interpretation) described above. Throughout the whole process, induction, deduction and verification is continuously occurring.

Briefly, Strauss and Corbin's method of data analysis involves *data collection*, *data coding* and *memoing*. The researcher goes back and forth between each of these phases that together make up the 'coding paradigm'. *Data collection* is the finding/gathering of information for the researcher to analyse. *Data coding* is a general term used by Strauss and Corbin to mean conceptualising data: careful examination and thinking about the data, often in conjunction with experiential insights, which leads to asking generative questions. Generative questions make comparisons and distinctions between the information collected and stimulate the line of inquiry in profitable directions. Strauss and Corbin use the term *coding* to refer to any product of this sort of analysis that creates categories, as well as exploring the relationships between them. Three types of coding are discussed below.

Memos are separate analytical notes that the researcher makes to help think theoretically about their findings: notes that record theoretical questions, concepts, hypotheses, summaries of codes, insights, clues for further data collection, etc. Memos keep track of coding results, stimulate further coding and integrate theory.

Strauss and Corbin note that qualitative researchers from a grounded theory perspective use the coding paradigm in a very different way to other qualitative researchers. Whereas more positivist qualitative researchers move forward in a linear way from data collection through to coding and hypothesising and then collect new data to verify their hypotheses, grounded theory researchers move back and forth between data collection, coding and memoing from very early in the process and continue to do so throughout the project. The developing theory is grounded in the data because it develops through intensive and systematic analysis of data, sometimes sentence by sentence or phrase by phrase (Glaser [1978] cited in Strauss [1990, p. 22]). Data collecting quickly leads to coding, which may soon lead to memoing, either of which will guide the researcher to more data collecting, or more coding and memoing, or even to re-inspection and analysis of old data that has already been analysed. Strauss points out that grounded theory research can return to old data at any point in the research process, even when researchers are writing the last page of their final report!

The process by which researchers collect more data as a result of their coding and memoing activities is termed *theoretical sampling*. This is sampling of people, situations, events or activities that is guided by the need to compare ideas or answer questions in the process of developing theory. This type of sampling is very different from sampling in quantitative research because it is driven by the emerging theory. The basic question behind theoretical sampling is: 'What groups or subgroups of populations, events, activities (to find varying dimensions, strategies, etc.) does one turn to next in data collection? And for what theoretical purpose?' (Glaser [1978] cited in Strauss [1990, pp. 38–9]). It is useful when sampling theoretically to look at the deviant or atypical cases, or what might be referred to as the 'outriders'. In assessing these cases you are better able to illuminate the norms emerging from your data.

The early phases of data analysis in this approach are more open than later ones, although it may take long periods of data collection, coding and memoing before the researcher decides on which categories and concepts are the most important (the most important categories are termed *core categories*). As theoretical sampling guides the collection of more data, memos become more theoretical and 'integrative', and core categories emerge. Once core categories have been established, the researcher concentrates on relating other categories to them and gradually making the developing theory more 'dense'. Additional categories and properties related to the core categories will continue to be 'discovered' throughout this process. As the research proceeds, memos become more elaborate and conceptual, making links and integrating earlier ideas so that the entire theory can be written up in the final report. Strauss and Corbin emphasise that each research project will be unpredictable in how the steps of data collection, analysis (coding) and interpretation (memoing) evolve. However, there are several essential operations you should note when undertaking qualitative analysis from a grounded theory perspective.

Managing data

Padgett (1998) and Miles and Huberman (1994) refer to qualitative data analysis as an 'hierarchical typology of abstraction' where the researcher moves from the raw data (field notes, documents transcripts and memos) to coded transcripts and analytical memos to a conceptual map of the emerging theory. To achieve the transition between stages cleanly you need to deal with your data in a systematic way. The following guidelines are the result of our experience managing large amounts of qualitative data.

- The main advice we can give is to begin early!
- Organise and store your data for maximum efficiency and retrieval.
- Transcribe any taped interview material as soon as is practical so that this precious material is not lost or corrupted. If this process is delayed make copies of tapes immediately and keep them in separate locations. You should try and have the transcribing done as you go to minimise the delay in analysis and to keep abreast of the costs.
- Mark each tape, document, field note and memo with the date, time, place and source of information.
- Once you have had your taped material transcribed make backup copies of your files and again keep copies in separate places.
- When formatting your file leave a wide margin on the left side of the paper allowing you to make notations as you read.
- Read and reread your transcript, marking preliminary codes in the margins. After reading several transcripts, write your codes on a large sheet of paper, noting linkages between codes and sub-codes. Note that this beginning schema will change several times during the course of your analysis before you are completely satisfied with the emerging theory.
- During your analysis write memos noting the linkages between codes, questions that arise, ideas for theoretical sampling and any other issue that is significant.

As the conceptual framework becomes clearer you will note that some data is more relevant than others and it is okay to focus on the more relevant material.

A final piece of advice is to use a computer program to store and retrieve your material. Several programs are available including *INVIVO* and *Ethnograph*, that allow ease of data management. If you are conducting a large project the purchase of one of these programs is very worthwhile.

Data collection

We have already seen how qualitative data can be collected from a range of sources, including interviews, group meetings, documents and field observations. Beginning the data analysis as early as the first, second or third interview or day of observation helps prevent the richness of the data from becoming overwhelming. This is because early analysis guides the direction of the next interviews or observation by providing analytic questions and hypotheses about categories and their relationships. As the analysis of new data develops, so the guidance of the analysis becomes more explicit.

Just as coding and memoing begin early in the process of data collection and continue throughout the life of the project, so data collection continues because coding and memoing raise fresh questions that need to be addressed through either gathering new data or re-examining old data. Theory-guided data collection (theoretical sampling) often also leads to new methods of data collection, for example, a series of directed interviews to supplement the more casual ones already done during fieldwork.

Coding

'The excellence of the research rests in large part on the excellence of the coding' (Strauss 1990, p. 27). The ability to code well and easily is one of the keys to successful qualitative data analysis. Coding involves much more than simple description—it is important that it become analytical as quickly as possible. One of the most difficult aspects of qualitative data analysis is learning to move from the data to the more abstract level of theory. To assist researchers code data in a way that is relevant and helpful in forming categories, Strauss (1990) and Strauss and Corbin (1998) suggest the following paradigm for what to look for in the data when coding:

- Conditions
- Interaction among actors
- Strategies and tactics
- Consequences

Conditions become easy to recognise when the researcher looks for cues in words such as 'because', 'since' and 'as'. Similarly *consequences* can be revealed by phrases such as 'because of that', 'the result was' and 'in consequence'. *Strategies and tactics* are usually easy to discover and observe, and *interactions* among actors consist of all other interactions that are not strategies or tactics. While this paradigm may be useful to you in analysing your data, the most important thing you should be looking for are the emerging *themes*, the issues that are important to the people from whom the data is collected.

As the data collection and analysis progress, so coding changes as concepts are developed. Strauss and Corbin identify three types of coding that occur at different phases in the research: *open coding*, *axial coding* and *selective coding*. Other authors may use different terms to describe this process. For example, Tutty et al. (1996) refer to coding stages as 'first level coding', 'second level coding' and 'theory building'.

Open coding

Open or first level coding is the initial type of coding that is done early in the research. It is the unrestricted coding of data that aims to produce provisional concepts and dimensions which seem to fit the data. These in turn will result in many more questions and provisional answers about conditions, strategies, interactions and consequences. As the researcher proceeds through the data, the process snowballs, with more information raising new questions that in turn lead to the search for more information. From this description, it can be seen that the skill and training of the researcher in 'opening up' the data to tentative interpretation is a crucial part of the process.

At this early stage, Strauss and Corbin reassure us, it does not matter if the codes are 'right' or not, as further inquiry will soon establish which categories are more or less useful in describing what is happening in the data. Thus, codes are modified, and even discarded, as data collection and coding continue. Because this process of modification and elaboration is central to the analysis, it is important not to become committed to particular codes too early. Be careful not to be swayed by pre-existing theoretical understandings—remain open to all possibilities. Although it may seem as though codes are proliferating in the early stages, this slows down and some codes are eliminated as the data are checked for verification (that is, checking that the code really does fit). Gradually the code becomes saturated and is placed in relationship to other codes. The important function of open coding is to help the researcher move quickly to an analytic level by 'fracturing the data' or breaking it apart so that the exciting process of developing grounded theory can begin.

There are two main types of codes: *Invivo* and *constructed*, or sociological, codes. *Invivo* codes come directly from the language of the people being studied and are usually vivid in imagery as well as being analytically useful. They are terms or descriptions that explain the basic problems or processes faced by the people being researched and can lead to associated theoretical codes. For example, in Strauss's study of people–machine interactions in hospitals, people often used the term 'monitoring'. This is an *Invivo* code that describes a set of behaviours by patients and nurses. It implies various conditions under which the monitoring is done, the consequences of monitoring or not monitoring, etc. (that is, the items in the coding paradigm above).

Constructed or sociological codes, on the other hand, are codes formulated by the researcher that are based on the researcher's own knowledge as well as the data being studied. Constructed codes can add more sociological meaning to the analysis than in-vivo codes because they go beyond local meanings to broader concerns and because they are constructed systematically.

Strauss offers several guidelines for open coding which are summarised as follows.

Guidelines for open coding of qualitative data (Strauss 1990, pp. 29–31)

- Look for *Invivo* codes
- Give each code a provisional name (whether *Invivo* or constructed) without worrying too much about whether it is right—this can be modified later
- Move quickly to dimensions that seem relevant to given words, phrases, etc.
- Concentrate on finding comparative cases to explore the dimensions
- From the beginning, continually ask a series of questions of the data including:
  What study are these data pertinent to?
  What category does this incident indicate?
  What is actually happening in the data? (What's the main story here and why?)
- Analyse the data minutely (line by line or phrase by phrase) until the category seems saturated. Ask many questions about words, phrases, sentences and actions in the line by line analysis as you go
- Pay attention to the coding paradigm: conditions, interactions, strategies and consequences
- Frequently interrupt the coding to write a theoretical memo
- Do not assume the relevance of traditional variables such as age, race or sex until they emerge in the data

Once a particular code seems to be relatively saturated, the researcher may move more quickly through the data, noting repetitions and scanning the pages for something new. At that point, the minute examinations begin again. Thus, the intense form of open coding occurs at various stages throughout the analysis. Saturation is achieved when your data fits into established codes and no new codes emerge. It is wise to reflect upon your coding at this point before moving to the next level to ensure that your analysis reflects the data. Have you missed anything? Does your interpretation cover all the major ideas presented by those interviewed? Is there a need for further theoretical sampling?

Axial coding

The next stage, axial or second level coding, is an important, particular aspect of open coding which occurs in the later stages of the open coding process and is different from the looser kinds of open coding which occur earlier. (Other kinds of open coding can also alternate with axial coding.) Axial coding occurs once the researcher decides to code more intensively and concertedly around one category at a time (hence its name, as the analysis revolves around the axis of one category). It is more abstract and involves interpretation on the part of the researcher (Tutty et al. 1996). Look for relationships between codes and themes. Link codes and work towards a higher level of abstraction. Axial coding increases in intensity as the researcher moves towards developing core categories, and precedes selective coding. It also runs parallel to the increasing number of relationships being specified among categories (although not all this coding will be done as intensively as axial coding).

Selective coding

Once the researcher has decided on the core categories that are central to the research, they move into selective coding. Selective coding means that the researcher codes systematically only for the core codes and those codes that are related to them. The core code, once decided upon, becomes the guide to further theoretical sampling and data collection. Thus, selective coding is different from open coding but occurs within the context developed while doing open coding. Selective coding becomes increasingly dominant as the analysis progresses. During selective coding, analytic memos become more focused and theory becomes integrated.

In summary, Strauss notes seven rules for coding data.

Seven rules of thumb for coding data (from Strauss 1990, p. 81)

- Do not merely describe or summarise the phrases of the data—discover genuine categories and name them (at least provisionally)
- Relate categories as specifically and variably as possible to the four items in the coding paradigm (conditions, consequences, strategies and interactions)
- Relate categories to subcategories, all to each other: that is, make a systematically dense analysis
- Do all of the above on the basis of specific data. Frequently reference this data by page, quote or precis
- Underline, for ease of scanning and sorting later
- Once the core category or categories are decided upon, relate all categories and subcategories to the core: that is, move from open coding through axial to selective coding so that the analysis becomes integrated
- Later, minor or unrelated categories and hypotheses can be discarded as more or less irrelevant. Otherwise, the researcher must attempt to specifically relate them to the major core of his or her analysis

---

Core categories

During qualitative data analysis, the researcher is constantly searching for the 'main story', concern or theme that accounts for most of the variation in the patterns of behaviour being observed/talked about. Strauss and Corbin write that the researcher should repeatedly ask themselves 'What is the main story here?' as a kind of motto question throughout the research, to remind themselves that what they are searching for is the *core category* (or categories—there can be more than one). They also advocate that researchers should begin to label potential core categories as early as possible.

A core category is related to most other categories and their properties. It is the key category around which theory generation occurs by making the grounded theory *dense* and *saturated* as relationships between the core category and subcategories are discovered. Theoretical sampling further saturates the categories because they are related to many others and recur often in the data. 'The core category must be proven over and over again by its prevalent relationship to other categories' (Glaser [1978] cited in Strauss [1990, p. 35]). The more data that supports the core categories, the more the researcher can be sure of having chosen the core categories accurately. Core categories should integrate theory and have explanatory power if the research is to be successful. To facilitate the process of theory building around core categories there are some pictorial strategies you can use. We are not alone in suggesting you make some form of graphical representation of your data (Miles & Huberman 1994; Tutty et al. 1996). Try drawing a diagram of your codes and the way they fit together, count the number of times core categories occur, look for missing links and, importantly, note contradictory evidence.

Criteria for selecting core categories (from Strauss, 1990, p. 36)

- The core category must be the most central category, and related to as many other categories and their properties as possible
- It must appear frequently in the data (that is, the indicators pointing to the concept of the core category must appear frequently). Thus it is seen as a stable pattern
- It relates easily to other categories
- It has clear implications for a more general theory
- As the details of the core category are worked out, so the theory is developed
- It allows for building in maximum variation to the analysis, since the researcher is coding in terms of its dimensions, properties, conditions, consequences and so on

---

Memos

Memos are analytic notes that are kept separately from coding notes and which are made throughout the research project. As the project progresses, so different types of memos are written. Early in the research there may be initial orienting memos, preliminary memos and 'memo sparks'. Later on, memos deal with initial discoveries, new categories, distinguishing between two or more categories, and other relationships between categories. As the research progresses, so memos become more elaborate, analytic and theoretically dense. They may include integrative diagrams as well as recording theoretical questions, hypotheses, summary of codes, further directions, etc. Memos provide a way of keeping track of coding and of the researcher's thoughts. They are the major means of integrating theory in grounded theory analysis.

Strauss provides many rules for writing memos, some of which are described below.

Rules for writing memos (from Strauss 1990, Strauss & Corbin 1998)

- Keep memos and data separate
- Record the date of the memo
- Write down memos as ideas occur, even if it means interrupting coding
- Include references and important sources
- Don't force memo-writing (though writing a code can assist memo-writing if stuck)
- Label memos according to the codes to which the memo relates
- Modify memos as research develops (Strauss notes that the data is more precious than the theory. If the theory doesn't fit, it should be modified to fit the data)
- Keep a list of codes handy to check that you have not missed any relationships
- When writing memos, talk about the codes as they are theoretically coded, not individual people (this helps maintain the level of analysis as relationships among concepts)
- Write ideas up one at a time
- Use diagrams in memos to explain ideas
- Mark memos 'saturated' when the categories are saturated
- Always be flexible in your techniques of writing memos
- Keep multiple copies

In order to ensure the credibility of your findings and theory development, Tutty et al. (1996) suggest you document your processes fully, that you consider asking a colleague to assess your data to see if they arrive at the same results and/or that you check the results with the research participants to see if they agree with your analysis. Additionally, they suggest you look to conduct further research with people with markedly different views to balance any bias and that you carefully assess atypical cases. In these ways you act to ensure the validity of your findings.

USE OF COMPUTERS IN QUALITATIVE DATA ANALYSIS

The process of qualitative data analysis has become far more manageable with the recent appearance of qualitative data analysis software. Two packages that we would recommend are *INVIVO* and *Ethnograph*. Both allow for large amounts of data to be managed more effectively by enabling sorting and coding. What used to be an arduous chore, involving massive amounts of interviews and observations recorded on paper, has now become streamlined. You should take the time to learn to use one of these packages. It will be time well spent. It is particularly important to consider purchasing a program if the project is large and you are likely to use the program again.

Case study—women on the land

In 1991 Alston undertook a major qualitative study of farm women to gain insight into their lives and experiences. She was concerned to understand the dynamics that rendered them a particularly invisible group.

Two different and geographically distant areas were selected and snowball samples of farm women were drawn from each. Women were interviewed using semi-structured interviews about their lives, their work roles, their expectations for themselves, their children and their families, their opinions and political persuasions, their interactions with others on and off the farm. As the study progressed memos were kept, alerting Alston to significant issues, categories and theoretical concepts which were emerging. Coding proceeded throughout the data gathering phase.

All interviews were taped and transcribed for entry to the *Ethnograph* program. *Ethnograph* is a 'set of interactive, menu-driven computer programs designed to assist the ethnographic/qualitative researcher in some of the mechanical

---

aspects of data analysis' (Seidel et al. 1988, pp. 1–1, 1–2). By allowing data files to be coded and sorted, and by allowing text to be reviewed, marked, displayed, sorted and printed, *Ethnograph* and programs like it remove the burden of the 'cut and paste' tasks of qualitative research.

The program allows the input of a number of variables relating to each interview script. Consequently each woman was identified by age, marital status, size of farm, industry, number of children and several other significant indicators. Using *Ethnograph*, transcripts are firstly formatted in a compatible way. They are then run through the program so that previously established codes can be inserted in the text. As the data were coded and entered the core categories which emerged included power differentials, interpersonal relationships, changing work roles, differing work inputs, lack of political power, stress and changing expectations.

Ethnograph allowed these core categories and related ones to be examined and broken down by variables. For example, major differences were evident between women over 40 and younger women in their expectations and acceptance of differential power relations. Differences also were noted between more geographically isolated women and those closer to regional centres (and job opportunities). One of the major advantages of computer packages in qualitative data analysis is the ability to 'crunch' data quickly and effectively, allowing a clearer picture of themes and patterns and relationships between issues and variables to emerge.

The use of computer technology in this study demonstrated the very useful contributions such technology can make to the mechanical processes of data analysis. Of course, it must be remembered that computers cannot take over the analytical process, a process that remains very much under the researcher's control.

Alston, Margaret 1991, *Women on the Land: The Hidden Heart of Rural Australia*, University of New South Wales Press, Sydney.

SUMMARY

In this chapter we have considered the differences between qualitative and quantitative data analysis and examined in detail the processes of qualitative data analysis involved in Strauss and Corbin's grounded theory approach. We have seen how qualitative data analysis requires rigorous interaction with the data in order to develop new theory which, at all stages in the process, is 'grounded' in data through a continuous, cyclical process between data collection, coding (analysis) and memoing (interpretation). Three types of coding have been discussed and handy hints for coding and memoing provided. We have also provided an example of how the computer program *Ethnograph* was used to analyse qualitative data in Margaret Alston's study of farm women.

In chapter 1 some criticisms of qualitative research as being too microscopic and focused only on interaction rather than larger social/political or structural issues were raised. Strauss and Corbin (1998) answer such criticisms by maintaining that proper coding can encompass both interactional (micro) and structural (macro) analysis and even link the two theoretically, although this takes much time and thought. In their edited book *Grounded Theory in Practice* (1997), they provide detailed examples of the way grounded theory researchers develop detailed codes leading to theoretical explanations. Analysis of close-in connections between contextual conditions and interactions can be widened to coding which analyses the impact of broader institutions, social and political forces on individual experience. The ultimate balance between the relative focus on macro and micro level analysis will be up to the individual researcher and research project. Thus, qualitative data analysis is an exciting prospect with potential applications across a wide range of research activities, not just those micro interactional studies that have traditionally been seen as the appropriate place for qualitative analysis.

QUESTIONS

1 What are some differences in the ways qualitative and quantitative researchers analyse their data?
2 Describe the different ways qualitative and quantitative researchers use induction, deduction and hypothesising, and develop indicators, dimensions and concepts.
3 What are the three general stages in qualitative research according to Sarantakos?
4 What does Strauss mean by the terms data collection, coding and memoing?
5 What are the four aspects which should be looked for when coding data to develop categories?
6 Describe the differences between open coding, axial coding and selective coding. What are their purposes and when do they occur in the research process?
7 What is theoretical sampling?
8 What is the role of core categories in qualitative data analysis?

EXERCISES

1 There are a number of books and journal articles presenting the findings of qualitative research. Locate one such study, preferably by a researcher who used the grounded theory approach in your library.

   What are the core categories in the study? How was the grounded theory developed? How do the researchers present their results? How do they verify their conclusions?

2 Select another piece of qualitative research from a sociological journal. How explicit are the authors about their methods of data analysis? Was a computer program used? How are the results presented? Could you replicate this study? Comment on the validity of the findings.

FURTHER READING

Berg, B. 1995, *Qualitative Research Methods for the Social Sciences*, 2nd edn, Allyn & Bacon, Boston.

de Vaus, D. A. 2002, *Surveys in Social Research*, 5th edn, Allen & Unwin, Sydney.

Miles, M. B. & Huberman, A. M. 1994, *Qualitative Data Analysis: An Expanded Source Book*, 2nd edn, Sage, Newbury Park.

Padgett, D. K. 1998, *Qualitative Methods in Social Work Research: Challenges and Rewards,* Sage, Thousand Oaks.

Reissman, C. K. (ed.) 1994, *Qualitative Studies in Social Work Research,* Sage, Thousand Oaks.

Sherman, E. & Reid, W. J. (eds) 1994, *Qualitative Research in Social Work,* Columbia University Press, New York.

Strauss, A. 1990, *Qualitative Analysis for Social Scientists*, Cambridge University Press, Melbourne.

Strauss, A. & Corbin, J. (eds) 1997, *Grounded Theory in Practice*, Sage, Thousand Oaks.

Strauss, A. & Corbin, J. 1998, *Basics of Qualitative Research: Techniques and Procedures for Developing Grounded Theory,* Sage, Thousand Oaks.

Tutty, L. M., Rothery, M. A. & Grinnell, R. M. Jr 1996, *Qualitative Research for Social Workers,* Allyn & Bacon, Boston.

13 PRODUCING RESULTS: QUANTITATIVE RESEARCH

In the previous chapter we saw that there were four major differences between qualitative and quantitative data analysis. First, unlike qualitative research, quantitative research has clearly defined rules about how to go about data analysis. Second, quantitative data analysis involves mathematics and statistics. Third, quantitative research usually follows a single method of data analysis that has been worked out in advance as part of the design of the study. Finally, data analysis occurs after all the data has been collected in quantitative research.

Noting that most studies will incorporate both quantitative and qualitative methods, some of the differences in data analysis mean that in these days of computer analysis, quantitative data analysis can be relatively easy, even though it involves the use of statistics. In this chapter we set out some fundamental principles of data analysis for quantitative research as well as a guide to coding your results for computer entry. Examples from the *SPSS* program for data analysis are used. This is because *SPSS* is the most common program used in universities and large welfare organisations. There are many other programs which are easy to use, such as *Minitab* and *SAS*.

FACTORS AFFECTING QUANTITATIVE DATA ANALYSIS

Three factors determine the type of quantitative data analysis you choose (de Vaus 2002). These are the number of variables, the level of measurement and the purpose of the statistics (whether descriptive or inferential).

The number of variables

The first factor is the *number of variables* being analysed. This depends on the type of research questions the study addresses. Data analysis involving one variable at a time is termed *univariate analysis*, data analysis involving two variables is called *bivariate analysis* and data analysis involving three or more variables *multivariate analysis*.

Examples of questions involving different numbers of variables

- *Univariate*—one variable
('How many', 'What type' . . .)
- *Bivariate*—two variables
('Does living in the country or city affect the sort of service provided to income-support agency clients on their initial visit?')
- *Multivariate*—more than two variables
('Does age affect the different experiences people from the country or city have when they visit an income-support agency for the first time?')

Often the reporting of quantitative results begins with descriptions of the sample and results using univariate statistics to paint a general picture. Following this general description, more complex statistics are performed to investigate relationships between two or more variables.

Level of measurement

The second factor that must be taken into account when planning quantitative data analysis is the *level of measurement* of the variables being analysed. Review chapter 3 for definitions of *nominal, ordinal, interval* and *ratio* levels of measurement.

Choosing the appropriate level of measurement for each variable depends on several factors. In general, it is best to measure variables at the highest level of measurement possible. Higher levels of measurement provide more information and allow more powerful statistical techniques to be used. In addition, it is always possible to reduce the level of measurement after data is collected (for example, from interval to ordinal), but it is mostly not possible to increase the level of measurement once you have collected data at a lower level.

On the other hand, asking for too much detail (too high a level of measurement) may lead to inaccurate or untruthful replies. For example, if you asked how often people attended an income-support agency during the last two years (interval level), they may be unable to give an exact number of times and either make up an answer or not answer the question at all. However, they may respond with reasonable accuracy to an ordinal range of responses (*'at least weekly'*, *'approximately once per fortnight'*, *'between fortnightly and monthly'*, *'three or four times a year'*, *'twice a year'*, *'once only'*). From this brief example it can be seen that deciding on the appropriate level of measurement for each variable is an art in itself which requires consideration of a range of issues.

Descriptive and inferential statistics

The third factor in deciding which types of data analysis should be performed is whether the researcher wants to use the data for *descriptive* or *inferential* purposes. *Descriptive statistics* are those which summarise the patterns of information or data which is obtained from the sample. *Inferential statistics* tell us whether the patterns found in the sample we have studied are likely to be found in the general population from which the sample was drawn. That is, can the information that we have discovered from analysing the results from our sample (descriptive statistics) be generalised to the wider population? Inferential statistics are used when we have a random sample from the population. They rely on assumptions drawn from probability theory, which in turn assume that each element in the sample has an equal chance of being selected.

Three issues which determine what data analysis procedures to use (from de Vaus 2002)

- The number of variables to be analysed (univariate, bivariate or multivariate analysis)
- The level of measurement of the variables (nominal, ordinal, interval or ratio)
- Whether descriptive or inferential statistics are required

The rest of the chapter provides an introduction to computer coding and data entry, showing how quantitative data are entered into a computer for analysis. We also show how variables at different levels of measurement are coded.

CODING, DATA ENTRY AND COMPUTER PACKAGES

Coding at different levels of measurement

You should note that the unit around which you code is the variable. Answers addressing each variable are coded for each possible response. In earlier chapters we introduced the idea of coding results for data entry into a computer by using numbers as codes. With interval and ratio data, coding is relatively simple because the code is usually the same as the answer and can be entered directly into the computer. Variables in which the code numbers refer to actual numbers are termed *numeric* variables in computer packages such as *SPSS*.

Ordinal level data is coded according to each response, for example, small, medium, large, with 1 representing small, 2 medium, and 3 large. With nominal data, coding becomes more complex, especially with open-ended questions. We have discussed how the nominal variable 'gender' has two categories which may be coded 1 for female and 2 for male and that these numbers differentiate categories but do *not* imply 'greater or less than'.

Coding open-ended questions (nominal level)

Coding open-ended questions often means that you have to group answers into categories. How you do this depends on the purpose of your question. When coding open-ended questions you can code for more than one answer to each question. You will need to check the manual of the program you are using for specific instructions on how to do this.

A handy hint for coding nominal data is to use coding systems that have been devised by large research organisations (such as the Australian Bureau of Statistics). Coding schemes for information such as 'occupation', 'qualifications' and 'type of household' are already available from these organisations at different levels of specificity. It saves a lot of work (and reduces error) if you use a coding system that has been tried and tested by others. This will also allow you to compare your results with other large studies and census findings. However, this is not essential. If you are devising your own code you should remember to ensure that your response categories are mutually exclusive, exhaustive and unidimensional (see chapter 6).

Missing data

Whether you are coding nominal, ordinal, interval or ratio data, it is important to code all answers, even when the respondent did not answer some questions. It is also important to be able to distinguish non-responses, or refusals to answer particular questions, from 'no' and 'don't know'. We suggest a different code for each of these answers. When codes are classified as 'missing data' they are not included in the statistics which the computer calculates, but the numbers of 'missing cases' are recorded in the results. It is important to use the same missing data categories for each research project so that you do not become confused. What has worked for us has been to use 777 for 'don't know' (some questionnaires do not provide this option and respondents may write this over the question), 888 for 'not applicable' and 999 for 'no answer' where an answer is not given. The missing data can then be included as part of your data entry and programs such as *SPSS* will ignore them when calculating statistics and frequencies.

Principles of entering your results

Codebooks

Before beginning to enter your data into the computer you should ensure that you have noted all possible response categories. While closed-ended questions will have been worked out when the survey instrument was developed, it is useful to record for yourself and data entry assistants all possible response categories so that no confusion arises during the data entry process. Usually researchers have a codebook into which they enter all the codes for various questions. Codebooks are especially important if there is more than one person entering data or if there are open-ended questions.

What to include in your codebook (from de Vaus 2002, p 158)

- The question asked
- The 'mnemonic' or short name for the variable that is used in the computer program
- The type of data used for that variable (numeric, alpha-numeric)
- The first and last columns in which the variable is located
- The codes for each variable
- The 'missing data' codes for each variable
- Any special coding instructions

An example of coding and a data matrix for entry into a computer

Coding variables—developing a variable by case matrix

We will use questions from chapter 6 to show how data is coded into a matrix for computer entry, using a codebook.

Note that *questions 1, 3* and *4* are variables at the nominal level of measurement. *Question 2* is at the ordinal level of measurement. All the questions are closed-ended except *question 4*, which is open-ended. Thus the codes for the first three questions could have been worked out in advance as we know what the range of answers will be.

Examples of closed-ended questions, including scaled questions

1   Please tick the box which describes the social security payments you were receiving when you first visited the office of the Department of Social Security:

Sole parent pension ☐
Young homeless allowance ☐
Aged pension ☐
Disability support payment ☐
Special benefit ☐
Unemployment benefit ☐
Other ☐
Not receiving payments at the time ☐

2   Please indicate how you felt about your first interview with departmental staff by circling a rating out of 5 for the following statements. On the scales, 1 = strongly disagree and 5 = strongly agree.

From my first interview at the Department of Social Security I would say:

a. staff listened carefully to what I had to say:

1_____2_____3_____4_____5
strongly   neutral   strongly
disagree   agree

b. staff acted as though I was lying:

1_____2_____3_____4_____5
strongly   neutral   strongly
disagree   agree

c. staff treated me with respect:

1_____2_____3_____4_____5
strongly   neutral   strongly
disagree   agree

d. staff attitudes need to improve:

1_____2_____3_____4_____5
strongly   neutral   strongly
disagree   agree

e. staff provided me with the information I required:

1_____2_____3_____4_____5
strongly   neutral   strongly
disagree   agree

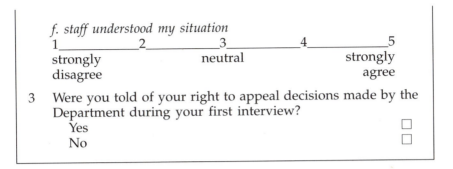

f. staff understood my situation

1_____2_____3_____4_____5
strongly   neutral   strongly
disagree   agree

3   Were you told of your right to appeal decisions made by the
    Department during your first interview?
    Yes   ☐
    No   ☐

Table 13.1   **Answers to the questions from the example in a variable by case matrix**

Respondent (ID)	Type payment (PAY)	Staff respect (ATTIT3)	Info re appeal (APPEAL)	Staff behaviour (BEH1, BEH2)
J. Smith (001)	Sole parent	3	No	Formal, rushed
P. Collins (002)	Disability support	5	Yes	friendly, took time for me
M. Chapman (003)	Young homeless	1	No	Rude
A. Jones (004)	Unemployment	3	Yes	OK, friendly
T. Black (005)	Sole parent	2	Yes	In a hurry, didn't seem interested in my questions

In Table 13.1, the names of the five respondents and their answers to the four questions are summarised. This table is called a variable by case matrix because it shows how five respondents (cases) answered four questions (variables). We have also begun two sorts of coding for the computer in this table. Listed under each question heading is the short name (mnemonic or variable name) that will be listed in the computer to name each variable. Note that two mnemonics are listed for question 4. This is because we have decided to allow two answers from each respondent to be entered for this question. We have also given each person an identity code (ID) which will also be entered into the computer to make sure we know which answers belong to which respondent.

There are two ways of looking at Table 13.1. First, it is possible to obtain a holistic 'snapshot' of each respondent by looking across the rows (or record). For example, J. Smith is a sole parent who thought that the staff treated him or her with respect, but was not given information about his/her right to appeal and found the staff's behaviour formal and rushed. T. Black, on the other hand, is also a sole parent who felt less respected by staff than J. Smith, but was given information about his/her right to appeal decisions. T. Black also found staff to be rushed and further reported that they did not seem to be interested in him/her.

The other way of looking at this table, instead of looking across the rows for each individual respondent, is to compare the answers down the columns, thus gaining a picture of the range of answers for different variables. For example, we can see from column 2 that we have answers from two sole parents, and one of each from the following groups: disability support payment, unemployment benefit and young homeless. Similarly, people's experience of whether staff acted respectfully towards them (column 3) ranged from 1 (not at all respectful) to 5 (very respectful), with three people being somewhere in the middle. As we shall see in the following chapter, these sorts of 'pictures' or summaries of the data are exactly what descriptive univariate statistics provide, but on a larger scale involving all the cases in our sample.

Developing a data matrix

We now move to the second stage of our coding demonstration, by transforming the same information that appeared in words and numbers in Table 13.1 into numerical computer codes for each variable. When these numerical codes are entered into a computer, together they are termed a data matrix.

The first step in transforming data into a data matrix is to create a codebook, as discussed above. In your codebook, you should record for each variable the aspects identified by de Vaus (2002) listed on page 225. Each variable needs at least one page, and for open-ended questions several pages should be left if you are expecting a large number of different answers.

An illustration of a codebook entry for the first variable in Table 13.1 (type of payment) appears in Example 1. This variable could have been precoded, as it is a closed-ended question from which respondents choose one of the options.

Example 1: Codebook entry for question 1

Question 1: What social security payments were you receiving when you first visited the office?

Mnemonic: PAY	*Record:* 1	
Value labels:	No payment	00
	Sole parent	01
	Young homeless	02
	Aged pension	03
	Disability support	04
	Special benefit	05
	Unemployment	06
	Other	**
** *codes for other:*	Veteran's payment	07
	Carer's pension	08
	etc.	
Missing values:	Don't know	777
	Not applicable	888
	No response	999

Note that there is a choice marked 'other' in this question. The coder can choose whether to just consider all answers of 'other' as a single category, or whether instead to record the details of each other sort of 'other' payment separately. The answers to 'other' can then be coded as for other open-ended questions, within the existing structure of the closed question.

This exercise is repeated for each variable until all have been entered into the codebook and you have a comprehensive record of the coding you are putting into the computer. The page for question 2 may look like Example 2.

Example 2   Codebook entry for question 2

Question 2c: Scale rating (1–5) about agreement with whether staff treated me with respect

Mnemonic: ATTIT3	*Record:* 1	
Value labels:	Strongly disagree	1
		2
	Neutral	3
		4
	Strongly agree	5
Missing values:	Don't know	777
	Not applicable	888
	No response	999

The codebook entry for the third question would be even simpler because there are only two values for this variable. (Having only two values, this variable is called a dichotomous variable. Dichotomous variables have special properties for statistical purposes.) Note that when deciding on different codes, we recommend that you use similar codes for each variable that way coding is easier to remember. For example 'no' could always be coded 1. Similarly, the codes for missing values are easiest if they are always similar across different questions (for example, 'don't know' as 777).

Example 3   Codebook entry for question 3

Question 3: Were you told of your right to appeal decisions made by the agency during your first interview?

Mnemonic: APPEAL	*Record:* 1	
Value labels:	No	0
	Yes	1
Missing values:	Don't know	777
	Not applicable	888
	No response	999

The coding for open-ended questions is more complicated, depending on the range of answers that are received. Note that because we will code both the variables BEH1 and BEH2 with the same value labels we can include them both in the same entry in the codebook, as demonstrated in Example 4. (Remember that we are allowing ourselves the opportunity to record two answers to this question. The codes will be the same in both variables so that we can add them up later.) When coding multiple variables as one entry in your codebook, make sure that you have allowed sufficient space for, or ability to distinguish between, each variable.

If the person has given more than two answers, you will need to decide how to deal with this and record it in the codebook so that all coders follow the same rule for each survey or questionnaire (see Example 4). There is no right or wrong approach to this situation; what is important is to be consistent. In the example we have decided to use the first two answers the person gives.

Example 4   Codebook entry for question 4

Question 4: Please describe how the staff behaved towards you during your first interview at Centrelink
Mnemonic: BEH1, BEH2

**Value labels:*	No comment	0
	Formal	1
	Rushed, hurried	2
	Friendly	3
	Took time for me	4
	Rude	5
	OK	6
	Uninterested	7
Missing values:	Don't know	777
	Not applicable	888
	No response	999

**Note: If more than two options are listed, code the first two only.

Coding open-ended questions requires skill and careful thought. Even in this simple example it can be seen that there are some similarities in these five respondents' comments about staff behaviour, and some subtle differences which may or may not be important to code. At this early stage, with only five responses, it is best to code the answers in as much detail as possible, and wait until more cases have been examined before deciding how to re-code open-ended questions into smaller numbers of categories.

Entering your data into the computer

Having decided on your coding frame or matrix for these four questions, you are now ready to enter the information into a computer. Different packages, and even different versions of the same packages, use different methods for entering the results of your study. However, the basic principles we have described—labelling each variable with a short mnemonic or variable name, then coding answers for each variable including non-responses (that is, listing value labels for each variable)—are general principles which apply to most databases and statistics packages.

When research results are entered into a computer, they are entered as a data matrix. The answers from each person (respondent) are systematically recorded so that the computer can count, collate and compare different answers to the same question (univariate analysis), or the way different answers vary for different people between different questions (bivariate and multivariate analysis).

In order for the computer to do this, each respondent's answers are recorded across a line of columns. The same questions are answered for each respondent in the same order, and the computer is told which columns refer to which variables.

Thus, researchers must enter into the computer the name of each variable (giving it a short label called a mnemonic or variable name). They must also enter all the different codes or answers/values for each of these variables in the appropriate columns or spaces provided for each respondent.

Example of data matrix (with variables labelled)

ID	PAY	ATT3	APPL	BEH1	BEH2
001	01	3	0	01	02
002	04	5	1	03	04
003	02	1	0	05	00
004	06	3	1	06	03
005	01	2	1	02	07

Using the codes that we have identified above, the data matrix which the computer would read to analyse the data is given in the example. See if you can relate the information from this matrix to the information that was listed in words in Table 13.1, using the codebook examples to de-code the numbers.

Entering into SPSS

Note that when you are entering your own results, some packages are more user-friendly and will provide prompts for each variable. *SPSS* for Windows is very easy to use. A useful reference to keep on your shelf is Pallant's *SPSS Survival Manual* (2001). This book provides easy-to-follow directions to allow you to deal with common data analysis issues.

SUMMARY

In this chapter we have presented three factors which determine the types of quantitative data analysis you will perform. We then discussed how to code your results (at different levels of measurement) ready for computer analysis, showing how to develop a data matrix using a codebook. For more detailed instructions on how to enter data and set up a statistics package, you will need to consult the manual of the package which is available to you, and probably seek the assistance of someone who has experience with that particular package. The principles of data entry and the thinking behind them that are presented here, however, are generally applicable to all computer packages.

QUESTIONS

1 What are the three factors affecting quantitative data analysis?
2 List whether the following questions require univariate, bivariate or multivariate analysis:
   (a) Are people from non-English speaking backgrounds given the same information as native English speakers by income support agency staff?
   (b) What type of Social Security payments do you receive?
   (c) Do younger people have more satisfactory experiences than older people when they visit an income support agency?
   (d) What factors affect the experiences people have when they visit an income support agency?
3 Consider these two questions:

   i   How old are you? Please write your age in years in the space provided.
   ii Please indicate your age by ticking the box which shows the range within which your age falls:
       Under 15 years   ☐
       16–25 years   ☐
       26–35 years   ☐
       36–45 years   ☐
       46–55 years   ☐
       56–65 years   ☐
       66 years and over   ☐

   (a) Are the questions open- or closed-ended?
   (b) At what level of measurement are the two questions?
   (c) Which question do you think is preferable and why?
4 What is the difference between descriptive and inferential statistics?

EXERCISES

Create a codebook and write a data matrix for three hypothetical respondents in answer to the following questions:

1 In what area do you live? (Please write your postcode only)
2 Do you think this area needs an after-school leisure centre?
  Yes ☐
  No ☐
  Maybe ☐
  Don't know ☐
3 If you have children, please answer these questions:
  (a) How many children live in your house under the age of 12?
  (b) Are your children interested in:
      aerobics?
      pottery?
      creative writing?
      computer games?
  (c) Would they use an after-school leisure centre if it was properly supervised and these kinds of activities were provided?
  (d) What other after-school activities might your children want to do at an after-school leisure centre?

FURTHER READING

Alreck, P. L. & Settle, R. B. 1995, *The Survey Research Handbook*, 2nd edn, Irwin, Burr Ridge, Ill. Chapter 9 offers a clear guide to coding.

Argyrous, G. 2000, *Statistics for Social & Health Research with a Guide to SPSS*, Sage Publications, London. This book provides a useful guide to Version 9 of *SPSS*. You should note that Version 10 has some slight format changes.

Babbie, E. 2001, *The Practice of Social Research*, 9th edn, Wadsworth, California. This book offers a history of computers in social research and then some good ideas for codebooks, coding and data cleaning.

Betts, K., Hayward, D. & Garnham, N. 2001, *Quantitative Analysis in the Social Sciences: An Introduction*, Tertiary Press, Croydon, Vic.

de Vaus, D. A. 2002, *Surveys in Social Research*, 5th edn, Allen & Unwin, Sydney. See chapters 9 and 10 for an overview of analysis and a guide to coding which is particularly good on coding open-ended questions.

Kumar, R. 1999, *Research Methodology*, Sage, Melbourne. See chapter 4 for a detailed account of setting up codebooks and how to code.

Mark, R. 1996, *Research Made Simple: a Handbook for Social Workers*, Sage, Thousand Oaks, California. Chapter 17 sets out a good introduction to computers in social work research, including the use of databases and spreadsheets.

Pallant, J. 2001, *SPSS Survival Manual*, Allen & Unwin, Sydney.

Sarantakos, S. 1998, *Social Research*, 2nd edn, Macmillan, Melbourne. Contains a guide to quantitative data analysis and coding.

14 STATISTICS FOR SOCIAL WORKERS

Having examined coding procedures, we now introduce you to a range of statistical techniques and tests that social workers are most likely to use in their research. It is important for you to understand the three factors introduced in the previous chapter—level of measurement, number of variables, and whether statistics are intended to be inferential or descriptive—as these are significant elements in any data analysis. Our aim in this chapter is to introduce the main concepts in quantitative analysis, so that you know how to analyse your data and the possibilities that such analysis offers you as a researcher. We want to help you think through what data analysis you will perform in your own research, and to enable you to critically examine the analysis reported in other studies.

Statistical analyses used properly provide powerful arguments for many of the battles you face in your everyday work life. In this chapter we describe complex statistical processes in plain English. We have assumed that you are interested not so much in complicated mathematical proofs, but in the logic of the processes and how you can use the results in your own research to improve the quality of your conclusions. Sometimes, therefore, we will present formulae without the long mathematical explanations that are beyond the scope of this book.

In particular, this chapter introduces you to the following factors in statistical analysis:

- Continuous and discrete variables
- Frequency distributions
- Describing a distribution (central tendency, dispersion, taking into account levels of measurement)
- The normal distribution
- Testing hypotheses—levels of significance
- Relating two variables (correlation and regression)

In order to explain statistics and what they mean in relation to the population you want to know more about (termed the *target population*), we have invented a fictitious example. Our example uses small numbers so that we can demonstrate with simple calculations the logic of statistics and how they estimate what is actually going on in the target population.

In our example, Nancy Wilson is a social worker at a hospital. She works in an outreach service provided for mothers after discharge from hospital following the birth of their child. She is part time and her caseload consists of 20 babies. For the purposes of this example, the target population may be Nancy Wilson's caseload of new babies, or more likely, it would be all the new babies in the hospital's catchments area.

As we saw in chapter 5, we often have a target population in mind but it is very difficult to collect a random sample from this population. Instead, we may decide to select our random sample from a subset of the target population that we consider to be typical in some way. This subset is called the *sampled population*. In our example, the sampled population is Nancy Wilson's caseload. We must remember that any conclusions we draw from our research are actually only statistically valid for babies in Nancy's caseload although we may feel comfortable about extending our conclusions to all children in the local area.

CONTINUOUS AND DISCRETE VARIABLES

A variable is called *discrete* if the set of possible values it can take is a discrete number of values or categories (the value of the variable is often called a score). The number of times a baby wakes during the night is a discrete variable—each value of the variable is a whole number, representing the number of times a baby woke on a particular night. If the baby woke five times, we say the variable has a value or score of five. Other examples include eye colour, gender and number of siblings. A *dichotomous* variable is a discrete variable with only two categories such as gender (female or male). Remember that when variables have categories as their values (for example, female and male) we usually assign each category with a numeric value for ease of processing (female = 1, male = 2). In this case the numeric values are labels only and do not indicate order in themselves.

A variable is called *continuous* if it takes any numerical value in a given interval. This means it does not just have whole number values like 3 or 4, but can take on intermediate values like 3.345 . . ., for example. We could say that the 'length of time a baby is awake' is a continuous variable because in theory, we could say the baby was awake 3.356 minutes.

The distinction between variables is important because, like levels of measurement, it guides the selection of appropriate statistical techniques.

STATISTICS WITH ONE VARIABLE—UNIVARIATE ANALYSIS

Frequency distributions

One of the most common ways of presenting descriptive statistics (that is, data that describes or summarises your findings) is through the use of frequency distributions. Frequency distributions allow us to record the frequency of each value of the variable being reviewed.

Table 14.1 Nancy Wilson's caseload sample—number of times children woke Wednesday/Thursday, March 27/28, 2002

Name	Number of times child woke during night
Rosie	3
Tom	4
Nick	1
Peter	2
Meredith	3
Mary	2
Jessica	1
Wendy	5
John	2
David	3
Steven	7
Susan	5
Sarah	3
Phillip	1
Trent	9
Daniel	0
Kate	3
Dominique	0
Alison	2
Dylan	1
Total: 20 children	57

In our fictitious example, Nancy has noticed that one of the most pressing concerns for mothers is the number of times babies wake during the night. She has decided to ask the mothers in her caseload to keep records to allow her to record patterns of waking behaviour. The first step in constructing a frequency table is to record the *raw data*. Table 14.1 shows the number of times each child woke on a particular night in Nancy Wilson's caseload.

Table 14.2 Population frequency distribution—number of times children woke Wednesday/Thursday, March 27/28, 2002

Name	Number of times awake	Frequency
Daniel + Dominique	0	2
Nick + Jessica + Philip + Dylan	1	4
Peter + Mary + John + Alison	2	4
Rosie + Meredith + David + Sarah + Kate	3	5
Tom	4	1
Wendy + Susan	5	2
	6	0
Steven	7	1
	8	0
Trent	9	1
Total 20 children		Total 20

We can summarise the information recorded by the raw data to make it more comprehensible. The simplest way to summarise raw data is in a frequency distribution that shows, in our case, the number of children who woke the same number of times. Table 14.2 shows the frequency distribution of the number of times children in Nancy Wilson's caseload woke on a particular night. We call it a population frequency distribution because Nancy Wilson's caseload is the population we are interested in and from which we will take a sample later.

Table 14.3 Cumulative frequency distribution—number of times awake

Name	No. of times awake	Frequency	Cumulative frequency
Daniel + Dominique	0	2	2
Nick + Jessica + Philip + Dylan	1	4	6
Peter + Mary + John + Alison	2	4	10
Rosie + Meredith + David + Sarah + Kate	3	5	15
Tom	4	1	16
Wendy + Susan	5	2	18
	6	0	18
Steven	7	1	19
	8	0	19
Trent	9	1	20

Cumulative frequency distribution

A *cumulative frequency distribution* can be constructed when the data is measured at an ordinal or higher level of measurement. It allows frequencies to be summed down the column, giving a 'rolling count'. From Table 14.3, for example, we can see that ten babies woke up to two times during the night.

Percentage frequency distributions

A *percentage frequency distribution* adds percentage values to your data. The frequency percentage column in Table 14.4 indicates for each entry the percentage of the whole group or sample represented by that particular piece of data. Thus we can see that 25 per cent of the group woke three times. The cumulative percentage data column, which is added as you go down the column, allows us to ascertain that, for example, 50 per cent woke up not more than two times. Note that cumulative percentage columns always end with 100 as their total.

Table 14.4   Percentage frequency distribution—number of times awake

Name	No. of times awake	Frequency	Frequency %	Cumulative frequency	Cumulative %
Daniel + Dominique	0	2	10	2	10
Nick + Jessica + Philip + Dylan	1	4	20	6	30
Peter + Mary + John + Alison	2	4	20	10	50
Rosie + Meredith + David + Sarah + Kate	3	5	25	15	75
Tom	4	1	5	16	80
Wendy+ Susan	5	2	10	18	90
	6	0	0	18	90
Steven	7	1	5	19	95
	8	0	0	19	95
Trent	9	1	5	20	100
Total		20	100	20	100

Grouped frequency distribution

When dealing with interval and ratio level data, where there may be a large number of possible scores, it is often simpler to divide the range of possible values into equally spaced intervals and to calculate the frequency with which the scores fall within each interval. It may be necessary to have a final open-ended interval to include all remaining possibilities. Grouping the data in this way often makes patterns more obvious. When deciding the groupings to use it is important to reduce the number of values to a small number while still maintaining some level of measurement precision. If the values are spread evenly then groupings should also be evenly spread. Table 14.5 shows a grouped frequency distribution for the 20 cases in our example. Note the way that the categories have been grouped so that they are of equal size, include all cases and do not overlap.

Table 14.5   Grouped frequency distribution table—number of times awake

Number of times awake	Frequency
0 – 3	15
4 – 7	4
> 7	1

Representation of frequency distributions

The simplest representation of a frequency distribution is a table. If we examine Table 14.2 we see that all the different possible values for the variable (number of times awake) are listed in the second column. When you construct frequency distributions for ordinal and interval/ratio data, it is most important to arrange the possible values of the variable in numerical order (as in the tables above). The next column (called the frequency column) shows the frequency with which the variable has this value. Other optional columns can then be added. Sometimes researchers work solely in percentages and leave out the raw frequency column altogether, because it is much easier to see patterns in the data when it is represented in this way.

Note that if you are writing up a frequency distribution table from a sample instead of from the whole population, you must include a line underneath the table recording the number of cases in the sample for which a score was not recorded. This is called 'missing data' (see Table 14.6). For example, if one of the families in Nancy Wilson's caseload was away on the night the data was collected and did not record the data, there would be one missing case which would be noted beneath the table. This is important information to include as it may affect the validity or reliability of any conclusions drawn.

de Vaus (2002, p. 214) provides a handy list of the information which must be included in frequency tables.

Information which should be included in a frequency table (from de Vaus 2002, p. 214)

- Table number and title
- Labels for the categories of the variable

239

- Column headings to indicate what the numbers in the column represent
- The total number on which the percentages are based
- The number of missing cases
- The source of the data (particularly important if the data are from a different source than your own survey, e.g. census data for comparison with your findings)
- Sometimes footnotes are needed which provide the actual question or working definitions on which the table is based

Graphical representations of data

Sometimes a graphical representation provides a more concise and more easily interpreted representation of data than a frequency distribution table. While graphs reduce the detail available to the reader, they may be more readily accessible to a non-research savvy audience. There are several types of graphs and pictorial representations of data. In this section we provide a description of the most common.

Histograms and bar charts

Histograms and bar charts have two axes that intersect at right angles. One axis (usually the horizontal one) is divided into intervals representing the various possible values of the variable. The other axis (usually the vertical one) is divided into intervals representing frequencies. Histograms depict the data graphically with vertical bars

Figure 14.1 Histogram

Frequencies of payment type

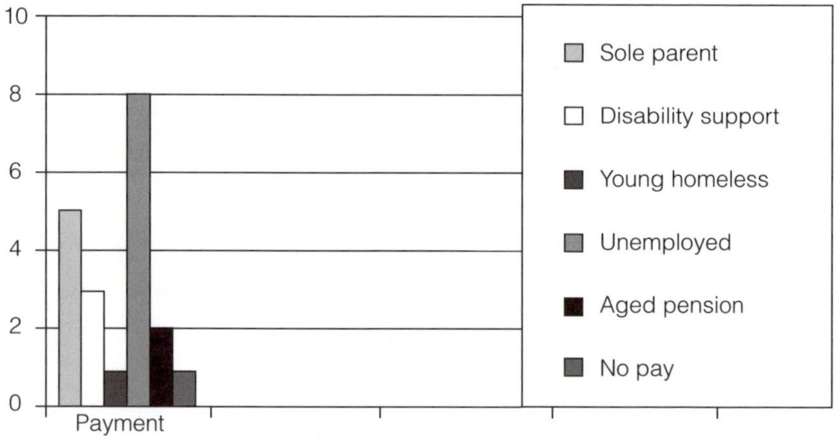

Figure 14.2 Bar chart

Frequencies of payment type

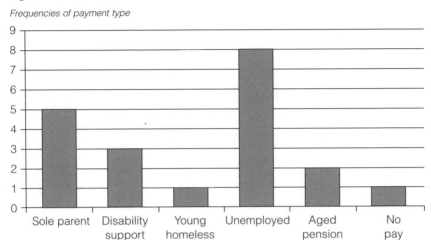

adjacent to each other, as shown in Figure 14.1. Bar charts are very similar to histograms except that the bars are separated (Figure 14.2). Bar charts can be used for nominal level data to show different variables.

Pie charts

Pie charts are circular charts divided into slices. Each slice represents a possible score and its size is proportional to the occurrence of that score in the sample (see Figure 14.3).

Figure 14.3 Pie chart

Frequencies of payment type

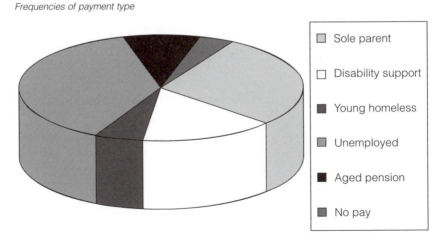

Figure 14.4 Pictograph

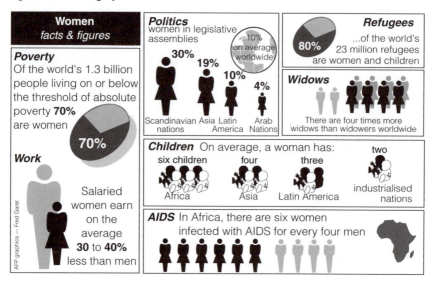

Pictographs

Pictographs are an exciting way to summarise data and are often used in newspapers. Figure 14.4 is an example of a detailed pictograph.

Frequency polygons and curves

The frequency polygon is another type of graph which is useful when dealing with ratio or interval level variables that can be regarded as continuous (age, height, salary, etc.). Frequency polygons can be drawn from histograms by joining the mid-point of each bar to create a polygon (Figure 14.5). Polygons show the shape of the data very well.

For other methods of visually presenting data, see Weinbach and Grinnell (1995, chapter 2), Kumar (1996, chapter 16) or Sarantakos (1998, chapter 14).

Summarising frequency distributions: descriptive statistics

In social research it is rare to have a whole population to use for statistics. Instead we use a sample—in quantitative statistics we use a random sample. Sample statistics estimate the statistics for the whole population. As we saw in chapter 5, they are more or less accurate depending on how well the sample reflects or represents the population. To illustrate how statistics from samples estimate the values found in the population, a random sample was taken from Nancy Wilson's caseload, with replacement, as the population of this

Figure 14.5 Frequency polygon—ages of students in social work research methods on-campus class

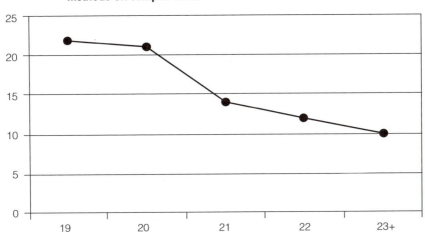

caseload is so small (see chapter 5). Table 14.6 shows the frequency distribution of this random sample of seven cases.

While frequency distributions display the range of answers to questions, descriptive statistics go further in providing critical information about data. This is particularly important when we want to understand how much variation there is in our data. Two descriptive statistics are particularly useful in this context. They are the statistics that tell us:

- The most typical response, called *measures of central tendency*
- The spread or variation of responses, called *measures of dispersion*

There are several different ways of measuring central tendency and dispersion. The most common measures of central tendency are the *mode, median* and *mean*.

Table 14.6 Sample frequency distribution—random sample of number of times awake

Number of times awake	Frequency	Frequency%	Cumulative frequency	Cumulative frequency%
0	1	14.3	1	14.3
1	1	14.3	2	28.6
2	2	28.6	4	57.3
3	1	14.3	5	71.6
4	0	0	5	71.6
5	1	14.3	6	85.9
7	1	14.3	7	100
Total	7			

Note: No. of missing cases = 0

Measures of central tendency

The mode

The mode is the only measure of central tendency for nominal data. It can, however, be calculated for all types of data if required. It is the score that occurs most often in the sampled population. In Table 14.2, for example, the mode from the sampled population is waking three times in the night. However, the mode in our sample is two times per night (Table 14.6)—a close estimate of the actual population mode. Note that the mode does not tell us anything about how typical this most common category is, or about the shape of the frequency distribution.

The median

The median can be calculated for ordinal, ratio and interval data. It is the usual measure of central tendency for ordinal level variables. If the scores for each member of the sample population are arranged in numerical order, then the median value is the middle value. We estimate this by finding the middle value for our sample. When there is an even number of scores, as in the following example, then the median is the average of the two central scores:

1, 2, 2, 3, **4, 6,** 7, 8, 10, 11

In this case the median is calculated by averaging 4 and 6. Thus 5 is the median of this grouping even though 5 is not one of the scores listed.

If there are an uneven number of scores then the median is the central number:

1, 3, 5, 8, **9,** 12, 14, 16, 18

In this case the median is 9.

You will note in Table 14.2 that there are 20 babies, therefore the median is the score between the 10th and 11th subjects. Note that as the score for the 10th is waking two times, and the score for the 11th is waking three times. Therefore the median for this group is waking 2.5 times.

An easy way to estimate the median is to use the cumulative percentage column in your frequency distribution table. The median is found in the 50th percentile (or the point where 50 per cent of cases fall). In Table 14.4, for example, the median waking is two times—an approximation of the median that was more precisely calculated above. In the sample, the median is also two waking times (Table 14.6).

The mean

The mean can be calculated for interval and ratio level variables only, and is the most commonly used statistic for these levels. The mean is the arithmetic average value of the variable over the sampled population. To calculate the mean we add up the scores for all the members of the sample and then divide by the sample size. You will note from Table 14.1 that the babies woke a total of 57 times. As there are 20 babies, the mean number of times the babies in the sampled population woke is 57/20 = 2.85 times. For the sample, the mean is 20/7 = 2.9 times (Table 14.6).

Sometimes a random sample of a population will contain 'outliers'. These are values of the variable which are quite extreme in that they have a very low frequency in the sampled population. If such outliers appear in your sample, they will distort your sample statistics, particularly if the sample is small.

In many cases that you will uncover during the course of your research career you will have good reason to suspect that the variable you are measuring is 'normally distributed' over the population (see below for a description of the normal distribution). In such a case, if you feel that 'outliers' have distorted your estimate of the mean, the median of the sample may be a better estimate of central tendency as it is unaffected by extreme scores. This is because the mean, mode and median of a normally distributed population are equal.

Measures of dispersion

While measures of central tendency can give a great deal of information about the distribution of scores, measures of dispersion are used if we wish to understand the degree of variability, or how widely our scores are dispersed.

Variation ratio

The variation ratio is defined as the fraction of members of the population which are outside the mode of the variable's distribution. For example, the variation ratio of the population in our example is 15/20 = 0.75. If we estimate this using our sample, the variation ratio is 5/7 = 0.71. The higher the variation ratio, the more poorly the mode describes the distribution. In our example, in the population, the mode only describes 25 per cent of the population. When we took a random sample, our estimate for the mode was wrong. The higher the variation ratio, the more likely it is that the estimated mode in your sample will be wrong.

The variation ratio is the only measure of dispersion for nominal data.

Range

The range is the difference between the highest and lowest value of the variable. In our example of the number of times the babies woke during the night, in Table 14.3 we can see that the highest number is 9 and the lowest is 0, so the range is 9 − 0 = 9. The range, like the mean, can easily be distorted if there are 'outliers', extreme scores at either end.

Decile and interquartile ranges

Both the decile range and the interquartile range are ways of assessing the effectiveness of the median as the summary measure of the distribution. Both measures avoid the distorting effect of extreme cases by 'dropping off' the cases at the edges of scores. The decile range shows the range of the middle 80 per cent of the cases, while the interquartile range shows the range of the middle 50 per cent of cases. They are calculated from the cumulative percentage columns by dropping the top and bottom 10 per cent of cases (for the decile range) or the top and bottom 25 per cent of cases (for the interquartile range). You can see how this will give you a measure of dispersion that is uncontaminated by outliers. Decile and interquartile range are the usual measures of dispersion for ordinal level variables. In our example, the interquartile range of the population is 1–3 times awake (we drop off the top and bottom 25 per cent), and the decile range is 1–5 (we drop off the top and bottom 10 per cent). (You should check this at Table 14.4.) If we use our sample, we would estimate that the interquartile range is 1–5 as is the decile range (Table 14.6).

Variance and standard deviation

The standard deviation and variance are the most frequently used measures of dispersion for interval and ratio level frequencies. When used in conjunction with the mean they tell us a lot about the spread of the distribution without having to use the raw figures. Like the mean, the standard deviation takes all values into consideration when it is calculated. In fact, in the case of a normally distributed variable (see below), the distribution is completely defined if we know the mean and the standard deviation.

> The variance is the average square distance from the mean of all the scores in the sampled population.
>
> For a population size of N and where μ represents the mean of the set of scores, the variance σ^2 can be calculated using the formula:
>
> $$\sigma^2 = \Sigma (X - \mu)^2 / N$$

Why average square distance, you may ask, why not just average distance? The reason for this is that the distance from the mean may be positive or negative; if we average these values, negative and positive values will cancel each other out.

When we have a sample, the estimate we use for the population variance is not what we might expect. Instead of dividing by n (the number in the sample) we divide by n − 1. Why do we do this? It can be shown mathematically that dividing by (n − 1) gives us an unbiased estimate of the population variance. If we divide by n we get an estimate that tends to always be less than the real value.

The sample variance s^2 for a sample of size n uses the following formula:

$$s^2 = \Sigma\,(X - \overline{X})^2/(n - 1)$$

The standard deviation of the distribution is the square root of the variance. This is useful because standard deviation is measured in the same units as the values of variables (in our example, number of times waking per night).

The standard deviation of the distribution is the square root of the variance. Therefore standard deviation or σ is calculated using the following formula:

$$\sigma = \sqrt{\Sigma\,(X - \mu)^2/N}$$

or in the case of a sample:

$$s = \sqrt{\Sigma(X - \overline{X})^2/(n - 1)}$$

where s is the standard deviation of the sample, $\overline{X}$ is the sample mean and n the number of cases in the sample.

Table 14.7 shows an example of variance and standard deviation using our example of waking babies and using the scores listed in Table 14.6. Remember that the average number of times awake ($\overline{X}$) calculated above is 20/7 = 2.9.

To calculate standard deviation of a population you must list scores, determine the mean, subtract the mean from the score, square the result, add the sum of this column, divide this sum by the number of cases to calculate variance, and determine the square root of the variance to calculate standard deviation.

The standard deviation allows us to determine how widely our scores are spread. A small standard deviation indicates a small variation in scores while a large standard deviation reflects wide variation.

247

Table 14.7 Calculating the variance and standard deviation

No. of times awake (X)	No. of times awake minus the mean (X – X̄)	No. of times awake minus the mean squared (X – X̄²)
0	−2.9	8.41
1	−1.9	3.61
2	−0.9	0.81
2	−0.9	0.81
3	0.1	0.01
5	2.1	4.41
7	4.1	16.81
Total 20		34.87
X̄ 20/7= 2.9		
s^2		34.87/6 = 5.81

Variance is $\Sigma (X - \bar{X})^2/ (n - 1)$ 34.87/6 = 5.81

To illustrate in a different way, let us take two samples of social workers working for a department of community services. One sample works in the city and the other in a rural area. The workers are asked to list the number of cases of child abuse seen in a single week.

Sample A—city workers:

6, 9, 1, 13, 16

Note there are five cases, so n = 5 and the mean is calculated by summing the scores and dividing by n.

6 + 9 + 1 + 13 + 16 = 45
Mean = 45/5 = 9

Sample B—country workers

1, 3, 2, 7, 2

Again we sum the scores and divide by n (5) to calculate the mean.

Mean = 15/5 = 3

Tables 14.8 and 14.9 are calculations of the standard deviations of the two groups.

We can deduce from these two examples that there is greater variation in the city workers' scores and that the country workers' scores are grouped more closely together.

It is most unlikely that you will have to perform these calculations these days, given that most advanced calculators and statistical packages will do it for you; however, it is important to understand variance and standard deviation and what, together with the mean, they tell us about the distribution.

Table 14.8 Calculating the standard deviation of the city workers' cases

No. of cases (X)	Mean	No. of cases minus the mean (X – X̄)	No. of cases minus the mean squared (X – X̄)²
6	9	–3	9
9	9	0	0
1	9	–8	64
13	9	4	16
16	9	7	49
			Total Σ(X – X̄)² = 138

Table 14.9 Calculating the standard deviation of the country workers' cases

No. of cases (X)	Mean	No. of cases minus the mean (X – X̄)	No. of cases minus the mean squared (X – X̄)²
1	3	–2	4
3	3	0	0
2	3	–1	1
7	3	4	16
2	3	–1	1
			Total Σ(X – X̄)² = 22

Variance = 22/4 = 5.5
Standard deviation = $\sqrt{\text{variance}}$ = 2.35

The normal distribution

Much of your future research will deal with data which is approximately 'normally' distributed over the population. What does this mean? Essentially it means that the values of the variables are spread across a range of scores in a particular pattern in a way that sees them cluster around a common mean, mode and median. If we draw the pattern we will see the bell-shaped curve. The distributions of many continuous variables can be described as normal distributions. If the distribution of a particular variable is 'normal', its probability curve is an example of a 'normal curve'. A normal curve can be described simply by a mathematical formula which uses the mean and the variance. This means we can know a great deal about our data, once we have good estimates of the mean and variance.

Three normal curves are shown in Figure 14.6 on page 250. The probability curves of normally distributed variables all have a typical bell shape, and in fact the normal curve is often called the bell curve. The first thing to note is that the mean, mode and median are all the same for each curve (0 for one, 2 for second and 0 for the third). Second, when you compare the curves, you can see that the larger the standard deviation is, the greater the spread of the curve.

There are some other important properties that you should note.

Once we know that a variable has a normal distribution, the standard deviation becomes a powerful tool. In the case of a normal curve, the area under the curve between plus or minus 1 standard deviation from the mean is 0.68. That is, the probability of X having a value within plus or minus 1 standard deviation from the mean is 0.68. This means that 68 per cent of scores lie within plus or minus 1 standard deviation of the mean.

For example, if the average age of people in a nation is 25 years and the standard deviation is 8 years, then 68 per cent of people in that country will be aged between 17 and 33 years. In a similar way 95 per cent of scores lie between plus or minus 2 standard deviations from the mean and 99.74 per cent lie between plus or minus 3 standard deviations from the mean. In our example of a nation, 95 per cent of people would be aged between 9 and 41 years (25 plus or minus 2 x 8) and 99.74 per cent would be between 1 and 49 years (25 plus or minus 3 x 8). So if we can get good estimates for mean and variance, we can speak meaningfully about the spread of the data.

The importance of normal distributions in statistics: the sampling distribution of the mean

We have created a population of 5000 imaginary students studying History. The students' scores were normally distributed, with a mean of 50 (a bare pass) and a standard deviation of 11.2. From these examination scores we took a number of simple random samples—

Figure 14.6 Examples of normal curves

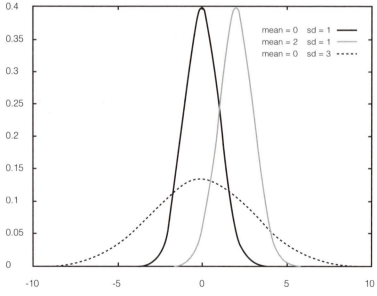

Figure 14.7 The area under the normal curve

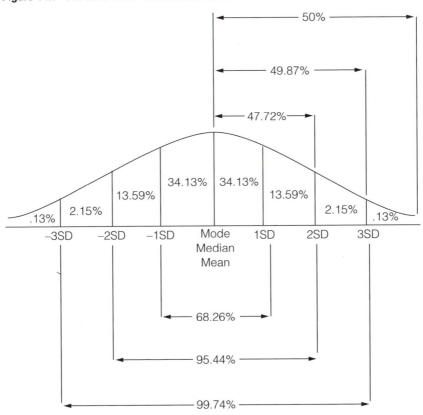

Source: R. W. Weinbach & R. M. Grinnell Jr, *Statistics for Social Workers*, 3rd edn, Longman, New York. 1995.

three samples of 30 students and three samples of 100 students. The means and standard deviations of the samples are shown in Table 14.10.

From Table 14.10, we can see that each time we take a sample, we get different estimates for the mean and the standard deviation which are close to, but not the same as, the actual mean of the population (50 marks) and the actual standard deviation (11.2 marks).

Further, we can see that the sample means are closer to the actual population mean in the larger samples (samples 4, 5 and 6). If we had taken every possible sample of size 30, calculated all the sample means, and drawn a relative frequency curve of the sample means, we would have seen that these means were distributed approximately normally, with a mean of 50. When we do the same for the larger samples of 100, the sample means will again approximate a normal curve but with a much smaller standard deviation.

Figure 14.8 Relative frequency curves for sample means size 30 and 100

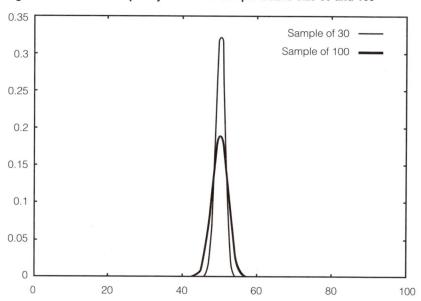

Figure 14.8 shows relative frequency curves for the sample mean for samples of size 30 and 100. The graph for the sample of 100 is very tall and thin (a very small standard deviation), showing that the probability that our estimate of the mean will be near the population mean is very high.

In summary, there are three important points to be learned from this example, which are graphically depicted in Figure 14.8:

- The distribution of the sample means are distributed normally (and this will happen even if the original population from which the sample is taken is not normally distributed, or skewed in some way).
- The mean of the sample means is equal to the population mean from which the samples were drawn (notice how the peak of each curve is at 50).

Table 14.10 Means and standard deviations of samples from History students—sample sizes 30 and 100

30 students	Sample 1 (30)	Sample 2 (30)	Sample 3 (30)
Mean	47.3	50.7	49.6
Standard deviation	12.4	13.2	12.2

100 students	Sample 4 (100)	Sample 5 (100)	Sample 6 (100)
Mean	48.85	50.25	50.4
Standard deviation	10.129	12.52	10.99

- The distribution of sample means is less dispersed as sample size increases (the sample of 100 is taller and thinner).

If the distribution of sample means is less dispersed as sample size increases, it follows that the mean of any single sample is likely to be closer to the mean of the population as sample size increases. This is why we advised you to take as large a sample as you can, in chapter 5.

Together these three points illustrate a most important theorem in statistics, the central limit theorem.

Central limit theorem

If random samples of a certain size n are drawn from any population (regardless of its distribution or shape), as n becomes larger, the distribution of the sample means approaches normality.

This theorem can also be used to show that for a large population and sample, it is often safe to assume that the variable is distributed normally.

Standard error

We have seen that when we take all the possible samples of size n, the sample means have an approximately normal distribution. If we take the mean of all these sample means, we get the mean of the population. The standard deviation of all these sample means gives us an estimate of the spread of the error that we would encounter if we estimate the mean from just one sample of size n (which is what you would normally do in research). This standard deviation is called the *standard error* and indicates the potential error in the sample statistics by comparison with the population statistics. It can be shown that the standard error is $\sigma/\sqrt{n}$ (where σ is the standard deviation and n the sample size). In our example with samples of size 30 the standard error is $11.2/\sqrt{30} = 2.04$. In the case of our samples of size 100 the standard error is $11.2/\sqrt{100} = 1.12$. This suggests that the greater the sample size the closer it will approximate the population statistics.

Standard error

For a sample of size n and a population with mean μ and standard deviation σ, the standard error of the sample mean E is given by the formula:

$$E = \sigma/\sqrt{n}$$

In our second set of samples, we used a sample size of 100. We could see that our estimates for the mean were closer to the actual population mean in these larger samples. This is confirmed by the standard error—that is, $(11.2/\sqrt{100} = 11.2/10 = 1.12)$, which is much smaller than the standard error for a sample size of 30 (2.04). This is demonstrated in the graphs of distributions of sample means for different sample sizes (Figure 14.8). Thus, larger samples give more accurate estimates of the actual population mean.

The standard error is inversely proportional to the sample size and hence we see what common sense already tells us, that our sample mean will be much more likely to be close to the population mean if we use a large sample.

Standard error is also used to calculate sampling error. As the sample mean is itself a variable from a normal distribution we know that 95 per cent of the time it will have a value within two standard deviations (2 x standard error) of its mean, which is in fact the population mean. So we can be 95 per cent confident that our sample mean is an accurate estimate of the population mean to within two standard errors. Thus, when you read tables that tell you the sample sizes required for various sampling errors at the 95 per cent confidence level, the sampling error reported is in fact two standard errors. We discuss the concept of confidence intervals in more detail below.

Converting scores to Z-scores

The standard deviation has another important function. It can be used to tell us where an individual is situated in relation to the group. Sometimes we might wish to compare the values of interval or ratio level variables taken from different samples or populations. If we know the means and standard deviations of the sample scores we can do this by calculating a standard score, or Z-score.

The Z-score transforms our original variable into a new variable which is distributed normally and has a mean of 0 and a standard variable of 1. This distribution is very well tabulated. We can convert any normal distribution to the Z or standard distribution and then use tables to look up probabilities of individual Z-scores. This means that we can reduce two (or more) quite different normal distributions to the same distribution and compare them.

The Z-score will tell us the number of standard deviations that the score is from the population mean. Z-score is calculated by taking the mean from the raw score and dividing by the standard deviation.

Calculating the Z-score

$$Z\text{-score} = \frac{\text{raw score} - \text{mean}}{\text{standard deviation}}$$

Example

Imagine you wish to contrast the results of two students in two different subjects to see which student did better. Imagine that Ruth scored 65 in her Social Work Theory subject and Emma scored 51 in Social Policy. You cannot be entirely sure that Ruth is the better student because the grades reflect the students' work on different subject material. However, if we can calculate the Z-scores for each student in relation to the rest of the students taking each subject, we can calculate how each fared relative to their group, and this allows us to compare our two students.

Suppose that the mean for the Social Work Theory group is 70 and the standard deviation 10. Ruth's Z-score is therefore:

$$Z = \frac{65 - 70}{10} = -\tfrac{1}{2} = -0.5$$

Therefore Ruth's score falls 0.5 standard deviations *below* the mean for her group.

On the other hand the mean for the Social Policy group was 50 and the standard deviation is 5. Emma's Z-score is therefore:

$$Z = \frac{51 - 50}{5} = \tfrac{1}{5} = 0.2$$

This tells us that Emma's score is 0.2 standard deviations *above* the mean.

In relation to the two groups of students, Emma's score of 51 is thus a better score.

How to use tables of the standard normal distribution (Z-scores)

To determine the percentage of the population that fell below the Z-score we look up a table of areas under the normal curve, such as Table 14.11.

In examining where Emma's score (0.2) falls, and describing what this information tells us, we have taken one cell from Table 14.11, as shown in Table 14.12. Emma's score lies in row 0.2 and column 0.00. We can see that 7.93 per cent is the percentage of values of the random variable Z which will fall in the interval between 0 and 0.2 + 0.00 = 0.20. If you prefer, 7.93 is the percentage of the total area under the normal curve between 0 and 0.20. The table only gives the value between 0 and 0.20 because the standard normal curve is symmetrical about 0, so we can immediately say that the percentage of values of Z lying between −0.20 and +0.20 is 7.93 x 2 = 15.86 per cent. We also know that 50 per cent of values of Z are less than 0, so we can now say that 50 + 7.93 = 57.93 per cent of values of Z are less than 0.20.

Table 14.11 Percentage areas under the normal curve

Z	.00	.01	.02	.03	.04	.05	.06	.07	.08	.09
0.0	00.00	00.40	00.80	01.20	01.60	01.99	02.39	02.79	03.19	03.59
0.1	03.98	04.38	04.78	05.17	05.57	05.96	06.36	06.75	07.14	07.53
0.2	07.93	08.32	08.71	09.10	09.48	09.87	10.26	10.64	11.03	11.41
0.3	11.79	12.17	12.55	12.93	13.31	13.68	14.06	14.43	14.80	15.17
0.4	15.54	15.91	16.28	16.64	17.00	17.36	17.72	18.08	18.44	18.79
0.5	19.15	19.50	19.85	20.19	20.54	20.88	21.23	21.57	21.90	22.24
0.6	22.57	22.91	23.24	23.57	23.89	24.22	24.54	24.86	25.17	25.49
0.7	25.80	26.11	26.42	26.73	27.04	27.34	27.64	27.94	28.23	28.52
0.8	28.81	29.10	29.39	29.67	29.95	30.23	30.51	30.78	31.06	31.33
0.9	31.59	31.86	32.12	32.38	32.64	32.90	33.15	33.40	33.65	33.89
1.0	34.13	34.38	34.61	34.85	35.08	35.31	35.54	35.77	35.99	36.21
1.1	36.43	36.65	36.86	37.08	37.29	37.49	37.70	37.90	38.10	38.30
1.2	38.49	38.69	38.88	39.07	39.25	39.44	39.62	39.80	39.97	40.15
1.3	40.32	40.49	40.66	40.82	40.99	41.15	41.31	41.47	41.62	41.77
1.4	41.92	42.07	42.22	42.36	42.51	42.65	42.79	42.92	43.06	43.19
1.5	43.32	43.45	43.57	43.70	43.83	43.94	44.06	44.18	44.29	44.41
1.6	44.52	44.63	44.74	44.84	44.95	45.05	45.15	45.25	45.35	45.45
1.7	45.54	45.64	45.73	45.82	45.91	45.99	46.08	46.16	46.25	46.33
1.8	46.41	46.49	46.56	46.64	46.71	46.78	46.86	46.93	46.99	47.06
1.9	47.13	47.19	47.26	47.32	47.38	47.44	47.50	47.56	47.61	47.67
2.0	47.72	47.78	47.83	47.88	47.93	47.98	48.03	48.08	48.12	48.17
2.1	48.21	48.26	48.30	48.34	48.38	48.42	48.46	48.50	48.54	48.57
2.2	48.61	48.64	48.68	48.71	48.75	48.78	48.81	48.84	48.87	48.90
2.3	48.93	48.96	48.98	49.01	49.04	49.06	49.09	49.11	49.13	49.16
2.4	49.18	49.20	49.22	49.25	49.27	49.29	49.31	49.32	49.34	49.36
2.5	49.38	49.40	49.41	49.43	49.45	49.46	49.48	49.49	49.51	49.52
2.6	49.53	49.55	49.56	49.57	49.59	49.60	49.61	49.62	49.63	49.64
2.7	49.65	49.66	49.67	49.68	49.69	49.70	49.71	49.72	49.73	49.74
2.8	49.74	49.75	49.76	49.77	49.77	49.78	49.79	49.79	49.80	49.81
2.9	49.81	49.82	49.82	49.83	49.84	49.84	49.85	49.85	49.86	49.86
3.0	49.87									
3.5	49.98									
4.0	49.997									
5.0	49.99997									

Source: From R. W. Weinbach & R. M. Grinnell Jr 1995, *Statistics for Social Workers*, 3rd edn, Longman, New York. The original data for Table 14.11 came from *Tables for Statisticians and Biometricians*, K. Pearson (ed.). Imperial College of Science and Technology, London. The adaptation of these data is taken from E. L. Lindquist, *A First Course in Statistics*, rev. edn, Houghton Mifflin, Cambridge, Mass.

We can see from this example that 57.93 per cent of Emma's class scored lower than she did.

We can also see where Ruth's score falls. Remember that Ruth scored −0.5, therefore is in the bottom half of her class. If we look at the table we can see that the area equating to 0.5 is 19.15. Because Ruth's score is negative, we take 19.15 from 50 to determine where she came in her group, that is, 50 − 19.15 = 30.85 per cent. We can deduce from this that only 30.85 per cent of the class scored below Ruth's score.

Table 14.12 Extract of percentage areas under the standard normal curve between 0 and Z (from Table 14.11)

Z	.00	.01	.02	.03	.04	.05	.06	.07	.08.	.09
0.0										
0.1										
0.2	07.93									
0.3										
0.4										
0.5	19.15									

Confidence intervals

We have seen how statistics from samples give us an estimate of population parameters. We hope they are close, but we need to know how likely it is, or how confident we can be, that the result from our sample reflects the actual statistic in the population. The confidence interval specifies a range of values within which the actual population mean lies.

Once we know our sample mean and standard deviation, and using the fact that 95 per cent of scores from a normal distribution lie within 2 standard deviations of the mean, we can calculate a *confidence interval*. This confidence interval tells us the range within which we can be 95 per cent confident that the actual population mean lies. The range of scores is called the *confidence interval* and the degree of certainty we have that the population percentage will fall within that range (in this case 95 per cent) is called the *confidence level*.

While we will not explain how to calculate confidence intervals because computer packages do this for us, it is important to know how to read and interpret them. For example, take Sample 1 from Table 14.10. The mean of the sample was 47.3. We can calculate the 95 per cent confidence interval using Z-scores and our knowledge that 95 per cent of normal scores lie within two standard deviations of the mean ($-2<Z<+2$). When calculated, the 95 per cent confidence interval for Sample 1 is 43.22–51.38. This means that we are 95 per cent confident that the population mean lies between 43.22 and 51.38. In fact we know that the population mean is 50, which does lie within our 95 per cent confidence interval.

BIVARIATE ANALYSIS

It is a very common problem in research to need to determine whether there is or there is not an association between two variables and, if there is, to explore the nature of that relationship. The first task is to examine the two variables to see if there appear to be patterns or associations between them. One way to do this is to draw up crosstabulations.

Crosstabulations

Crosstabulations are tables showing the relationship between two variables. Table 14.13 shows the crosstabulation between the two variables in the example in chapter 6—the relationship between location (whether people live in the country or city) and their experience of staff treatment (good, satisfactory or bad) at income support agency offices. This table is called a 'three by two' table, indicating that there are three rows and two columns. For the purposes of illustration, we have increased our hypothetical sample to 300 people, 150 from the country and 150 from the city.

Note that the table has a title and a number. Both the columns and rows are labelled. The independent variable (location) is across the top of the table in columns, and the categories of the dependent variable are in the rows. The box at the intersection of a column and row is called a *cell*. Cells contain the number of cases from the sample that have the values of both the row and column at which they intersect. Thus, 33 people from the country had a good experience at agency offices, while 43 rural people had bad experiences. The end row and end column are called marginals and show the totals for each row and column. We can see that there were 150 people each from the country and the city, 90 who felt the service was good, 135 who felt it was satisfactory, and 75 who had a bad experience. This makes 300 people in all, as shown in the bottom right-hand marginal cell.

From Table 14.13, it appears that people in the city could be more satisfied overall with their experiences at an agency office than people in the country, but it is difficult to tell. An easier way is to use percentages. Technically there are three kinds of percentages that we could calculate, each of which provides different information. These are:

- Percentages across the rows
- Percentages down the columns
- Percentage of each cell compared to the total of all the cells

Table 14.13 **Experience at income support agency offices by location (observed frequencies: raw scores)**

Experience at agency office	Location		
	Rural	City	Total
Good	33	57	90
Satisfactory	74	61	135
Bad	43	32	75
Total	150	150	300

If you are not sure which percentages are being used in a table, work out which way they add to 100. This information should be in the table (as marginals), but sometimes it is omitted.

In this example, we are interested in the effect the independent variable has on the dependent variable (that is, does living in the country or city affect the experiences people have when they visit an agency office?), so it makes sense to examine how subgroups of the independent variable vary in terms of the dependent variable. In this example, because the independent variable is across the top of the table, we calculate percentages down the columns, so that we can see how the dependent variable changes with the independent variable (Table 14.14).

From Table 14.14 we can see that 22 per cent of rural dwellers felt that their experience at the agency office was good, compared to 38 per cent of city people. On the other hand, 29 per cent of rural people had bad experiences compared to 21 per cent of city dwellers. In these statements we are comparing the percentages for each category of the independent variable (location) across the categories of the dependent variable (experience visiting an agency office).

From this brief glance at the percentages, it does appear that country people are less satisfied than city people with their treatment when they visit an income-support agency office. To find out if these differences are significant, we need to perform statistical tests. Firstly, however, de Vaus (2002) summarises the steps in detecting association between two variables in a table. These are important for you to learn and to understand.

Steps in detecting relationships in cross-tabulations (from de Vaus 2002, p. 245)

1 Determine which variable is to be treated as independent
2 Choose appropriate cell percentages:
   a. Column percentages if the independent variable is across the top
   b. Row percentages if the independent variable is on the side
3 Compare percentages for each subgroup of the independent variable within one category of the dependent variable at a time
4 If the independent variable is across the top, use column percentages and compare these across the table. Any difference between these reflects some association
5 If the independent variable is on the side, use row percentages and compare these down the table. Any difference between these reflects some association

Table 14.14 Experience at income support agency offices by location (percentages)

Experience at agency office	Location	
	Rural %	City %
Good	22	38
Satisfactory	49	41
Bad	29	21
Total	100	100
	(n = 150)	(n = 150)

Tables are only useful as ways of presenting information when there are relatively few cells. They are most useful when variables have a maximum of six or seven categories each (de Vaus 2002). If variables have too many categories, it may be possible to collapse some of the categories. This can be done for nominal, ordinal and interval level variables.

Note that Table 14.14 is fairly simple to read (compared to one, say, which included all the different percentages possible, as well as raw frequencies in each cell). It contains all the important information in skeleton form, from which it is possible to calculate any other information as needed (such as raw figures or row percentages). Presented in this way, it also gives us an indication of the answer to our question: that is, does living in the country or the city affect the experiences people have when they visit an income support agency office? de Vaus (2002) provides a useful summary of what information to include in crosstabulations so that they are simple and clear to read, and yet any other calculations can be made from the skeleton information provided in the table.

Information to include in bivariate tables

- Table number
- Title (dependent variable by independent variable, e.g. Table 14.12: Experience at income support agency)
- Label clearly each variable and each category of each variable
- Use '%' to head percentage columns
- Define variables in footnotes to avoid lengthy titles
- Footnote how many were in the 'missing data' category (don't know, refusals, no answers)
- If the independent variable is across the top (as has become the convention), use column percentages only
- Place a 100 per cent figure beneath the column to show that percentages have been used

> ■ Place the column marginal frequency beneath each column (this shows what numbers the percentages are based on and enables the re-calculation of cell frequencies and the grand total)
>
> From de Vaus, p. 249 (2002)

TESTING FOR STATISTICAL SIGNIFICANCE

In this section we introduce you to some key concepts in testing for statistical significance, provide an overview of the tests you can choose from and then discuss in more detail the logic behind the more common tests.

Statistical significance

When investigating a relationship between two or more variables we are looking for evidence that the relationship is clear and not just the effect of chance. Usually we only undertake one study of a research question, drawing only one sample. We need to be reasonably clear that any detected relationship cannot be dismissed as simply the result of sampling error and that the patterns we can see in the variables taken from our sample actually occur in the population from which the sample came.

Remember chapter 3 and our discussion of the null hypothesis, which assumes that there is no relationship between variables? This is the implicit assumption on which research is based. If we find, contrary to the null hypothesis, that there is a relationship between the variables in our sample, we are faced with two possibilities— either we have drawn a poor sample which does not reflect the trends in the population (sampling error) or there actually is a relationship between the variables in the population from which we took our sample, and we have some evidence on which to reject the null hypothesis. Tests of statistical significance give us a way of working out which is the correct explanation for our findings.

When testing for significance, we choose what risk we are willing to take that the relationship we observe between the variables in our sample has been caused by sampling error. This risk (probability) is called the level of significance of the test and is a figure ranging from 0 to 1 (usually represented as p). For example, if we get a p of 0.05, we know that in 5 out of 100 samples, the results in our sample would be due to sampling error. The closer the p value is to 0, the more likely it is that the results are *not* due to sampling error. Thus, the lower the significance level, the more confident we can be that the results in our sample are due to real differences in the population.

In most research reports significance levels are represented as 'ρ'. When you read research reports and articles you will no doubt come across this type of statistical shorthand. Consider the following statement that reflects the way much statistical evidence is reported.

> The average number of cases of child abuse dealt with by city social workers in the Department of Community Services is 12 and for country workers it is 5. This difference is statistically significant at the 0.05 level. (Or it could also be written as $\rho < 0.05$).

The writer is suggesting that the probability that these results could have occurred through sampling error is 5 in 100 and so she/he is reasonably confident that there is in fact a relationship between location and number of child abuse cases.

Having understood what level of significance level (or ρ) means, we now have to choose an appropriate level for our research. In other words, at what level do we reject the original assumption that there is no relationship between the variables (or null hypothesis)? Social researchers, by convention, usually choose either the 0.05 or 0.01 significance levels. There are problems with both of these levels. These are best discussed in the context of Type I and Type 2 errors.

Type 1 and Type 2 errors

If we are too easy on ourselves and choose too large a level of significance, we run the risk of rejecting the null hypothesis when in fact our results are due to sampling error. This is called a Type 1 error. With the standard 0.05 significance level, 5 in 100 chances that our results are due to sampling error could be too many to risk and mean that we conclude that there is a relationship between variables when in fact there is not. de Vaus (2002) writes that this type of error is most likely with large samples. Thus he recommends that it is best to use the 0.01 level of significance with larger samples.

On the other hand, if we are too tough, and choose too small a significance level we might not reject the null hypothesis, assuming our results are due to sampling error, when in fact they do represent a relationship between variables, that occurs in the population. This is called a Type 2 error. Selecting the 0.01 level means that we could mistakenly conclude that there is no relationship, when in fact there is.

All the statistical tests in the following discussion are tests of significance, or ρ, for the sample results we obtain. The art (and danger) of choosing the level of significance we are happy with, and interpreting our results accordingly, is balancing the risks of Type 1 errors against those of Type 2 errors. Much of this assessment depends on the type of study we are doing. For example, if our study involves risks to health, for example comparing the effects of different types of treatments for alcohol abuse, we would choose much smaller levels of significance than for another study, say on the preferences of holiday makers.

For a fuller discussion of the logic of testing for statistical significance, see de Vaus (2002) or Sarantakos (1998) or Babbie (2001).

Two other important concepts to understand before discussing statistical tests, are the notions of one- and two-tailed hypotheses.

One-tailed and two-tailed research hypotheses

When formulating a research hypothesis we specify a relationship between two (or more) variables. Sometimes we nominate the direction of the relationship. This is called a *one-tailed hypothesis*. An example of such an hypothesis might be:

> Clients are more likely to have a positive experience in rural income support agency offices.

When we do not specify the direction of the relationship (thus in our example we are not saying if the experience is positive or negative), we have a *two-tailed research hypothesis*. An example might be:

> Clients are likely to have a different experience in rural income support agency offices.

Selecting the right statistical test

The credibility of a research project will stand or fall on the selection of the most appropriate statistical test. There are many statistical tests we can use; choosing the right one requires serious thought. Weinbach and Grinnell (2001, pp. 118–25) note that there are five factors that should guide your choice of a statistical test. These are:

- The sampling method used
- The distribution of the variables within the population
- The level of measurement of the independent and dependent variable
- The amount of statistical power that is desirable
- Tthe robustness of the tests being considered

There are two main types of statistical tests: *parametric* and *non-parametric*. *Parametric* tests are more powerful. They require that a random sample be drawn, that the variables are normally distributed within the population, and that at least one variable is at the interval or ratio level of measurement. Parametric tests are used when the probability distribution of the variable is known. Weinbach and Grinnell (2001) suggest that if the mean and standard deviation describe a study's findings fairly well (which means that the variables are normally distributed within the sample), then parametric statistics *may* be appropriate for examining the relationships between variables within the study.

263

Non-parametric tests are generally less powerful than parametric tests but can be used in studies where the conditions for parametric tests cannot be met. For example, if variables are at nominal or ordinal level, or if samples have been drawn from different populations or the samples are very small, non-parametric tests may be the most appropriate. Sometimes the lesser power of non-parametric tests can be compensated for by using larger samples. Often when we do not know the distribution of the variable, and have reason to suppose that it is not normal, we use non-parametric or distribution-free tests. Non-parametric methods are the only ones available for nominal and ordinal level data. Both methods are used for interval/ratio data depending upon what we want to know.

The chart on page 265 (Figure 14.9) reproduced from Weinbach and Grinnell (2001) provides a useful guide to selecting the appropriate statistical test. Note that the use of computers in statistical analysis makes the task of nominating the most appropriate test based on your study conditions much simpler.

Tests of significance

Chi-square

Chi-square is one of the most commonly used statistics in social work research because it measures the association between variables at the nominal or ordinal level. Like many other measures of association, chi-square can tell us if two variables are related. It is a non-parametric test. We will begin our discussion of significance tests with this test.

Measuring association at nominal level

From Table 14.13, the cross table of raw scores from a survey to measure people's experience when they visit an income support agency office, we would like to know whether there is a significant difference between the rural and urban experiences.

In order to find out if there is a significant difference, we first form two hypotheses, as discussed in chapter 3. These are the null hypothesis and the alternative hypothesis. Remember that in conducting tests of significance we are attempting to disprove the null rather than actually 'prove' the alternative.

- H_0 The null hypothesis—there is not a significant difference between the urban and the rural experience
- H_1 The alternative hypothesis—there is a significant difference between the urban and the rural experience

We first consider the case where H_0 is true.

If H_0 is true we would expect the proportions of people having a

Figure 14.9 Parametric and non-parametric statistical tests

Parametric statistical test			Non-parametrical statistical test		
Test	Dependent (criterion) variable	Independent (predictor) variable	Test	Dependent (criterion) variable	Independent (predictor) variable
–	–	–	Chi-square	Nominal	Nominal
–	–	–	Fisher's exact	Nominal	Nominal (2 categories)
–	–	–	McNamar's	Nominal (before)	Nominal (after)
One sample t	Interval/ratio	–	Goodness of fit	Nominal	Nominal
Independent t	Interval/ratio	Nominal	Mann-Whitney U	Ordinal/skewed interval	Nominal
Dependent t	Interval/ratio	Nominal	Kolmorogov-Smirnov	Ordinal/skewed interval	–
One-way ANOVA	Interval/ratio	Nominal	Wilcoxon Sign	Ordinal plus	(2 repeated measures)
			Kruskal-Wallis	Ordinal/skewed interval	Nominal
Pearson's r	Interval/ratio	Interval/ratio	Spearman rho	Ordinal/skewed interval	Ordinal/skewed interval
			Kendall's tau	Ordinal/skewed interval	Ordinal/skewed interval
Simple linear regression	Interval/ratio	Interval/ratio	Logistic regression	Nominal	Nominal

Source: From R. W. Weinbach & R. M. Grinnell Jr 2001, *Statistics for Social Workers*, 5th edn, Allyn & Bacon, Boston

Table 14.15 Experience at income support agency offices by location—observed (and expected) frequencies

Experience at agency office	Location		
	Rural	City	Total
Good	33 (45)	57 (45)	90
Satisfactory	74 (67.5)	61 (67.5)	135
Bad	43 (37.5)	32 (37.5)	75
Total	150	150	300

good experience to be the same in both locations. What we look for is that the *observed frequencies* differ from the *expected frequencies*. If they do, then the null hypothesis does not ring true. To determine this we firstly calculate the expected frequency using the following equation:

$$\text{Expected value} = \frac{\text{row total} \times \text{column total}}{\text{number of cases}}$$

There are 90 people overall with a good experience (row total). There are 150 people in the rural sample (column total). The total number of cases is 300. Calculating the expected frequency for the first cell:

$150 \times 90/300 = 45$

We would expect 45 rural people to have had a good experience. We can similarly calculate 'expected' values for the different levels of experience in the two locations (Table 14.15) using this formula.

We now look at a sample statistic, chi-square, that we will represent using the symbol χ^2.

To calculate chi-square we sum the observed values minus the expected values squared and divide by the expected value:

$\chi^2 = \Sigma$ (observed value – expected value)^2/expected value

$$\chi^2 = \frac{\Sigma (O - E)^2}{E}$$

where:

χ^2 = chi-square value, O = observed frequency, E = expected value and Σ = sum of (for all cells).

Table 14.16 illustrates the working out for each cell in our example.

In assessing the statistical significance of chi-square we need to look up the result in a chi-square table. First, we need to note that

Table 14.16 Example of calculation of chi-square value for income support agency office experience by location

O	E	O – E	(O – E)	$\dfrac{(O-E)^2}{E}$
33	45	–12	144	3.2
74	67.5	6.5	42.25	0.63
43	37.5	5.5	30.25	0.81
57	45	12	144	3.2
61	67.5	–6.5	42.25	0.63
32	37.5	–5.5	30.25	0.81
				$\Sigma = 9.28$

our assessment is affected by the number of *degrees of freedom* (df). If you examine the data in the table of raw scores Table 14.13 you will note that there are six cells. The value of chi-square is affected by the number of cells in our table, such that the larger the number of cells the more likely it is that the chi-square value will also be high. It is important that we do not jump to the conclusion that our results are significant before we consider the dimensions of our table. This is where the degrees of freedom come in. To calculate degrees of freedom we multiply the number of rows (r) minus 1 by the number of columns (c) minus 1. Thus:

$$df = (r - 1)(c - 1)$$

From Table 14.13

$$df = (3 - 1)(2 - 1)$$
$$= 2 \times 1$$
$$= 2 \text{ degrees of freedom}$$

We now look up our value in a chi-square table (Table 14.17). We need to be aware of our degrees of freedom and our level of significance, or ρ. If we take 0.05 as an acceptable level of significance, this suggests that we are willing to accept that our results are flawed in five out of 100 cases.

To look up our result in the chi-square table we look down the left-hand side of the table under 2 degrees of freedom and then across to our accepted level of significance. In the table you will note that the result for chi-square at 2 degrees of freedom and a probability level of 0.05 is 5.99. If our result is greater than 5.99 we can be 95 per cent confident that a relationship exists. Since our result of 9.28 is greater than 5.99, we can be fairly confident that a relationship does exist (especially as this result is also significant at the 0.01 level).

Table 14.17 is a subsection of the χ^2 table supplied as Table 14.18 (a fuller table which will allow you to assess chi-square results in detail).

Table 14.17 Portion of a table showing the two-tailed area of a χ^2 distribution

df	.20	.10	.05	.02
1	1.64	2.71	3.84	5.41
2	3.22	4.60	5.99	7.82

Level of significance for a two-tailed test

As Table 14.17 shows us that χ^2 for our sample is > 5.99, we say that we will reject hypothesis H_0 at 0.05 level of significance and accept H_1. What does this mean?

> The significance of a test is the probability that we reject H_0 when H_0 is actually true (Type 1 error).

In this case the probability that H_0 is true is 0.05. Another way of saying this is that there are five chances in 100 that we conclude that there is a relationship between the two variables when there is no relationship.

In our example $\chi^2 = 9.28$. As 9.28 is much bigger than 5.99, we reject H_0 at the 0.05 level of significance and accept that there is a relationship between experience at the income support agency and location. Usually in social work or social science research we say that 0.05 is an acceptable level of significance. If we wish to be more rigorous we might choose a 0.01 level.

If we were to present our chi-square findings in a report of our work, we would list it in the following way:

$\chi^2 = 9.28$, df = 2, $\rho < 0.05$

That is, we list our chi-square result, the number of degrees of freedom and the probability that sampling error may have produced the result.

Chi-square is a non-parametric test. It can be used to test association between two variables at nominal or ordinal level when we don't know what their distribution is, or when samples have been drawn from different populations, or when sample size is small. Although less powerful than the parametric tests described below, this can sometimes be compensated for by using larger samples.

For references to other ways to measure association between variables measured at the nominal level see de Vaus 2002 (chapter 14) and Sarantakos (1998).

Parametric tests for interval/ratio data

Parametrical statistical tests are more powerful tests than non-parametric tests. However, certain conditions must be met before these tests can be used. Parametric tests require that we know the distribution of the variables (usually normal) and that at least one variable is at the interval or ratio level of measurement.

Table 14.18 Critical values of χ^2

	Level of significance for a one-tailed test					
	0.10	0.05	0.025	0.01	0.005	0.0005
	Level of significance for a two-tailed test					
df	0.20	0.10	0.05	0.02	0.01	0.001
1	1.64	2.71	3.84	5.41	6.64	10.83
2	3.22	4.60	5.99	7.82	9.21	13.82
3	4.64	6.25	7.82	9.84	11.34	16.27
4	5.99	7.78	9.49	11.67	13.28	18.46
5	7.29	9.24	11.07	13.39	15.09	20.52
6	8.56	10.64	12.59	15.03	16.81	22.46
7	9.80	12.02	14.07	16.62	18.48	24.32
8	11.03	13.36	15.51	18.17	20.09	26.12
9	12.24	14.68	16.92	19.68	21.67	27.88
10	13.44	15.99	18.31	21.16	23.21	29.59
11	14.63	17.28	19.68	22.62	24.72	31.26
12	15.81	18.55	21.03	24.05	26.22	32.91
13	16.98	19.81	22.36	25.47	27.69	34.53
14	18.15	21.06	23.68	26.87	29.14	36.12
15	19.31	22.31	25.00	28.26	30.58	37.70
16	20.46	23.54	26.30	29.63	32.00	39.29
17	21.62	24.77	27.59	31.00	33.41	40.75
18	22.76	25.99	28.87	32.35	34.80	42.31
19	23.90	27.20	30.14	33.69	36.19	43.82
20	25.04	28.41	31.41	35.02	37.57	45.32
21	26.17	29.62	32.67	36.34	38.93	46.80
22	27.30	30.81	33.92	37.66	40.29	48.27
23	28.43	32.01	35.17	38.97	41.64	49.73
24	29.55	33.20	36.42	40.27	42.98	51.18
25	30.68	34.38	37.65	41.57	44.31	52.62
26	31.80	35.56	38.88	42.86	45.64	54.05
27	32.91	36.74	40.11	44.14	46.94	55.48
28	34.03	37.92	41.34	45.42	48.28	56.89
29	35.14	39.09	42.69	46.69	49.59	58.30
30	36.25	40.26	43.77	47.96	50.89	59.70
32	38.47	42.59	46.19	50.49	53.49	62.49
34	40.68	44.90	48.60	53.00	56.06	65.25
36	42.88	47.21	51.00	55.49	58.62	67.99
38	45.08	49.51	53.38	57.97	61.16	70.70
40	47.27	51.81	55.76	60.44	63.99	73.40
44	51.64	56.37	60.48	65.34	68.71	78.75
48	55.99	60.91	65.17	70.20	73.68	84.04
52	60.33	65.42	69.83	75.02	78.62	89.27
56	64.66	69.92	74.47	79.82	83.51	94.46
60	68.97	74.40	79.08	84.58	88.38	99.61

Source: From R. W. Weinbach & R. M. Grinnell Jr 1995, *Statistics for Social Workers*, 3rd edn, Longman, New York. This material was originally from Table IV of R. A. Fisher & F. Yates, *Statistical Tables for Biological, Agricultural and Medical Research,* Longman, London (previously published by Oliver & Boyd, Edinburgh)

Scattergrams

To get a good working hypothesis of the type of relationship (if any) between two interval/ratio variables which have been measured in pairs we use a *scattergram*. We plot pairs of points on a graph, one variable (usually the independent variable) being measured on the horizontal axis and the other (the dependent) on the vertical. We mark the point corresponding to each pair with a cross. The kinds of results to be expected are shown in Figure 14.10. There are various possibilities.

1 There is a linear relationship between the two variables, and Y increases as X increases—the line has a positive gradient.
2 There is a linear relationship between the two variables, and Y decreases as X increases—the line has a negative gradient.
3 There is no relationship.
4 There is a relationship—that is, the crosses do form a definite pattern, but it is not linear. It is a curvilinear relationship. Most of the tests we do will be concerned with linear relationships.

Correlation co-efficients

The association between two variables can be summarised by a single figure known as the *correlation co-efficient*. There are many types of correlation co-efficients which are used at different levels of measurement. Knowing what they mean, and which one is appropriate for your situation, is the most important thing to understand, as computers usually do the mathematics for you. The following aspects of correlation co-efficients are important factors.

Characteristics of correlation co-efficients

- Correlation co-efficients vary between −1.00 and 1.00. If the size of the correlation co-efficient is large (approaching 1 or −1), the relationship is strong; if the value is low (approaching 0), the relationship is weak. Correlations of 0 indicate that there is no correlation between the variables.
- Having a strong (high value) correlation co-efficient does not indicate causality. Correlation co-efficients only show whether two variables are associated (vary together), not that one caused the other.
- At ordinal and interval levels of measurement, correlation co-efficients also show the direction of a relationship using either a minus sign (indicating a negative relationship— variables change in different directions), or no sign (indicating a positive relationship—variables change in the same direction).
- Some co-efficients only indicate whether there is a linear relationship; some can also measure non-linear relationships.
- Different levels of measurement require different measures of association.

From de Vaus (2002)

Figure 14.10 Scattergrams and corresponding values of r

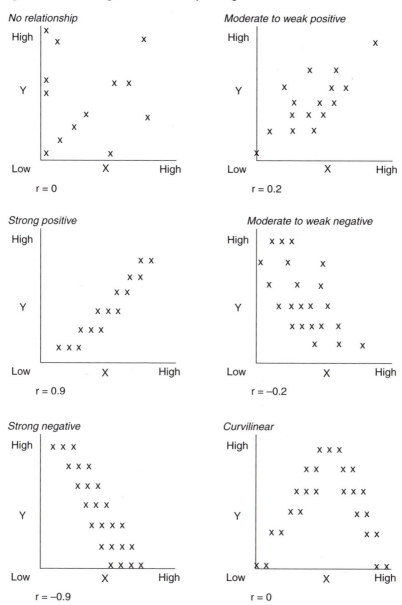

Source: Adapted from de Vaus (2002, p. 281)

Pearson's product-moment correlation co-efficient

If a scattergram seems to indicate a linear relationship between two variables X and Y, then we may wish to investigate the relationship further. Pearson's product-moment correlation co-efficient is a useful measure (this is commonly called *the* correlation co-efficient or Pearson's r).

Pearson's r is calculated using the following formula:

$$r = \frac{N\Sigma XY - (\Sigma X)(\Sigma Y)}{[N\Sigma X^2 - (\Sigma X)^2][N\Sigma Y^2 - (\Sigma Y)^2]}$$

where:
r = Pearson's r
N = number of cases
ΣXY = sum of the XY column
ΣX = sum of the X column
ΣY = sum of the Y column
ΣX^2 = sum of the X^2 column
ΣY^2 = sum of the Y^2 column

From Weinbach and Grinnell (2001, p. 147)

This co-efficient always has a value between −1 and 1. A value of 1 means that there is a perfect positive linear relationship between the two variables; a value of −1 means that there is a perfect negative linear relationship between the two variables; while 0 means that there is no relation. (Note that we are talking about data that we have already ascertained is *not* curvilinear. The correlation co-efficient is not particularly meaningful in the case of a curvilinear relationship.)

It should be noted that very little reliance should be placed on correlation co-efficients for small samples.

We use as an example the data in Table 14.19 and Figure 14.11. Table 14.19 lists the results in two examinations of a class of 58 students. We are interested in whether there is a relationship between each student's two sets of marks.

We first look at the scattergram (Figure 14.11). We note that there is a possible positive linear relationship between the two sets of marks. It is thus worth looking at the correlation co-efficient to verify this. If we calculate Pearson's correlation co-efficient using the above equation we find that r = 0.722005. A correlation co-efficient of .72 represents quite a strong linear relationship.

To determine an expression describing this relationship we need to look at lines of regression.

Pearson's product-moment can be calculated in a number of different ways. For three clear and readable accounts refer to de Vaus (2002), Sarantakos (1998) or Weinbach and Grinnell (2001).

Table 14.19 Class marks for two examinations with scattergram

Exam 1	Exam 2
10 12 7 13 6 10 13 10 5 9 10 12 13 7	54 79 56 86 53 71 84 70 41 62 76 84
12 12 10 11 12 13 12 11 11 12 12 9 8 89	50 69 74 68 78 78 86 87 79 73 28
10 12 11 7 12 8 11 7 13 9 13 11 11 10	71 77 60 64 77 72 50 72 56 83 48 92
12 9 10 8 12 11 10 7 11 10 7 9 10 13	66 91 75 75 76 79 68 65 65 70 73 63
12 6 8	60 66 88 62 75 64 93 83 52 66

Regression

If we find that there is good reason to suppose that two variables (X, Y) are linearly related, we can use this fact to predict the value of the dependent variable based on the value of the independent variable. For example, r can tell us how likely it is that higher education will mean higher income, but regression analysis tells us how much the difference is likely to be. The regression co-efficient, or b, is the slope of the line and predicts how much a change in the independent variable (X) will cause a change in the dependent variable (Y). The regression co-efficient b is always expressed in the units of measurement of the dependent variable.

Figure 14.11 Scattergram showing relationship between two sets of examination marks

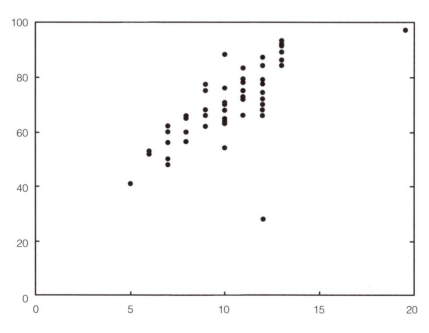

The equation of a straight line is given by

$Y = a + bX$

where:

Y = the value we want to predict on the basis of a particular value of X

a = the point at which the regression line crosses the Y axis

b = the slope of the line or the regression co-efficient (it is always expressed in the units of measurement of the dependent variable)

X = the value of X on the X-axis

Relationships between variables at the ordinal data level

Data at ordinal, ratio and interval level can be arranged in rank order and can thus be associated with a set of ordinal numbers (1st, 2nd, 3rd, . . .). If we use cardinal numbers instead of ordinal numbers we assign a number n to each rank. A common measure of association for random variables at these levels is Spearman's rank correlation co-efficient.

If R_x is the set of ranks for variable X, and R_y the set for Y, then the Spearman rank correlation co-efficient is given by

$S = 1 - 6\Sigma(R_x - R_y)^2/(N(N^2 - 1))$

This correlation co-efficient again has values between –1 and 1, and can be used in a similar way to Pearson's correlation co-efficient. It has the advantage that it can be used with ordinal level data and also with ratio and interval level data that may be related in some non-linear fashion.

Table 14.20 presents a sample of ten pairs of examination marks. (Note that ten is not really a very realistic sample size for this kind of work, and has been used merely to demonstrate the method.)

The scattergram for the scores listed in Table 14.20 looks like Figure 14.12. The relationship is certainly not linear, but it looks as

Table 14.20 Sample of pairs of examintion marks

Practical exam rank	Practical exam score	Theory exam rank	Theory exam score
10	74	1	22
9	70	2	35
8	68	3	41
1	15	4	48
7	60	5	60
6	59	6	62
2	22	7	63
5	48	8	76
4	47	9	77
3	38	10	79

Figure 14.12 Scattergram of relationship between pairs of scores

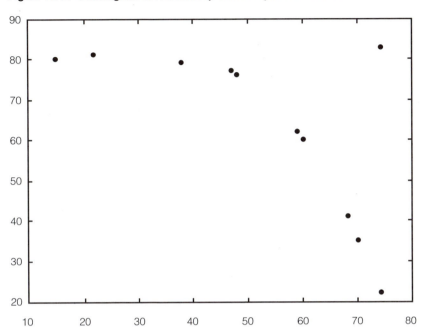

if there is a possibly curvilinear relationship. Spearman's rank correlation co-efficient for this data is –0.7, indicating quite a strong relationship.

OTHER WAYS TO MEASURE BIVARIATE RELATIONSHIPS

There are other ways to test for statistical significance, but detailed discussion of them is beyond the scope of this book. You can go on to read for yourself about these other statistical tests, all of which use similar reasoning to these basic examples we have provided.

To conclude our overview of statistics for social workers, two of these other methods, t-tests and ANOVA, are briefly described, and examples of how these tests are used to interpret results is provided.

T-tests

The t-test, another parametric test that can be used in a number of ways, is an interval/ratio level test. We will briefly consider how to use it to test whether statistics of a sample can be compared to populations (a one-sample t-test), and how it can be used to test the differences between values of two populations (a two-sample t-test).

One-sample t-test

T-tests can be used to test whether sample results can be generalised to the population, that is, to establish confidence intervals. The one-sample t-test is used to calculate whether there is a significant difference between the sample mean and the population mean. It can be used in situations where the population parameters are unknown. Similarly to the chi-square test, t-tests depend on the number of degrees of freedom. In the case of one sample t-tests, the number of degrees of freedom is (n–1) where n is the sample size.

Originally, t-tests were used with small samples and Z-scores were used for large samples, but these days t-tests are used for both large and small samples (Argyrous 1996, cited in Sarantakos 1998, p. 420). The t-test follows the same logic and uses tables in the same way as the Z-score described earlier in this chapter. Once you have the sample mean and standard deviation, you can calculate a t-score using a computer or a formula, then compare the t-score with the table value of t, using degrees of freedom (n – 1) and the confidence level (usually 0.05) you wish to accept. If the value of t is equal to or greater than the value in the table, H_0 is rejected.

Two-sample t-test

T-tests can also be used to compare the means of two different populations. The logic for calculating the t-statistic and using degrees of freedom and a confidence level is the same, but the methods of calculating the t-statistic are different, depending on whether the samples you are comparing are independent (unrelated) or dependent (paired or matched).

For a more detailed discussion of how to calculate one- and two-sample t-tests, see Sarantakos (1998), chapter 18. In addition to describing the calculation of these tests using formulae, Sarantakos discusses how to undertake and interpret these tests using *SPSS*.

ANOVA

Analysis of variance (ANOVA) is a common and powerful test that is used when we want to make multigroup comparisons, or when there is more than one variable we wish to compare—a common occurrence in social work research. In such situations we cannot use multiple t-tests, because in so doing we increase our likelihood of making Type 1 errors. Instead of having to make many calculations comparing different sets of means, ANOVA allows us to make an overall comparison of the difference of the means among various groups.

Most commonly, ANOVA (or analysis of variance), is used when there are three or more categories of the independent variable or when more than two variables are studied. While t-tests produce a t-value which can be checked in a table for statistical significance, ANOVA tests produce an F-ratio which is checked against its own table. ANOVA tests can be one-way (when there is one independent variable), two-way (when there are two independent variables) or N-ways (for N numbers of independent variables, also called factorial ANOVA).

ANOVA analyses the ratio of variance between groups (between-group variance or difference between the means) and the variation within groups (the within-group variance). If the between-group variance is large compared to the within-group variance, the F-ratio is large. As for t-tests and chi-square tests, degrees of freedom are important in calculating ANOVA results.

$$\text{F-ratio} = \frac{\text{between-group variance}}{\text{within-group variance}}$$

See Weinbach and Grinnell (1995, chapter 10) for explanations of these tests, Sarantakos (1998, chapter 18) or Mark (1996, chapter 16).

Example of use of statistical tests

In 1995 Wendy Bowles studied the quality of life of adults with spina bifida in New South Wales (NSW) (Bowles 1995). From her experience as a social worker, she was concerned that people with spina bifida were often disadvantaged but did not protest about the conditions in which they were living.

As part of the reading she did to try to explain this, Bowles discovered a model of quality of life which proposed that the lowest quality of life was defined by a condition termed 'adaptation', in which people were objectively disadvantaged, but reported no dissatisfaction with their circumstances because they had no hope that things would improve (Zapf 1986, 1987). According to this model, people only report dissatisfaction when they have had some experience that things can be better—having objectively poor conditions and being dissatisfied (deprivation) is one step higher than adaptation because people in this category have some belief that it is possible for their situation to improve.

If this model could explain the situation Bowles had observed in the course of her work, it also had important implications for the uncritical use of subjective-only measures of need in needs analyses. Indeed, it pointed to how dangerous it could be to use subjective measures of need without objective measures when dealing with severely disadvantaged groups of people.

Bowles conducted structured interviews with a stratified random sample of 117 adults with spina bifida, and compared these with the results from postal surveys from 180 Technical and Further Education students and with 1991 census data.

Table 14.21 Annual income of the spina bifida group, NSW population aged 15–44 years and comparison group

Annual income range $	Spina bifida group %	NSW population 15–44 years %	Comparison group %
0–14 999	70		23
0–12 000		38	
15 000–29 999	25		50
12 001–30 000		42	
30 000 +	5		27
30 001 +		20	
Total	100	100	100
	(n = 113)	(n = 2 380 775)	(n = 171)

SB grp x NSW popn
Chi-square = 50.44
Significance: $p < 0.001$ (Sig)

Comp. grp x NSW popn
Chi-square = 15.57
Significance: $p < 0.01$ (Sig)

SB grp x Comp. grp
Chi-square = 63.089
Significance: $p = 0.000$ (Sig)
Strength: Cramer's V = 0.471

People with spina bifida were found to be disadvantaged in every area of life studied, being in the 'adaptation' category for many domains. In this situation, the spina bifida group had significantly lower objective life conditions than the comparison group, yet were as satisfied or more so with their circumstances, having adapted their expectations downwards. Qualitative results revealed that people with spina bifida suffered high levels of discrimination, social exclusion and isolation. They wanted jobs, leisure opportunities, relationships and to form their own families. Having little hope of attaining these, however, they had become resigned to their disadvantaged situations.

An example from this study of how t-tests and ANOVA were used comes from the domain of income.

People with spina bifida experienced significantly lower levels of income than the general population of NSW aged 15 years and over (see Table 14.21). The median annual individual income for all people in the NSW population in 1991 was $12 001–$16 000 (Australian Bureau of Statistics, 1994); the annual median income for adults with spina bifida was $5000–$9999. The comparison group, on the other hand, had a higher median annual income than the overall population ($20 000 to $24 000).

When income levels were grouped into three categories, the proportion of people with spina bifida in the lowest income range was twice that of the general population of adults in NSW aged 15 to 44 years; the proportion in the middle income range was half the NSW figure, and less than a third of the NSW percentage was earning

Table 14.22 Subjective income scales: spina bifida group by comparison group, t-test results

Variable	Group cases	Number of cases	Mean*	t-value	2-tail probability	Signficance**
Income satisfaction	SB	115	3.2	2.76	0.006	**
	Comp.	179	2.8			
Expectation gap	SB	113	2.7	1.49	0.138	NS
	Comp.	178	2.5			

* Mean represents the group mean on a scale of 1–5 where 1 = not at all satisfied, or low/worse than, and 5 = very satisfied, or high/better than
** NS = not significant, * = $p < 0.05$, ** = $p < 0.01$, *** = $p < 0.001$

incomes in the highest bracket (Table 14.21). While the income levels of the comparison group were higher than the general population, they were not as different from the NSW population as were the incomes of people with spina bifida.

The satisfaction scales for income level revealed results that were opposite to those that would be intuitively expected from the objective results. People with spina bifida, despite considerably lower average incomes than the NSW population and even lower incomes again compared with the comparison group, reported significantly greater satisfaction with level of income than did those in the comparison group (Table 14.22). People in both groups rated their present incomes as being a little under what they would have hoped for at this time in their lives (the 'expectation gap'). There was no difference in these expectation levels between the two groups.

Table 14.23 shows the highly significant differences in levels of satisfaction with income at all levels of actual income, between the spina bifida and comparison groups. Regardless of the amount of income received, people with spina bifida were more satisfied with their incomes than were those in the comparison group. This is clearly a pattern of adaptation. However, satisfaction with income also increased with increasing income in both groups, demonstrating that people were more satisfied with increasing income whether or not they had spina bifida.

Despite their considerably lower incomes than the NSW population, and still lower incomes than the comparison group, people with spina bifida were more satisfied with their incomes than the comparison group. In response to further questions, the majority of people with spina bifida in the sample also reported that their incomes were sufficient, regardless of level of income or source of financial support. However, satisfaction did increase with level of income for both groups. Such results place the spina bifida group in Zapf et al.'s (1987) 'adaptation' category of quality of life for income. Clearly, people

Table 14.23 Satisfaction with income by level of income and group: spina bifida and comparison groups

Income range	Spina bifida group		Comparison group	
($)	Mean	%	Mean	%
0–14 999	3.05	69	2.08	23
15 000–29 999	3.39	25	2.72	50
30 000 +	3.83	5	3.43	46
Total		100		100
		(n = 111)		(n = 171)

ANOVA			
Source of variation	F		Signif. of F
Main effects	13.683		0.000***
Income level	16.080		0.000***
Group	25.131		0.000***
2-way interactions			
Income x group	0.752		0.473
*$p < 0.05$	**$p < 0.01$		***$p < 0.001$

Note: Mean represents the group mean on a scale of 1–5 where 1 = not at all satisfied, or low/worse than, and 5 = very satisfied, or high/better than

with spina bifida are objectively disadvantaged in this life domain, yet subjectively are highly satisfied with their incomes.

As Sen (1985, p. 29, cited in Travers & Richardson 1993, p. 16) has written:

> A poor, undernourished person, brought up in penury, may have learned to come to terms with a half-empty stomach, seizing joy in small comforts and desiring no more than what seems 'realistic'. But this mental attitude does not wipe out the fact of the person's deprivation.

SUMMARY

In this chapter we have examined how to present your data, and some of the statistics most commonly used by social workers. We have presented some of the fundamental methods used in statistical analysis and have covered descriptive and inferential statistics, organising our discussion according to the level of measurement and the number of variables being analysed. The aim has been to explain the logic of different tests and how to interpret the information provided by computer calculations.

In particular, we have covered:

- Some basic analytical concepts
- Distribution (central tendency, dispersion, taking into account levels of measurement)
- The normal distribution
- Testing hypotheses—levels of significance
- Relating two variables (correlation and regression)

Of course, bivariate analysis is only the beginning of the statistics you can perform. Once you have explored the relationship between two variables, it is most likely that you will want to check on the effects of interfering variables, and how several variables relate or cluster together. To learn about this type of analysis, termed multi-variate analysis, you need to consult advanced statistical texts and computer software manuals.

QUESTIONS

1 What is a cumulative percentage column and when would you include one? What is its use?
2 What are the differences between a histogram, bar chart, pie chart and pictograph?
3 What is the measure of central tendency for nominal data?
4 What is a measure of dispersion for ordinal data?
5 If the mean, the median and the mode all fall at the one point in a distribution, what shape will it be?
6 If Susan scores 70 in an exam in which the mean is 60 and the standard deviation 20, and Sally scores 60 in an exam in which the mean is 45 and the standard deviation 15, who has done better relatively?
7 A study has found that age and income have a correlation co-efficient of 0.65, whereas age and number of qualifications have a relationship of −0.85. What do these correlation co-efficients say about the relationships between age and income, and age and number of qualifications, respectively? Which relationship is strongest?
8 What is the difference between parametric and non-parametric statistics?
9 A social worker studying domestic violence in the outer suburbs finds that in a table crosstabulating number of incidences of domestic violence by the type of couple relationship, the chi-square value is 4.23 in a table with 4 degrees of freedom. Is the relationship significant? What does this finding mean?

EXERCISE

Construct a cross table for the variables APPEAL (information re appeal) and gender in Table 14.24. Calculate the chi-square value from the table. Is there a significant relationship between someone's gender and whether they were given information about their right to appeal?

Table 14.24 Summary information

Respon-dent (ID)	Type payment (PAY)	Location	Gender	Age	Staff respect (ATTIT3)	Info re appeal (APPEAL)	Staff behaviour (BEH1, BEH2)
J. Smith (001)	Sole parent	City	Female	18	3	No	Formal, rushed
P. Collins (002)	Disability support	City	Male	19	5	Yes	Friendly, took time for me
M. Chap-man (003)	Young homeless	City	Male	16	1	No	Rude
A. Jones (004)	Unemployed	Country	Male	20	3	Yes	OK, friendly
T. Black (005)	Sole parent	City	Male	25	2	Yes	In a hurry, didn't seem interested in my questions
006	Unemployed	City	Female	21	2	Yes	Rushed, rude
007	Aged pension	City	Male	85	5	No	Polite, busy
008	Unemployed	Country	Male	26	1	No	Not interested, accused me of not seeking work
009	Sole parent	City	Female	23	3	No	OK, kids a nuisance
010	Sole parent	Country	Female	29	4	No	Just routine visit to ask if UB would be better, staff busy
011	Disability support	Country	Male	21	3	Yes	Staff kind, busy
012	Unemployed	City	Female	21	2	Yes	Rushed, formal
013	No payment	City	Female	53	4	Yes	Asking on behalf of my daughter, staff very nice
014	Aged pension	Country	Female	60	5	No	Very nice, very busy
015	Unemployed	City	Male	30	2	Yes	Formal, brusque
016	Unemployed	Country	Female	32	4	Yes	Formal but courteous
017	Sole parent	Country	Female	23	3	Can't remem-ber	OK
018	Unemployed	Country	Male	57	3	Yes	Very busy, no idea for jobs
019	Disability support	City	Female	40	3	Yes	Sympathetic but formal
020	Unemployed	City	Female	18	2	No	OK

FURTHER READING

de Vaus, D. A. 2002, *Surveys in Social Research*, 5th edn, Allen & Unwin, Sydney. Part IV, 'Analysing Survey Data' provides a clear and detailed account of the statistics in this chapter.

Mark, R. 1996, *Research Made Simple: A Handbook for Social Workers*, Sage, Thousand Oaks, California. Chapter 16 covers t-tests in the context of explaining statistical hypothesis testing.

Sarantakos, S. 1998, *Social Research*, Macmillan, Melbourne. Chapters 14 –17 provide further reading on the tests and procedures mentioned in this chapter.

Weinbach, R. W. & R. M. Grinnell Jr 2001, *Statistics for Social Workers*, 5th edn, Allyn & Bacon, Boston. This excellent text covers most of the topics in this chapter in a clear and easy to understand manner, using social work examples.

15 INFLUENCING POLICY AND PRACTICE

At last! Having written your research proposal, received ethical approval and funding, designed your study, collected and analysed the data, you are finally ready to release your results. Thought the hard work was over? In many ways it has just begun!

This final chapter covers two critical skills in the research process:

- Writing up your research
- Making an impact, or influencing policy and practice

The first step in doing either of these things, is to think about who you are presenting your research to. Most social work research projects have at least two audiences—the people who participated in the research and the people who sponsored it.

Usually a written report for sponsors is part of the research contract you agreed to in the first place. However, increasingly social work researchers also undertake to report back to the people who participated in the research. As well as being simple good manners in showing respect and appreciation for the effort and time participants have contributed, reporting back to participants can have many benefits. We have discussed how reporting back to participants in a series of stages can be part of the research process itself. When presented with results, participants often provide helpful comments which assist the researcher with the discussion and conclusions in their reports. Whether or not it is built into earlier stages of your research design, it is important to plan some report-back mechanisms to your participants at the end of the process, so that they can see the final outcome of their work. Apart from other benefits, reporting back to participants helps keep researchers honest! Remember our initial definition of research: the systematic observation and/or collection of information in order to find or impose a pattern *in order to make a decision or take some action*. Often the research participants have much invested in the outcome of your research and will be key people in pushing for action and/or change as a result of your findings.

Of course, all the key players we identified in chapter 1 are also potential audiences, as is the general community. Thus, when you are planning where to publish your findings, you will find that it might be best to use several of the avenues discussed in this chapter, in order to gain maximum impact and the outcomes you want. In addition to writing a full report of your research for your sponsors, you may be publishing a summary in the local paper, discussing your results on television or radio, and holding meetings with organisations and community or consumer groups to discuss the implications. Whichever way you do it, there is no point in conducting research if you do not ensure that the results are made public and that the people who need to hear about them do so in the way that will have the most impact (whether decision makers, policy people, funding bodies, agency personnel or the people involved in the study). Your choice of how and where you will publish your results is important in making sure that your research leads to decisions and action and does not end up just another report sitting quietly on a shelf gathering dust.

In addition to reporting their results to research participants and sponsors, most social workers aim to report their results at conferences and publish them in journals whose readers are other professionals and colleagues. In this way you can contribute to the growing social work research culture and the knowledge base of our profession. The more we publish the results of our research in venues accessible to our colleagues, the more we will develop an evidence-based culture for our work and increase confidence in our profession.

In this chapter we prepare you for publishing your research for the purposes and audiences outlined above, so that it has maximum impact. First we present a structure for writing up your report, which can be modified for most contexts for publication. Writing up your research is an important part of ensuring that the findings from your research become public knowledge. Whether you publish in academic journals, in books, write a report or monograph for publication or report your results in a newspaper or newsletter, there are several steps you must follow. Second, we discuss how you and your advisory group can develop an action plan to ensure that your research leads to decisions being made and action taken.

The first step is to write a full account of your research project. If you have followed the process which we have outlined in this book so far, writing up your report should be a relatively easy process. You will have already completed much of the work when you wrote your research proposal (Appendix A). The key to writing an effective report is to write for the particular context where it will be published.

WRITING YOUR REPORT

Contexts for publication

Journal articles

There is a range of avenues through which you can publish the results of your research. The most prestigious journals are called 'refereed journals'. The editors of these journals, such as national journals of social work, send your article out to readers, or referees, before they decide whether to publish your work. The readers, in turn, send in their comments and suggest changes you should make before your paper is published.

Monographs

Organisations which fund research may require a report or monograph that is published as a separate document in its own right. These stand-alone reports are longer than articles published in journals and usually involve more complex studies. The format for such reports follows the same general structure as for journal articles, although more detail can be included. Usually an executive summary and a list of recommendations are included in these reports. Methodology and results are both important in stand-alone reports, as they are for journal articles.

Conference presentations

Conferences are another important context for presenting research results. Unless you are a keynote speaker, usually no more than 20 minutes to half an hour is allowed for presentation time, sometimes with ten minutes for discussion and questions afterwards. At some conferences where many people want to present papers, you may not even be given a 20-minute time slot, but instead the option of presenting your research in poster form.

Newspapers, newsletters

At the more informal end of the publication spectrum, your results could be published in newspapers or newsletters read by people in your field. It is particularly important that tables, graphs and other presentations of the results in these contexts stand out and grab the readers' attention. They may then want to read about your study in more detail. Similarly, the title of your report should be catchy and readable, something that will whet readers' appetites to find out more about what you have been up to. Readers of informal or popular avenues for written research tend to be more interested in the results and implications of research than in the methodology, so you will need to tailor your writing accordingly. Make sure these articles are short enough so someone else does not edit your work down to size!

Media interviews

Media interviews are an important avenue for presenting research results. Researchers often send a news release highlighting their main findings to newspapers, radio and television stations, hoping to be invited for an interview as a way of publicising their research. This context for publishing research certainly reaches a wide audience, and depending on your motives for conducting the research, can lead to policy makers taking more notice of your results.

Seminars, meetings

Sometimes you or the organisation sponsoring the research will organise a seminar, public meeting or workshop specifically to publicise your research results. This is often an excellent opportunity to reach a wide range of people within an organisation, including the clients. We have seen how meetings and workshops to reflect on the results can be an intrinsic part of the research design in action research and some other types of qualitative research.

Of course, the nature of your contract with the organisation funding the research will determine who makes the final decision about where, how and by whom the research will be published.

Whether speaking at a conference, writing a paper for a journal or newspaper, or preparing for an interview on radio, it is imperative that you are succinct and present your ideas simply and within the word or time limit.

Research that is topical, lengthy and/or complex, and has an identifiable market, may be turned into a book. Some PhD theses end up as books. It is more likely, however, that such research is reported as chapters of books of collections of research on specific issues.

Contexts for publication of research results

- Books or book chapters

- Academic and professional journals (refereed or not refereed)
- Stand-alone reports published by sponsors
- Conference papers, posters
- Newsletters
- Newspapers, magazines
- Seminars about your research to organisations
- Media interviews, articles, press releases
- Internet

Whatever the context for your publication, the elements described in this chapter are present in nearly all forms of publication of research. The following discussion is tailored to research reports for journal articles, as this is the major avenue for publication of social work research results. However, all the elements mentioned are needed in all forms of publication to some extent, whether conference paper, media report or seminar. Whatever the context, when reporting your research you need to be able to give a succinct summary of your project (abstract), outline your aims and the significance of the research in the broader context (introduction/problem statement), describe your methodology and findings, discuss the limitations as well as the implications of your study and, finally, make conclusions and/or recommendations based on the evidence you have gathered.

Abstract

The abstract is written last and appears first. It is the brief summary which heads your report and is one of the most difficult parts of the report to write. In about 300–350 words you must summarise the aims of your study, the design and methodology, the key results and findings. Readers flipping through journals or searching databases use the abstract to find out if they wish to read the whole article. Therefore it is imperative that the abstract be written in clear and concise terms which motivate people to read further. The abstract should include key words that you expect other researchers to use if they are doing research in your area, so that librarians will classify your research correctly when they enter your abstract in a database.

The research report itself consists of five main elements, each of which includes several subsections. These are: introduction/statement of the problem, the methodology, the findings, the discussion and the conclusion/recommendations. When you are drawing up the outline or structure for your own report it is a good idea to divide the report into these five sections and write up subheadings within each of them. Usually the largest sections will be the 'findings' and 'discussion' sections so you need to allow plenty of space for these. Sarantakos (1998) suggests, as a general guideline, that the introduction and methodology section should not exceed 10 per cent of the report, unless there is something exceptional in the literature review, or there is a particularly complex methodology, which warrants extra attention. We now explore each of the five sections of a research report in more detail.

Introduction/statement of the problem

Most of the work for this section of the paper you have already completed in your original research proposal (see Appendix A). If you have done this correctly, all you need to do for the first part of your research report is a cut-and-paste job from several sections of your research proposal.

Context of study

The major task of the introduction/statement of the problem is to explain the context of your research, showing why it is important and how it is relevant to social work practice, theory, policy or social issues. In the introduction you set out the broad aims of the study as well as defining research questions and concepts (in quantitative studies), demonstrating through the literature search how and why you made the decisions that you did.

Auspices and assumptions

The auspices of the study are also clearly stated in the introduction, as well as the researcher's orientation, if this is appropriate. Some qualitative and feminist researchers are careful to state their own position in relation to the research—for example, how different or similar they are to the people they are researching, or what stake they have in the issues being examined, and what effects this might have on the research process. It is also important to make explicit any assumptions which underlie the approach you have chosen.

Literature review

In the introduction, the literature search is summarised and presented as an argument which leads up to and justifies the approach that you have taken. In only a few paragraphs you must demonstrate that you have read widely and understood the major debates in the literature, the research approaches which have been tried, and the gaps that exist (hopefully some of which your research is addressing). All the important concepts that you have used in your research should be located in the wider context of the literature as well as the theoretical approach which you have adopted. Most of this you have already completed in your research proposal. The only additions may be some more up-to-date literature about particular aspects of the research problem that have come to light as you analysed the data (but which you did not realise would be important when you wrote up the original literature search).

The literature review is not an author-by-author account describing what you have read. Rather, divide the literature into themes or issues which are related to the issue and questions in your study, and use this structure to justify the approach you have taken. Be critical of what you have read, especially if you detect biases or flaws in other studies which influence the results and/or conclusions.

What to include in the introduction/problem statement

- Statement of topic, aims, research questions
- Significance of the research, its contribution to social work practice, theory, policy or knowledge
- Summary and critical discussion of literature review, justifying the broad design (qualitative, quantitative, feminist), theoretical framework of the study and the definition of major variables and research questions
- Researcher's own position in relation to the research
- Assumptions clearly stated
- Auspices of the study
- Quantitative studies: identify dependent and independent variables, state hypotheses (as generated in the literature)

Methodology

The second major section of your research report is the methodology section. Again, much of this has been completed in your research proposal. There are several areas that you have to cover and it is important to distinguish between them. Subheadings in your report are an effective way to do this.

Design

This is a summary/overview of how your methodology addresses the research questions. Usually it begins broadly, indicating whether you have chosen qualitative, quantitative, feminist or a mix of approaches, and then narrows down to how you operationalised the variables (if quantitative), who you are going to research, and what kind of research techniques you will use. Review chapters 2, 3 and 4 for the sorts of information to put into your description of the design of your study.

Population and sample

Whether doing qualitative or quantitative research, it is important to report what population you are researching, how you drew your sample, what your unit of study is, and on what basis (theoretical or statistical) you will be generalising your results. When describing who was in your sample, acknowledge any limitations in the sampling process that might lead to biases in the findings. Tables and graphs are an effective way of presenting data about your sample. Take care only to include information about the sample which relates to how it was selected. For example, if you stratified your sample for age, gender or region, you could provide tables showing the breakdown of the sample in terms of these variables. If you did not stratify your sample according to certain criteria then much of this information is left to the section on findings (see chapter 5).

Instrumentation

Having spent so much time using your questionnaire or interview schedule, it is an easy mistake to forget to describe it to the reader. In longer reports it is expected that you will appendix the whole survey or list of questions as well as summarising the key aspects of it in the text of your report.

Describe how you developed the instrument, including sources from the literature, any pretests or pilot tests you performed, and major changes that were made as a result. Include some samples of the types of questions you asked, showing how they relate to the broader research questions. If you have not already provided the fine detail of how research questions and variables were operationalised, this is the place to do so. How you addressed questions of reliability and validity also should be included.

Data collection

Describe how the data were collected, where, how long it took and who collected it (for example, 'Interviews lasting from one to three hours were conducted by the researcher at locations convenient for the respondent, sometimes in the person's home, or at other places nominated by the respondent such as the local park, offices of the local X organisation or the respondent's workplace'). Include in this description the measures taken to address scope and coverage (number of callbacks, how refusals were dealt with, etc.—see chapter 6).

Ethical issues, limitations of methodology

As part of the methodology section, you should include a brief discussion of any ethical issues you anticipated in the research process and how you dealt with them. Again, this will have been written up already in your documents for ethics committees and will be a matter of cutting and pasting. If other ethical issues arose that you did not anticipate, this is the place to discuss them also, including how you dealt with them.

While you will most likely write a section in your report on the limitations of your study and areas for future research in the discussion section, it is also worth acknowledging any limitations in the methodology in this early part of the paper. Being constructively critical of your own work is a strength. It assists future researchers who wish to replicate your methodology. It also forestalls other critics if you have shown that you are aware of the weaknesses or limitations in your work. Providing a critique of your work enables your results to be interpreted in a wider context.

Data analysis

Finishing the methodology section with a description of how you analysed your data is a good way to lead into the results or findings section of the report. In this last subsection of the methodology section you need to 'take the reader by the hand' and guide them through the steps you took to analyse your data. Included in this part of the report could be an overview of which statistical techniques you used and how they were interpreted, mention of which computer software you used and an explanation of why these data analysis techniques were the most appropriate to address the research questions. In this section of the report you are providing the reader with a map of how to read the results you are about to present, and an explanation of how you arrived at them.

What to include in the methodology section of your report

- Design of the study
- Population and sample (including sampling techniques and sample description)
- Instrumentation (including how instrument was designed, pretests, pilot, reliability and validity, how variables were operationalised and how they relate to research questions)
- Data collection (including scope and coverage issues)
- Ethical issues, limitations of methodology
- Methods of data analysis

Findings

The section on your findings is usually one of the largest sections of the report. When planning how to present your results, it is a good idea to think of a series of subheadings which relate to the major themes in your findings, or to the research questions themselves, or to some other logical sequence, so that as you describe your results, a story unfolds. Sometimes researchers follow the same sequence in reporting results that they followed in asking the questions, if the

292

structure for the interview or questionnaire followed a logical sequence.

Before beginning on the story or sequence of the results related to the research issues, researchers usually present a description of the people in the research (the sample). Simple, univariate results are then described, followed by the more complex results from bivariate and multivariate analyses addressing various research questions about relationships between variables. In qualitative reports, the results are presented according to the themes that have been identified, often also in increasing order of complexity.

Remember that you don't have to include all your results when you report your findings. You should be selective in reporting your findings as you will have a great deal of information, all of which appears extremely interesting to you. However, much of this must be discarded in the interests of concise and precise reporting. This is a difficult issue for beginning researchers who want to tell all! However, you should extract the findings that directly focus on the relevant issue.

Do not selectively weed out the data that invalidate your hypothesis or point of view! You must allow contradictory data to emerge in the interests of the development of knowledge.

As a general guideline, if the results can be more simply and clearly put in words, then use text and don't bother about tables or graphs. On the other hand, if it is more effective to summarise large amounts of detailed information in tables, then do so, remembering to comment on the tables in the text. Readers can use the tables to check if your interpretations of the data are correct, or if you have overlooked something important. Remember that all tables or graphs require some explanation in the text as well. There is no need to state the obvious, but you should include an overview of the main points of the table, the meaning of statistics, or the highlights that you want to emphasise. Generally you do not have to explain the statistics you used—just list the results at the bottom of the table and comment on them in the text (see chapter 14 for examples).

Note that in the findings section the results are usually reported with little comment. This is saved for the discussion section, unless a decision has been made to combine the findings and discussion. Sometimes in qualitative research these two sections are combined in order to reduce duplication and to delineate the different themes more clearly. Similarly, in large, complex quantitative studies with many results to report, it is more sensible to combine the discussion and reporting of the findings according to particular themes or questions. Following such detailed discussion, the results and issues arising from them are summarised briefly to provide the 'big picture' or overview, before the final conclusions and recommendations are made.

What to include when presenting findings

- Present all findings relevant to the research issues or questions, including contradictory or unexpected results
- Not all the results have to be included
- Arrange the findings in a sequence, using logic or the order of interview questions so that the results tell a story
- Present a description of the sample of people involved in the research
- Start with simple descriptive findings and move on to the more complex explanatory results
- Use tables and graphs interspersed with text judiciously—choose between tables and text on the basis of what is the easiest, clearest and most accountable way of reporting findings

---

Discussion

This is the section where results are summarised, explained and interpreted. Often the discussion is conducted in the light of the issues identified in the literature search at the beginning of the paper, highlighting the contribution your own results make to these debates. If your results are different from findings in previous studies, try to explain why this may be so (using theory, other research or your own data) and hypothesise about future research to explore these differences further. If previous studies support your findings, discuss this and the implications.

The discussion is the place to comment on how your findings relate to theories about the issue you are researching, how the evidence you have gathered supports or does not support the hypotheses you made, and what implications arise from the findings. Reid (1993) notes that the discussion section is a balancing act between two negatives: not merely repeating the findings, and yet also not going off into flights of interpretation which are not supported by the evidence in your research. It is important that your discussion relates your findings back to the original research questions or issues which motivated the study in the first place.

Limitations

Usually the discussion includes a subsection or at least a few paragraphs on the limitations of the study and areas for future research that your study has identified. The limitations of the research often suggest areas for future research.

Acknowledging the limitations of the study is very important when you discuss the meaning of the findings and how they can be used in practice. You should include a discussion of the overall soundness of your study (its internal validity) as well as the degree to which the findings can be generalised (external validity). Discussing how findings can be generalised in quantitative research involves acknowledging the limitations of your sampling procedure. Very few pieces of social work research use random samples, the results of which can be generalised to the population in a straightforward way. However, while you may not be able to claim that the results apply directly to the population (within such-and-such a margin of error), you will undoubtedly be able to 'raise questions about', or 'suggest the possibility that' (Reid 1993), perhaps using theory and the results of other studies to add weight to your claims. In qualitative research, generalisability often relies on theoretical argument, as discussed in previous chapters.

As well as limitations in sampling, it is important to consider other methodological limitations, including the design of the instrument (survey, interview), drawbacks or effects on the study of interviewers, and other ways in which bias may have been introduced. In qualitative studies where bias is viewed as being inevitable, open discussion of this is again important.

Inevitably, your report contains bias based on your interpretation of data and selective reporting. The report is documentary evidence of your competence as a researcher, so you may be inclined in the interests of passing a subject or improving your career to overemphasise the strength of your work and to downplay the weaknesses. You should guard against this and allow readers to assess the merit of your work. Similarly, you should be on the lookout for data which not only support your stance, but also negate it. Do not overlook alternative interpretations in the interests of supporting your argument.

Remember that in some studies the discussion and findings sections can be combined. When this is the case, it is important that the points raised in this section are included somewhere in the report.

Discussion section

- Summarise, explain and interpret your findings
- Do not merely repeat findings and do not make interpretations which are not supported by the evidence in your study
- Discuss findings in the light of issues raised in the literature review
- Discuss implications of findings for current practice, policy and/or theory
- Acknowledge limitations of study
- Point to areas for future research

Summary, conclusion and recommendations

In long or complex studies, the conclusion begins with a summary of the key findings. This includes all the important aspects of the study. Sometimes this summary is placed at the beginning of the discussion section. There can also be an 'executive summary'. Executive summaries are usually placed at the beginning of government or stand-alone reports.

Whenever they are included, summaries and recommendations are sometimes the only parts of a research report which busy workers and decision makers read. This means that the message from your research, which you want the reader to understand, has to be clearly spelt out in the summary and recommendations. In shorter studies there is no need for a summary, and the conclusion and recommendations continue straight on from the findings.

After the summary (or after the findings section in the case of short reports), the conclusions about your study are made. Conclusions must, first, refocus the issue (relate to the original research questions), second, be justified in the light of your research design and the limitations of the study and, finally, remind the reader about directions for future research.

Following the conclusions, many social work studies end with a list of recommendations flowing from the conclusions. Recommendations may be about practice issues, policy matters, changes to existing services or advocating the need for new services. Often research recommendations are about changes in emphasis or priorities within existing services. Sometimes the sponsoring organisations which pay for the research specify that they have the right to approve, or at least to comment on, the recommendations made by researchers. Others consider this to be a breach of intellectual freedom and against the spirit of research. Wording recommendations is an important job for your advisory group. In action research designs, developing recommendations is an integral part of the research design.

Who has the final say over the recommendations of a research report is a political issue of ownership which should be understood by all parties from the beginning of the research process. If appropriate, negotiate this as part of the written contract with the sponsoring agency (see Chapter 1).

References

Research reports always include an alphabetical list of the references, books, articles and other sources of information (such as films) that you cited in the report. Most journals and publishers have specific requirements as to how you should present your references. There are several referencing systems and software packages available, as mentioned. If publishers do not prescribe a particular method, use one of the accepted means such as the Harvard system of referencing.

When listing your references, consistency and attention to detail is very important. Every source that you cite in the body of the report must be accurately referenced in this section.

Appendices

Research reports often include appendices. These are additional sections of the report and may include the original questionnaires or interview schedules, copies of letters, details about sampling and other procedural matters, and extra data which assist in the argument about the research or further support evidence for conclusions. In journal articles, there is usually not enough space for appendices. Appendices are more likely to be found in stand-alone reports, books or longer book chapters.

Acknowledgements

Acknowledgements are an optional extra for research reports. They often appear at the beginning of a report, either as a separate section, as part of the introduction, or as a footnote to the title. Acknowledgements thank others for their contribution to the research and are often personal statements by the author/s about the support they received during the project.

Tables of contents

Longer or complex research reports begin with a table of contents (listing section headings and page numbers), which acts as a guide to various parts of the report. Separate lists of tables, figures, maps or other important items in the report (for example, lists of abbreviations) may also follow the general table of contents and are placed before the introduction. Word processing packages usually include a Table of Contents function.

A structure for your research report

- Table of contents*
- Abstract
- Acknowledgements*
- Lists of figures*
- Lists of tables*
- Lists of abbreviations*
- Introduction/problem statement
- Methodology
- Findings
- Discussion
- Conclusion/recommendations
- References
- Appendices*

*Not generally included in journal articles

INFLUENCING POLICY AND PRACTICE

Report writing is a fundamental skill of the researcher, but is only one of the skills researchers need if their findings are to make an impact. In chapter 9 you read about action research, which aims to change injustice or address social problems as part of the research process. All research, according to our definition in this book, is undertaken in order to *make a decision or take some action*. While the action research approach is explicitly geared towards social change, all social work research should lead to change at some level, whether in deepened theoretical understanding or in the world of policy and practice.

Planning for maximum impact of your results is just as important as planning the research itself. There are many good reasons why you should plan the dissemination of your results as carefully as you plan the research. These involve political, ethical and practical issues. *Ethically*, it is important to be accountable to those who funded the research, those who were involved in the research and the key stakeholders who will be affected by the research. *Politically*, it is important for the goodwill of the community towards researchers generally that you plan some kind of report back to the people involved in the research process. Politically and ethically, social work is a profession committed to goals of social justice. If research does not lead to action and decision making, it is hard to justify why social workers should be involved in the research in the first place. *Pragmatically*, if you can demonstrate that the results of your research have led to specific outcomes in social work policy or practice, or have influenced decision makers in some way, you are more likely to get funded for further research. Thus, there are many good reasons why you should plan how to disseminate your results to a variety of audiences.

PLANNING FOR MAXIMUM IMPACT

There is no point going to all the trouble of completing a research project without also having in mind what you want to happen as a result. Anyone who has worked in the social welfare field will know that careful strategic planning is needed if we are to influence policy or decision making.

Wadsworth (1997a) suggests writing an action plan, once you know the results of your research. This is an excellent idea as the first step in influencing policy and practice and making sure that your results have an impact. If you used an advisory group throughout the research, writing an action plan and carrying it out is the final task that you will be undertaking with the group. If you did not use an advisory group, perhaps this is the time to form one. The advisory group consists of the key stakeholders in the research project, the people with an interest in the results (see chapter 2). An advisory group can help you to brainstorm the implications of your research and what should happen as a result of your recommendations. At this stage in the research, several heads are generally better than one.

There are six steps in forming an action plan, according to Wadsworth (1997a). We will briefly discuss each of these.

What to include in an action plan (Wadwsorth 1997a)

- *What* action should occur as suggested by the findings?
- *Who* needs to know in order for these things to happen?
- *Why* (how will they contribute to the process of getting the action taken)?
- *How* should the findings be presented to these people to get what we want?
- *What* is important to get across to them?
- *When* should this occur?

What needs to happen?

Often, your findings and the recommendations suggest directly what needs to happen as a result of your research. Some recommendations will be more specific than others. Specific recommendations usually imply decisions and action directly. More general conclusions require further discussion and brainstorming as to their implications for policy and practice. In the income support agency example, if you uncover that there are problems in the way some people are treated when they visit an office, there will be several things that you may want to occur as a result. You may want to raise the awareness of staff and management about the problem. You may also want additional training for the staff and to institute ways of monitoring their improvement in this area. You may recommend that a group within the agency be formed to decide the best ways that the problem can be dealt with.

Of course, the sorts of action/decisions which you and your advisory group may want to happen will be influenced by your position in relation to the issue you have researched. If you are researching from the 'outside'—for example, if you applied for funding to undertake the research as an independent researcher—the sorts of actions you will be able to plan will be very different from those you might select if you are a social worker within an organisation who has undertaken some research to decide something about a particular program. As an outside researcher, the actions you take might be limited to raising awareness and advocating the setting up of structures in which others will plan and carry out the changes that your research suggests. If you are within an organisation or community group, however, you may be in a position to participate in planning the action more specifically. For example, you may recommend broad goals, as well as specific objectives and strategies, including the key people who need to be involved. An outside researcher is usually not in a position to be so specific or as involved in the changes which occur as a result of the research.

Recommendations may also be long term or short term. You and your advisory group may formulate short-term objectives and also have in mind the long-term goals you wish to achieve as a result of the research. As you decide on what you want to happen, it is best to think in terms of long-term and short-term outcomes and to divide up your objectives accordingly.

Who do we tell?

Once you have decided what you want to happen, the next step is to decide who to tell. These decisions depend very much on your understanding of who has the power and influence to carry out your recommendations. Who controls the resources you need to achieve your goals? Who makes the decisions? Who will be your supporters and assist you? Who is likely to try to block you? Similarly, if your results are to have maximum impact, you must take into account the people who will support and oppose you. You need to decide who they are and what will be the most effective way of making your results known to them.

Understanding the formal and informal power structures of the key organisations relevant to your research topic (including organisations of 'the researched' as well as organisations controlling the funding, decision making or other resources) is a crucial ingredient in making good decisions about 'who do we tell?'.

Why we want to tell them

Part of deciding who you want to tell about your research results is being clear about what you want from these people. What do you want them to do? How do you want them involved? Researchers usually have few resources, so you need to carefully target which people you want to tell about your results. Being specific about why you want to tell the people you have chosen will help you to choose them and also to clarify further what you want to happen as a result of your findings.

How to present the findings

We have seen that written reports are fundamental to presenting your findings. The written report is the basis upon which you plan your action strategy and is necessary to justify your conclusions.

For maximum impact, you may need to write a simpler summary of your findings and recommendations as well as a full, more formal account of the research. People in the community, as well as policy and decision makers, may find a summary more accessible. Certainly for media interviews or news releases in local papers, you will need to be able to summarise your findings quickly and succinctly.

When planning how to present your findings, work out where and how your target group is most likely to see them. As well as written reports, there are many other ways to present your findings. How you present your results depends on what you want to happen, who you are telling, and why. Here is a list of some of the different ways that you could present your results, based on Wadsworth's (1997a) suggestions. A combination of methods is likely to be the most effective way of making sure that your research report does not lie on the shelf gathering dust:

- Present your results to meetings of key stakeholders (use visual aids such as overheads or PowerPoint and have a single-page summary for participants to take away). Be prepared to form follow-up action groups as a result of your meetings/discussions.
- Make displays in areas where the people you want to tell are likely to go—for example, displays in shopping centres, staff rooms, health centres, pamphlets or posters in doctors' waiting rooms, displays in shop windows.
- Make a videotape (with accompanying written summary).
- Photographic exhibitions or displays can be effective (with written or spoken commentaries).
- Produce sound/slide sets or a PowerPoint presentation.
- Undertake plays, puppets, revues, street theatre.
- You may choose to mount a campaign about a particular issue, or to mass-distribute material such as posters, pamphlets, leaflets, badges, stickers.
- Produce a news release.

What is important to get across

When you are thinking about who to tell and how to tell them, it is important to keep in mind your priorities. This is important when formulating an action plan. Different people will be targeted for different reasons and you will have different messages, or angles, for people in different positions. For example, if your results suggest that a youth refuge is needed in a particular area, you may want to reassure the local community about the safety of residents, and to dispel myths about young people who use refuges, as well as to gain support for the project. You might also want local funding bodies to understand the need for the service and provide examples of support from local organisations and the community.

When

Timing is always important in developing your action plan. It is important to know when the key decisions are being made which will affect the issues which you have researched, and to time your strategies accordingly. For example, just before an election can be an excellent time to ensure that politicians are interested in your results. Releasing your findings in time for key meetings, before budget decisions or while key people are *not* on leave, are also important considerations. The summer holiday period is not a good time to release your report!

Wadsworth (1997a) suggests the gradual release of information about your project, for example, at an early stage, again about half-way through, and finally at the end when you know what the results are and what you want to say about them. Such a timetable makes people aware of your project, helps people to 'own' it, and hopefully prepares them for the results when they emerge.

An example of an action plan, as devised by Wadsworth (1997a), might look like this:

What we want	Who we tell	Why	How findings will be presented	What to get over	When
Better treatment for country clients	a. Managers b. Country staff	To improve services and ensure efficiency with better access	Meetings, article in departmental newsletter, focus groups of staff to discuss how to monitor changes	Experiences of country clients	April: article in newsletter. May–Oct: meet with all country offices. April next year: evaluate action plan

SUMMARY

This final chapter has discussed various ways that you can make sure that your research has a maximum impact and leads to actions or decisions. Writing your report is a vital first step. The target audience and your purpose in undertaking the research will influence the structure of your report and the language you use. Whether your report is at the formal or informal end of the spectrum, several elements will make it more effective: a catchy title, logical structure, clear layout with well-spaced headings, plain English, graphics and charts, and finally an eye-catching cover.

Devising an action strategy is an important part of the research process which needs the same careful planning as other stages in your project. With an action plan in place and good follow-up procedures to monitor its success, you will be in an excellent position to make sure that your research is effective and that all your hard work has been worthwhile.

When devising your written reports and your action plan, remember that you are most likely to have maximum impact if you include a wide range of people in your advisory group. Reporting back to the research participants as well as the sponsors, and involving the participants in actions planned as a result of your research is an important aspect of social work research.

This brings to an end *Research for Social Workers*. We hope that the research process is now clear for you and that you are inspired to contribute your own research to the social work knowledge base. Societal change is rapid and inevitable. Research is a politically powerful means for critically analysing as well as creating change. Social work should be part of the debate about directions for change. Now is the time for you to take up the challenge of social work research, and become part of the new social work research culture which is working towards an equitable and just society.

QUESTIONS

1 What is the relative importance of the methodology versus the findings and conclusions sections of research reports in:
  a Professional journals or conference presentations?
  b Newspapers, newsletters, more informal sources of publication?
2 What is the purpose of the abstract?
3 List the main elements included in the introduction/statement of the problem section.
4 What are the six key aspects of the methodology section?
5 Should you discuss your findings as you present them?
6 What should be included in the discussion section?
7 What are the key elements to include in an action plan?

EXERCISES

1 Go to the library and select one quantitative and one qualitative research report in a journal, as well as one quantitative and one qualitative stand-alone report (either a book or a larger report):
  a List the structures of these four reports, noting similarities and differences.
  b Compare the structures of these reports with the suggested structure for report writing in this chapter:
    i Are the research question/s and the background literature

review clear? Do you understand the context of these studies?

ii How is the methodology section set out? Is all the necessary information included?

iii Are the findings related to the questions?

iv Is the evidence sufficient to justify the conclusions?

v Are the limitations of the studies acknowledged? How?

vi Are the recommendations/conclusions related to the original research questions and relevant for social work practice or policy?

2 Scan news reports and newspapers for some examples of how research is being reported and used to make decisions or take action. Is there evidence of an action plan on the part of the researcher?

3 Interview some researchers about how they formulate action plans, or try to ensure that the results of their research are known about in the right places. What strategies do they use to get their message across? How effective have they been?

4 Write an action plan for a piece of research in which you have been involved. Alternatively, select a piece of research from earlier exercises and write an action plan for that. You may use Wadsworth's framework or one of your own devising. Remember to include a time frame and to nominate who will be responsible for which strategy.

FURTHER READING

Allen, R. & Babbie, E. 2001, *Research Methods for Social Work* 4th edn, Wadsworth, California. Appendix C.

Kumar, R. 1996, *Research Methodology*, Longman, Melbourne. Chapter 17.

Mark, R. 1996, *Research Made Simple: A Handbook for Social Workers*, Sage, California. Appendix D.

Marlow, C, 1998, *Research Methods for Generalist Social Work*, 2nd edn, Brooks/Cole Publishing Co., Pacific Grove. Chapter 14.

Sarantakos, S. 1998, *Social Research*, 2nd edn, Macmillan, Melbourne. Part IV.

Royse, D. 1999, *Research Methods in Social Work*, Nelson-Hall, Chicago.

Wadsworth, Y. 1997, *Do It Yourself Social Research*, 2nd edn, Allen & Unwin, Sydney. Chapter 8.

APPENDIX

DEVELOPING A
RESEARCH PROPOSAL

Chapters 2 and 3 have introduced us to effective ways of transforming our problems into researchable questions. However, what *we*
think is a good research idea may not be so apparent to our agency
or to the funding source. A management committee or an external
funding body would be rightly sceptical if we wrote to them asking
for '$8000 to research domestic violence'! Our good idea must be sold
and, to do this, we must demonstrate that we have the skills and
knowledge to undertake a complex piece of research. The ability to
construct a detailed research proposal is an extremely important skill
in the current competitive environment. This appendix will discuss
funding sources and criteria which affect our research before outlining both the steps that must be followed to develop a well-crafted
research proposal and indicating the pitfalls to be avoided.

HAVE A GOOD IDEA—WHERE DO I FIND FUNDS?

The first step in preparing a research proposal is to target an appropriate funding source. Beginning researchers will often define their
researchable problem before turning to the practical question of
where to seek funds. Experienced researchers are more likely to
develop their proposals in response to guidelines from funding
bodies and thus may be more likely to attract funding. Students
would do well to begin collecting newspaper advertisements relating
to funds available and, as an exercise, send for funding guidelines so
that they become aware of the types of external funding available
and the priorities and areas of interest of available sources of funding.
This is an important part of your research training and will improve
your skills in the long term. You may have a good idea for a piece
of research on domestic violence but you are unlikely to receive funds
from a body which targets environmental issues. Examine the objectives of the funding programs available and decide where you might
find appropriate financial support.

You should also be aware of the budgetary limits of each funding program. Some bodies prefer to fund a number of small projects for less than, say, $20 000, while others invest their research funds in a few complex and more expensive proposals. We will examine budgetary issues later in this chapter. What is important to note here is that you should ensure that your budget matches the money available.

Don't be afraid to seek clarification from the funding body about its objectives and funding requirements. Remember, however, that most funding bodies are inundated with proposals for funding so you should be aware that the success rate is low (often as low as 10 per cent). Don't be disheartened if you are unsuccessful with your first proposal. Many bodies provide feedback and assessment of proposals and you should use this feedback to improve your chances at a later date.

Seeking funding

- Be clear about your research question
- Do your homework on funding bodies
- Seek funds from appropriate funding bodies
- Match your budget to available funds
- A minority of research proposals will be funded in any competitive round
- If your proposal is knocked back study the feedback and improve your proposal

---

DEVELOPING YOUR RESEARCH PROPOSAL

As we have already noted, many granting bodies have guidelines which include the categories of information required from you. If so, you should follow these carefully. You should also note that some funding bodies require a preliminary two-page summary of your proposal. These bodies then determine from the initial applications which applicants will be asked to submit full applications. All final applications for these organisations, and applications for other bodies, should include the categories to be discussed here. If funding guidelines do not include them, you should try to address them anyway by weaving the information into the set categories. Remember your research proposal will act like a road map alerting you and the funding body to the way the research will unfold. It will detail your aims and outcomes, the research plan and your budget. In addition, the first section in your proposal should be a brief background statement to introduce your topic area.

Background

The background statement should contain a statement that introduces your research issue and succinctly describes why this issue is important. What is it you wish to study? You should demonstrate the depth of your knowledge about the research question and indicate to the assessor that you have spent time researching the issue. If the issue has caused controversy lately, or proposed legislative reform is in the air, indicate that you are aware of this.

A literature review is an important part of your background statement. While this literature review will not necessarily be comprehensive, because there may be literally hundreds of sources of information, it should indicate that you are aware of the latest publications and reports. Additionally, if it is to be assessed by an academic committee, it should also include the current theoretical debate in the area you wish to address. You should also be cognisant of recent legislative reforms. If you are wishing to research aspects of domestic violence, or child protection, for instance, you will need to indicate an understanding of the latest legislative and policy developments and any proposed changes or problem areas.

Your background statement will provide information on existing knowledge in your topic area and will clearly outline how your proposed research relates to the existing knowledge base. Will it address theoretical development in the area? Will it challenge basic assumptions or treatment procedures? Will it test the relative benefits of one treatment procedure over another? Will it explore a new area where little information is available? Will it examine the effects of new legislation or policy development in unexplored areas—for example, in rural locations or among minority groups? Be clear about the value of your study and how it will contribute to our current understanding of the issues.

Aims and significance of the study

Following your background statement you should list your aims in undertaking the study and the significance of the work. These should be listed concisely and logically. Why are you proposing this study? Why is it so important at this particular point in time and who will directly benefit from your work? Note the importance of your work and how exciting it will be once the results are in! Remember you must sell the research, so do not be shy and hesitant in heralding its significance.

This section should also address the specific priorities of the funding body. Most will have three or four key areas—which may change from year to year—that are integral to the way the proposals will be assessed. If your funding body has specified that a priority for the current round is citizenship rights, and you are proposing to investigate child protection practices, then indicate how your research will contribute to enhanced rights for children. Addressing the funding organisation's current priorities is crucial to your ultimate success, so you should pay particular attention to the way you relate the significance of your work to these issues.

Outcomes

This section of your research proposal should detail the anticipated outcomes of your research. What will be the achievements of your work and how will these help the target group? What practice, policy or legislative implications will flow from your research? Note how these relate to the priorities of the funding body. In particular, you should detail how the results will be published, circulated or shared in order to achieve the proposed effects on practice, policy or legislation. Will this be in the form of a report, a conference paper, a journal article, a newspaper story or via a news conference? Be specific, because this is just as important a step as any other in the research proposal. You may conduct research that has the potential to markedly change society's thinking about an issue, but unless you disseminate the information, nothing will change.

Research plan

Having written a clear background statement and excited the reader with the potential significance of your work, your research will stand or fall on the detail provided in your research plan. A well-constructed and clear plan is critical to any research proposal and it is in this section that you must demonstrate an understanding of the research process.

Methodology

Begin with a statement on the type of methodology you have chosen, why this is the most satisfactory choice, and give a brief description of this methodology. We have outlined methodologies in chapter 1. This chapter should assist you to determine the most appropriate methodology, or combination of approaches, for any study you are proposing. Your research plan will outline the steps in the research process, all of which are discussed more fully in chapter 4. Should you choose a quantitative methodology then you should outline the hypothesis you propose to test and your operational definitions. If you choose a qualitative methodology you must outline your research problem.

Sampling

Your research plan will clearly define the population you wish to study and the sample to be drawn from that population (see chapter 5). How will this sample be chosen, and how is this relevant to the study aims? Be precise about your sampling procedure and why it is the best possible choice under the circumstances in which you will be conducting the study. Explain why this procedure will provide the most favourable examination of the issues.

In outlining your sampling procedure, you should indicate how you propose to gain access to the specified population group. If you are studying victims of domestic violence and your proposal suggests you will interview women entering refuges, your assessors will know you have not done your homework. It is standard practice in women's refuges to protect women from everyone, including well-meaning researchers! Make sure you have checked on your proposed access to your sample. This may involve including a letter from your agency or another source indicating that you have access to the group in question.

In the case of violence, for instance, there may be a group for victims of violence running at the local health centre. You might seek permission from the group leader to interview consenting members and include a letter from her/him indicating that this process is acceptable.

Method of data collection

Your research plan will include a discussion of the chosen method of data collection; that is, how you will be gathering the required information. Several chapters in this book have covered the type of method you might choose, including interviews, surveys, observations, secondary analysis and content analysis. You should indicate in your proposal which method or combination of methods you have chosen and why it is the most appropriate and effective. In particular, you should note any ethical considerations arising from your chosen method. How will you ensure confidentiality? What strategies are in place should your interviewees become distressed?

Data analysis

Your research plan will detail the type of data analysis to be employed. What will you do with the data once you have collected it? What procedures and statistical analyses, if any, will you use to find answers to your research question or patterns and themes in the data which relate to your research aims? You should always indicate any experience you may have had with the proposed methods and data analysis techniques.

In preparing this section do not restrict it to one sentence. 'Data will be analysed using *SPSS*' is not sufficient to inspire the confidence of assessors in your knowledge of data analysis. Indicate in a few

309

carefully crafted sentences that you actually understand the process of analysis and the way you intend to pursue it.

Limitations

The next section of your research plan will outline the limitations imposed by your proposed plan. The very nature of social research means that every study will have limitations, often due to factors that can never be entirely eliminated. For example, your sampling technique may limit your ability to generalise your findings. In the case of victims of violence, you may only have been able to interview those women confident and articulate enough to join a group. This limitation should be noted in your proposal, as should any limitation evident in your data collection method and data analysis. Do not ever try to hide limitations, but instead outline how you propose to minimise them.

Timetable

The final section of your research plan provides a timetable for the proposed project. This timetable should not only fit the funding guidelines (for example, some granting bodies require all research to be completed in one year) but should also fit your own schedule. Can you realistically meet the proposed timetable given your other commitments? Can you achieve the proposed aims? Be realistic in setting targets for yourself.

Ethical considerations

Ethical clearances are a major consideration of your proposal. Most agencies now have ethics committees as part of their organisational structure. If your agency is one of these, note that you will seek ethical clearance from this committee before you begin your study. You should note that most funding agencies and ethics committees require consent protocols. You should look over the example of the consent protocol in chapter 6. Your proposal should indicate the procedure to be used to address ethical issues.

Administration of the research

In this section of the research proposal, you should outline the way the study will be organised, and what resources are needed to successfully complete the research. You might indicate that your agency is allowing you to use your office and telephone and to have computing, typing, printing and photocopying done at no cost to the research funding body. Alternatively, if you are working independently, these costs will need to be factored into your budget. Note what staff are to be involved in the research. This may be agency personnel only, or you may need to employ a research assistant. If so, indicate what qualifications will be necessary and what their tasks and responsibilities will be. If you are the principal researcher, indicate this and list any consultants and others who will be contributing to the research.

Budget

Your budget is vital to the success or failure of your research project. If you have insufficient funds to complete the work you will fail to achieve your aims and your research record may be damaged.

Cost out all the items listed in your plan precisely. Which of the listed activities will cost money? These will generally fall under categories of personnel, travel, equipment and maintenance. Make sure these activities are accurately costed (seek quotes) and justified (is it really essential that you travel to London to compare your results with others researching in this field?). Do not pad your budget with unnecessary items but at the same time do not skimp.

Note from the funding guidelines what items the sponsoring body will financially support and make sure your requests are within reason. Finally, check and recheck your budget total to ensure you have not made a fundamental error in your adding up!

The following provides an example of a budget prepared for a small project to assess welfare service delivery changes in country towns. Note that there are no funds included for the principal researcher's time. If the project is part of your salaried position this is acceptable. If you require funds for your own time this should be added. Other personnel costs and travel costs should be computed on the current award rates. These may change periodically from what is listed in this proposal. You should also note that, depending on the size of the project, costs may include such items as lease of computers and other equipment items, and additional maintenance costs such as office lease, etc.

You should note that this example reflects Australian dollar values at 2001 levels. You should check the value of services in *your own currency at current prices.*

Budget justification

No matter what the size of your budget you should provide a short justification of all budget items. Why is it necessary to employ a level 6 research assistant? Why do you need 100 hours of transcription? Why do you need to travel to Canberra or Sydney or elsewhere? Why do you need a tape recorder? Assessors will expect each item to be justified with a brief statement. It may be that if this is not done well enough your proposal could be funded at a lower rate than requested.

Detailed budget items	Amount requested
2002	
Personnel	
Research Assistant, level 6, 1 day per week (7 hours) x 35 weeks@ $26.42 per hour	$6473
Transcriber—100 hrs @ $22.23 per hour	$2223
Equipment	
Tape recorder	$500
Maintenance	
Photocopying, disks, tapes	$2000
Telephone	$1000
Travel	
3 overnight trips to Canberra/Sydney x 2 researchers ($176 per night)	$1056
Car rates	
Canberra: 600 km @ 30c km x 2	$360
Sydney: 1000 km @ 30c km x 1	$300
Rural towns:1000 km @ 30c km	$300

			Financial summary			
Support requested	Personnel $	Equipment $	Maintenance $	Travel $	Other $	TOTAL $
2002	$8696	$500	$3000	$2016		$14 212

About you

You should include a section in your proposal that details your capability to conduct the research. Are you in a unique position to collect the data? For example, you may be a sexual assault counsellor in an area populated by people of diverse cultural backgrounds, and through your work have access to interviewees and to case material which puts you in a unique position to study the effects of sexual assault in multicultural groups. Note the importance of your position. Have you conducted research before? If so, say so. If not, you might outline any research training and higher degree study you have undertaken. Outline your publishing record, particularly in the areas of the proposed research. If you have not published, note any staff seminars or student supervision you may have given in this area. What experience do you have that makes it important that you are the one to be funded for this particular piece of research? Don't sell yourself short! Nominate people as referees who know your work and appreciate your skills. Be confident of your ability to conduct the project and be convincing.

Sections in your research proposal

- Background
- Aims and significance of the study

- Research plan
- Ethical considersations
- Administration
- Budget
- Outcomes
- About you

FINE-TUNING YOUR PROPOSAL

Having reached this stage you should now spend time going through and streamlining your proposal. Make sure you have not repeated yourself and that the proposal is clear, comprehensive and succinct. Make sure that there are no typing errors and that the proposal is well presented. Go back to the guidelines and check that you have kept within the page limits for the proposal. Some guidelines will indicate that they require nine (or six or 20) pages only. If this is the case you can be sure that any additional pages will not be read. Keep within the limits! Note from the guidelines the expected font size, spacing and number of copies to be sent. Particularly note the submission date and whether faxed or emailed copies are accepted. You can be sure that deadlines will be strictly adhered to. Before sending in your proposal ask colleagues to go through it and consider their advice on any modifications that should be made. Be sure you have done the best possible job you can.

ASSESSMENT OF RESEARCH PROPOSALS

Once your research proposal has been sent to your agency management committee or an outside funding body for assessment, you will have little to do but wait for feedback. The assessors will be particularly focusing on the merit of the proposed research and the ability of the researcher to conduct the work.

The merit of the proposed research will be judged by its potential outcomes. Will the research lead to a major advance in our understanding of the proposed issue, to an important advance in practice strategies, to the solution of a problem, or to policy development or legislative reform? If the answer to any of these questions is yes, then the assessment committee will be interested to read on.

The merit of the research will be further judged by the ability of the agency to provide the infrastructure to support the proposal and by the capacity of the researcher to devote the time and resources required to the project. If those points are soundly addressed in the proposal, the assessors will examine carefully the research plan for thoroughness and detail.

If the plan meets with approval, the assessors will finally examine the researcher's potential to successfully complete the project. Particularly relevant will be research experience, publishing record, work history and experience in the proposed areas. If you have covered all these sections effectively, your proposal has a very high chance of funding success. If so, it is now time for the hard work!

SUMMARY

This appendix has, first, examined the issues to be considered when developing a research proposal and, second, has illustrated how to develop a competitive proposal. You should note that there is a great deal of time and effort between a 'good idea' and an adequate proposal for funding support. You must deal with the agency, professional, personal and practical issues before developing a proposal for funding which will meet with approval.

The sections to be included in a proposal have been outlined in this appendix. You should bear in mind that only a limited number of proposals will be successful in the current restricted funding environment. You should therefore see the research proposal as a very important step in your research project and worthy of a great deal of your time and energy. Remember, you know the research is important but you must convince the funding body that you and your project are worthy of investment!

QUESTIONS

1 How should you investigate possible sources of funding for a proposed research project?
2 What are the constraints your agency might impose on your proposed research?
3 What professional issues will affect your proposal?
4 Outline the personal issues to be assessed before you begin developing your proposal.
5 What practical issues must be addressed before you submit your proposal?
6 Outline the sections to be included in your research proposal.
7 How might these differ depending on your methodology?
8 Why is an accurate budget so important to your research?
9 Given your current position, how might you go about gaining research experience?
10 What issues guide the assessors of your research proposal?

EXERCISES

1 Find an advertisement for research funding in the newspaper. Send for funding guidelines. Note the priorities of the funding body, the timeline for completion of the project and the funding limits.

2 Begin a file of advertisements as outlined in exercise 1. Collect funding guidelines for three different grant programs. Note how they differ.

3 Ask your agency supervisor or the management committee for a copy of any successful research proposals. Note how these are constructed. Why do you think they were successful?

4 Seek copies of unsuccessful research proposals. Why do you think they were unsuccessful? Here you may need to consult funding guidelines.

5 In your work situation you may have noticed that there are some issues that warrant further investigation. Make a list of these and determine how you might improve the situation through research.

BIBLIOGRAPHY

Allen, R. & Babbie, E. 2001, *Research Methods for Social Work*, 4th edn, Wadsworth, California

Alreck, P. L. & Settle, R. B. 1995, *The Survey Research Handbook*, 2nd edn, Irwin, Burr Ridge, Ill.

Alston, Margaret 1993, A Study of Farm Women, Unpublished PhD thesis, University of NSW, Sydney

——1995, *Women on the Land: the Hidden Heart of Rural Australia*, University of NSW Press, Sydney

——1996, *Goals for Women: Improving Media Representation of Women's Sport*, Centre for Rural Social Research, Charles Sturt University, Wagga Wagga, NSW

——1997, 'Violence against Women in a Rural Context', *Australian Social Work*, March, pp. 15–22

Andre, Marie & Vellozzi, Frank 1995, *United Views: Building a Stronger Community: HIV Community Development Project Needs Assessment Report*, AIDS Council of NSW, Illawarra Branch, Wollongong.

Argyrous, George 2000, *Statistics for Social & Health Research with a Guide to SPSS*, Sage Publications, London.

Australian Association of Social Workers 2000, *Code of Ethics*, Australian Association of Social Workers, ACT, Australia.

Australian Bureau of Statistics 1994, '1991 Census of population and housing basic community profile', ABS Catalogue No. 2722.1.

Babbie, E. 1990, *Survey Research Methods*, 2nd edn, Wadsworth, Belmont, California.

——2001, *The Practice of Social Research*, 9th edn, Wadsworth, Belmont, California.

Baldry, E. & Vinson, T. (eds) 1991, *Actions Speak: Strategies and Lessons from Australian Social and Community Action*, Longman Cheshire, Melbourne.

Beauchamp, Tom L. 1982, *Philosophical Ethics: An Introduction to Moral Philosophy*, McGraw-Hill, New York.

Belcher, John R. 1994, 'Understanding the process of social drift among the homeless: a qualitative analysis', in *Qualitative Research in Social Work*, E. Sherman & W. J. Reid (eds), Columbia University Press, New York.

Bell, C. 1978, 'Personal reflections on a research career,' in *Inside the Whale: Ten Personal Accounts of Social Research*, C. Bell & S. Encel (eds), Pergamon Press, Australia.

Bell, C. & Encel, S. (eds) 1978, *Inside the Whale: Ten Personal Accounts of Social Research*, Pergamon Press, Australia.

Bennett, B. & Zubrzycki J. 2001, 'Indigenous Social Workers: Putting stories into practice', conference paper, AASW National Conference, Melbourne.

Berg, B. L. 1995, *Qualitative Research Methods for the Social Sciences*, 2nd edn, Allyn & Bacon, Boston.

Bernstein, S. R. & Epstein, I. 1994, 'Grounded theory meets the reflective practitioner: integrating qualitative and quantitative methods in administrative practice', in *Qualitative Research in Social Work*, E. Sherman & W. J. Reid (eds), Columbia University Press, New York.

Betts, Katharine, Hayward, David & Garnham, Nick 2001, *Quantitative Analysis in the Social Sciences: An Introduction*, Tertiary Press, Melbourne.

Beyer, Barry K. 1971, *Inquiry in the Social Studies Classroom*, Charles E. Merrill Publishing Co., Columbus, Ohio.

Black, James A. & Champion, Dean J. 1976, *Methods and Issues in Social Research*, John Wiley & Sons, New York.

Bostwick, G. J. & Kyte, N. S. 1993, 'Measurement in research', in R. M. Grinnell Jr (ed.), *Social Work Research and Evaluation*, 4th edn, Peacock Publishers, Itasca, Ill.

Bowles, W. 1995, 'Quality of life of adults with Spina Bifida: An issue of equality', unpublished PhD thesis, Univeristy of NSW, Sydney.

Bradshaw, J. 1977, 'The concept of social need', in *Planning for Social Welfare: Issues, Models and Tasks*, N. Gilbert & H. Specht (eds), Prentice-Hall, Englewood Cliffs, pp. 29–96.

British Association of Social Workers 2002, *The Code of Ethics for Social Work*, <http://www.basw.co.nk/pages/info/ethics.htm>

Bronson, Denise E. 1994, 'Is a scientist-practitioner model appropriate for direct social work practice? The no case', in Walter W. Hudson and Paula S. Nurius (eds), *Controversial Issues in Social Work Research*, Allyn and Bacon, Boston. pp. 79–81, 86–7.

Burns, Robert B. 1994, *Introduction to Research Methods*, Longman Chesire, Melbourne.

Carr, Wilford & Kemmis, Stephen 1983, *Becoming Critical: Knowing Through Action Research*, Deakin University Press: Geelong, Victoria.

Cheetham, Juliet et al. 1992, *Evaluating Social Work Effectiveness*, Open University Press, Buckingham.

Coffey, Shaun 1995, *Action Research: The Process Phenomenon of Man*, CQ Extension Forum, April C1–C14.

Cournoyer, D. E. Klein, W. C. 2000, *Research Methods for Social Work*, Allyn & Bacon, Boston.

Craft, John L. 1990, *Statistics and Data Analysis for Social Workers*, 2nd edn, Peacock Publishers, Itasca, Ill.

Dangel, Richard F. 1994, 'Is a scientist-practitioner model appropriate for direct social work practice? The yes case', in Walter W. Hudson and Paula S. Nurius (eds), *Controversial Issues in Social Work Research*, Allyn & Bacon, Boston, pp. 75–9, 81–6.

Davis, I. P. 1994, 'Integrating qualitative and quantitative methods in clinical research', in *Qualitative Research in Social Work*, E. Sherman & W. J. Reid (eds), Columbia University Press, New York.

de Vaus, David 2001, *Research Design in Social Research*, Sage, London.

——2002, *Surveys in Social Research*, 5th edn, Allen & Unwin, Sydney.

Department of Health, NSW 1988, *Sexual Assault Services: Policy and Procedure Manual*, State Health Publication No. HSU 88–039, Sydney.

Dibb-Smith, Janet 1994, Grantsmanship, Unpublished Staff Seminar Notes, Charles Sturt University, Wagga Wagga.

Doyle, Robert 1996, 'Breaking the solitudes to improve services for ethnic groups: Action research strategies,' in *The Reflective Researcher*, Jan Fook (ed.), Allen & Unwin, Sydney.

Eckhardt, Kenneth W. & Ermann, M. David 1977, *Social Research Methods: Perspective, Theory and Analysis*, Random House, New York.

Einstein, Gilles O. & Nocks, Elaine C. 1987, *Learning to Use SPSSx*, Prentice-Hall, Englewood Cliffs, NJ.

Everitt, Angela et al. 1992, *Applied Research for Better Practice*, Macmillan, Hampshire.

Everitt, Angela & Hardiker, Pauline 1996, *Evaluating for Good Practice*, Macmillan, London.

Fanshel, David (ed.) 1979, *Future of Social Work Research*, National Association of Social Workers Inc., Washington DC.

Fawcett, B., Featherstone, B., Fook, J. & Rossiter, A. (eds) 2000, *Practice and Research in Social Work: Postmodern Feminist Perspectives*, Rontledge, New York.

Foddy, W. H. 1988, *Elementary Applied Statistics for the Social Sciences*, Harper & Row, Sydney.

Fook, Jan (ed.) 1996, *The Reflective Researcher*, Allen & Unwin, Sydney.

——2000, 'Deconstructing and reconstructing professional expertise', in Barbara Fawcett, Brid Featherstone, Jan Fook and Amy Rossiter (eds), *Practice and Research in Social Work*, Routledge, London, pp. 104–119.

Foote Whyte, William, 1991a, *Participatory Action Research*, Sage, Newbury Park.

——1991b, *Social Theory for Action*, Sage Publications, Newbury Park.

Fortune, Anne E. and Reid, William J. 1999, *Research in Social Work*, 3rd edn, Columbia University Press, New York.

Fox, Karl A. 1974, *Social Indicators and Social Theory: Elements of an Operational System*, John Wiley & Sons, New York.

Fredman, Norman & Sherman, Robert 1987, *Handbook of Measurements for Marriage and Family Therapy*, Brunner/Mazel Publishers, New York.

Freire, Paulo 1970, *Pedagogy of the Oppressed*, Herder & Herder, New York.

Garton, Leslie, Fenton, Joan & Paton, Annette 1992, *Review of Sexual Assault Services: Report on X Sexual Assault Service*, June, NSW Department of Health, Sydney.

Gibbs, L. E. 1991, *Scientific Reasoning for Social Workers: Bridging the Gap Between Research and Practice*, Macmillan, New York.

Gilbert, Nigel 1993, *Researching Social Life*, Sage, London.

Gillespie, David F. & Glisson, Charles (eds) 1992, *Quantitative Methods in Social Work: State of the Art*, Haworth Press, New York.

Gilley, Tim 1990, *Research for Action: Empowering Poor People*, Brotherhood of St Lawrence, Melbourne.

Girden, Ellen R. 1996, *Evaluating Research Articles: From Start to Finish*, Sage, Thousand Oaks.

Glaser, B. & Strauss, A. 1967, *The Discovery of Grounded Theory*, Aldine Publishing Co., Chicago.

Gray, M. 1995, 'The ethical implications of current theoretical development in social work', *British Journal of Social Work*, vol. 25, pp. 55– 70.

Grinnell, Richard M. Jr (ed.) 1988, *Social Work Research and Evaluation*, 3rd edn, Peacock Publishers, Itasca, Ill.

——1993a, 'Group research designs', in *Social Work Research and Evaluation*, R. M. Grinnell Jr (ed.), 4th edn, Peacock Publishers, Itasca, Ill.

——1993b, *Social Work Research and Evaluation*, 4th edn, Peacock Publishers, Itasca, Ill.

Grundy, S. 1990, 'Three modes of action research', in *The Action Research Reader*, 3rd edn, Deakin University Press, Geelong, Victoria.

Gunew, S. & Yeatman, A. 1993, *Feminism and the Politics of Difference*, Allen & Unwin, Sydney.

Harrison, W. D. 1994, 'The inevitability of integrated methods', in *Qualitative Research in Social Work*, E. Sharman & W. J. Reid (eds), Columbia University Press, New York.

Hart, Elizabeth & Bond, Meg 1995, *Action Research for Health and Social Care*, Open University Press, Buckingham.

Herbert, Martin 1990, *Planning a Research Project*, Cassell, London.

Heron, J. & Reason, P. 2001, 'The practice of co-operative inquiry: Research "with" rather than "on" people', in P. Reason and H. Bradbury, *Handbook of Action Research Participative Inquiry and Practice*, Sage, London, pp. 179–88.

Horn, Robert V. 1993, *Statistical Indicators for the Economic and Social Sciences*, Cambridge University Press, Cambridge.

Hornick, Joseph P. & Burrows, Barbara 1988, 'Program evaluation', in *Social Work Research and Evaluation*, R.M. Grinnell Jr (ed.), 3rd edn, Peacock Publishers, Itasca, Ill., pp. 400–20.

Howe, D. 1994, 'Modernity, postmodernity and social work', *British Journal of Social Work*, vol. 24, pp. 513–32.

Hudson, Walter W. & Nurius, Paula S. 1994, *Controversial Issues in Social Work Research*, Allyn & Bacon, Boston.

Humphries, B. & Truman, C. 1994, *Re-thinking Social Research*, Avebury, Great Britain.

Ife, Jim 1995, *Community Development: Creating Community Alternatives— Vision, Analysis and Practice*, Longman, Melbourne.

Kerlinger, F. 1973, *Foundations of Behavioural Research* (2nd Edn), Holt, Rinehart and Winston, London.

Kidder, L. H. & Judd, C. M. 1986, *Research Methods in Social Relations*, Holt, Rinehart & Winston, New York. Chapter 12, 'Observational and Archival Research'.

Kirilik, L. 1995, *Community Work Distance Education Notes*, Faculty of Arts, Open Learning Institute, Charles Sturt University, Wagga Wagga.

Kirk, J. & Miller, M. L. 1986, 'Reliability and validity in qualitative research', in *Qualitative Research Methods*, vol. 1, Sage, Newbury Park, California.

Kumar, R. 1999, *Research Methodology*, Sage, Melbourne.

Latting, J. K. 1995, 'Postmodern feminist theory and social work: A deconstruction' in *Social Work* 40 (6), pp. 831–33.

Leedy, Paul D. 1985, *Practical Research: Planning and Design*, Macmillan, New York.

Lewins, Frank 1992, *Social Science Methodology: A Brief but Critical Introduction*, Macmillan, Melbourne.

Loneck, B. 1994 'Commentary, practitioner–researcher perspective on the integration of qualitative and quantitative research methods', in *Qualitative Research in Social Work*, E. Sherman & W. J. Reid (eds), Columbia University Press, New York.

Maguire, P. 2001, 'Uneven ground: Feminisms and Action Research' in *Handbook of Action Research Participative Inquiry and Practice*, P. Reason & H. Bradbury (eds), Sage, London, pp. 59–69.

Mark, R. 1996, *Research Made Simple: A Handbook for Social Workers*, Sage, Thousand Oaks, California.

Marlow, Christine 1998, *Research Methods for Generalist Social Work*, 2nd edn, Brooks/Cole Publishing Co., Pacific Grove, CA.

Masters, J. 1995, 'The history of action research', in *Action Research Electronic Reader*. Internet address: <http://www.cchs.su.edu.au/AROW/masters.htm>.

McDermott, Fiona 1996, 'Social work research: Debating the boundaries', in *Australian Social Work,* vol. 49, no. 1, March.

McKillip, Jack 1987, *Need Analysis: Tools for the Human Services and Education*, Sage, Newbury Park.

McMurty, S. L. 1993, 'Survey research', in *Social Work Research and Evaluation*, R. M. Grinnell Jr (ed.), 4th edn, Peacock Publishers, Itasca, Ill.

McNiff, J., accompanied by Jack Whitehead 2000, *Action Research in Organisations*, Routledege, London.

McTaggart, R. (ed.), 1997, *Participatory Action Research: International Contexts and Consequences*, State University of New York Press, New York.

Meekosha, H. 1990, 'Is feminism able-bodied?', *Refractory Girl*, no. 36, August, pp. 34–42.

Meekosha, H. 2000 'Political activism and identity making: the involvement of women in the disability rights movement in Australia', *WWDA News*, vol 18, Sept. 2000, pp. 26–34.

Miles, M. B. & Huberman, A. M. 1994, *Qualitative Data Analysis: An Expanded Source Book*, 2nd edn, Sage, Newbury Park.

Morris, J. 1992, 'Tyrannies of perfection', in *New Internationalist*, July (233), pp. 16–17.

National Association of Social Workers 1999, *Code of Ethics,* <http://www.socialworkers.org/pubs/code/code.asp.>.

National Committee on Violence Against Women 1992, *Position Paper,* Australian Government Publishing Service, Canberra.

Nielsen, J. M. (ed.) 1990, *Feminist Research Methods: Exemplary Readings in the Social Sciences*, Westview Press, Boulder, Colorado.

Oakley, Ann 1985, *The Sociology of Housework*, Basil Blackwell, London.

Orcutt, B. A. 1994, 'Commentary on Reid's "Reframing the epistemological debate", in *Qualitative Research in Social Work*, E. Sherman & W. J. Reid (eds), Columbia University Press, New York.

Owen, John M. 1993, *Program Evaluation: Forms and Approaches*, Allen & Unwin, Sydney.

Owen, John M. and Rogers, Patricia 1996, *Program Evaluation: Forms and Approaches*, Allen & Unwin, Sydney.

Padgett, Deborah K. 1998, *Qualitative Methods in Social Work Research: Challenges and Rewards,* Sage, Thousand Oaks.

Pallant, J. 2001, *SPSS Survival Manual: A step by step guide to data analysis using SPSS*, Allen & Unwin, Sydney.

Peile, C. & McCouat, M. 1997, 'The rise of relativism: The future of theory and knowledge development in social work', *British Journal of Social Work*, vol. 27 (3), pp. 343–60.

Pieper, M. H. 1994, 'Science, not scientism: The robustness of naturalistic clinical research', in *Qualitative Research in Social Work*, E. Sherman & W. J. Reid (eds), Columbia University Press, New York.

Punch, Maurice 1982, *The Politics and Ethics of Fieldwork*, Sage, Beverly Hills.

Purches, L. & Jaeger, J. 1994, *Support Groups for Mothers in Wagga, Tumut, Leeton, Henty and Culcarim in Rural NSW*, Available from Wagga Community Health Centre, PO Box 159, Wagga Wagga NSW 2650 Australia.

Pyke, S. W. & Agnew, N. M. 1991, *The Science Game: An Introduction to Research in the Social Sciences*, Prentice-Hall, Englewood Cliffs, New Jersey.

Reason, P. & Bradbury, H. 2001a, *Handbook of Action Research: Participative Inquiry and Practice*, Sage, London.

——2001b, 'Introduction: Inquiry and participation in search of a world worthy of human aspiration', in P. Reason, & H. Bradbury, *Handbook of Action Research Participative Inquiry and Practice*, Sage, London, pp. 1–14.

Reference Group on Welfare Reform 2000, *Participation Support for a More Equitable Society*, Commonwealth Department of Family and Community Services, Canberra.

Reid, William J. 1993, 'Writing research reports', *Social Work Research and Evaluation*, R. M. Grinnell Jr (ed.), 4th edn, Peacock Publishers, Itasca, Ill.

——1994, 'Reframing the epistemological debate', in *Qualitative Research in Social Work*, E. Sherman & W. J. Reid (eds), Columbia University Press, New York.

Reinharz, Shulamit 1992, *Feminist Methods in Social Research*, Oxford University Press, New York.

Reissman, Catherine Kohler (ed.) 1994, *Qualitative Studies in Social Work Research*, Sage, Thousand Oaks.

Richards, Lyn & Richards, Tom 1990, Critiquing Qualitative Computing: Grounded Theory Method versus Code and Retrieve Technique, Paper presented to Social Research Conference, Queensland, December.

Roberts, Helen (ed.) 1981, *Doing Feminist Research*, Routledge & Kegan Paul, London.

Rogers G. & Bouey, E. 1996a, 'Phase two: collecting your data', in *Qualitative Research for Social Workers*, L. M. Tutty, M. A. Rothery & R. M. Grinnell Jr (eds), Allyn & Bacon, Boston.

——1996b, 'Reviewing the literature', in *Social Work Research and Evaluation*, R. M. Grinnell Jr (ed.), 4th edn, Peacock Publishers, Itasca, Ill.

Rossi, Peter H., Freeman, Howard E. & Lipsey, Mark W., *Evaluation: A Systematic Approach*, 6th edn, Sage Publications, Thousand Oaks, California.

Rossiter, Amy 2000, 'The postmodern feminist condition: New conditions for social work', in Barbara Fawcett, Brid Featherstone, Jan Fook & Amy Rossiter (eds), *Practice and Research in Social Work*. Routledge, London, pp. 24–38.

Rothery, M. 1993a, 'The positivistic research approach', in *Social Work Research and Evaluation*, R. M. Grinnell Jr (ed.), 4th edn, Peacock Publishers, Itasca, Ill., chapter 3.

——1993b, 'Problems, questions and hypotheses', in *Social Work Research and Evaluation*, R. M. Grinnell Jr (ed.), 4th edn, Peacock Publishers, Itasca, Ill., chapter 2.

Royse, David 1999, *Research Methods in Social Work*, 3rd edn, Nelson-Hall, Chicago.

Rubin, Allen 1993, 'Secondary analysis', in *Social Work Research and Evaluation*, R. M. Grinnell Jr (ed.), 4th edn, Peacock Publishers, Itasca, Ill.

Rubin, Allen & Babbie, Earl 2001, *Research Methods for Social Work*, 4th edn, Wadsworth, California.

Sands, R. G. & Nuccio, K. 1992, 'Postmodern feminist theory and social work', *Social Work*, vol. 37 (6), pp. 489–94.

Sarantakos, S. 1994, 'Trial cohabitation on trial', in *Australian Social Work*, 47, 3, pp. 13–25.

——1998, *Social Research*, 2nd edn, Macmillan, Melbourne.

Sarri, Rosemary C. & Lawrence, R. John 1980, *Issues in the Evaluation of Social Welfare Programs: Australian Case Illustrations*, University of New South Wales Press, Sydney.

Schmuck, R. A. 1998, *Practical Action Research for Change*, Hawker & Brownlow, Australia.

Schuerman, John R. 1983, *Research and Evaluation in the Human Services*, The Free Press, New York.

Seidel, John V., Kjolseth, Rolf & Seymour, Elaine 1988, *The Ethnograph: A User's Guide*, Qualis Research Associates, Corvallis.

Seigel, L. W., Attkisson, C. C. & Carson, L. G. 1987, 'Need identification and program planning in the community context', in *Strategies of Community Organisation Practice*, F. Cox et al. (eds), Peacock Publishers, Itasca, Ill.

Shaw, Ian & Lishman, Joyce (eds) 1999, *Evaluation and Social Work Practice*, Sage Publications, London.

Sherman, E. & Reid, W. J. (eds) 1994, *Qualitative Research in Social Work*, Columbia University Press, New York.

South Australian Community Health Research Unit 1991, *Planning Healthy Communities: A Guide to Doing Community Needs Assessment*, Flinders Press, Bedford Park, South Australia.

SPSS Inc. 1985, *SPSSx Tables*, McGraw-Hill, New York.

Stanley, Liz (ed.) 1990, *Feminist Praxis: Research, Theory and Epistemology in Feminist Sociology*, Routledge, London & New York.

Stanley, Liz & Wise, Sue 1990, 'Method, methodology and epistemology in feminist research process', in *Feminist Praxis: Research, Theory and Epistemology in Feminist Sociology*, L. Stanley (ed.), Routledge, London & New York.

Strauss, A. 1990, *Qualitative Analysis for Social Scientists*, Cambridge University Press, Melbourne.

Strauss, A. L. & Corbin, J. M. 1990, *Basics of Qualitative Research: Grounded Theory Procedures and Techniques*, Sage, Newbury Park, CA.

Strauss, Anselm & Corbin, Juliet (eds) 1997, *Grounded Theory in Practice*, Sage, Thousand Oaks.

——1998, *Basics of Qualitative Research: Techniques and Procedures for Developing Grounded Theory*, Sage, Thousand Oaks.

Taylor, J. B. 1993, 'The naturalistic research approach', in *Social Work Research and Evaluation*, R. M. Grinnell Jr (ed.), 4th edn, Peacock Publishers, Itasca, Ill., chapter 4.

Toseland, R. W. 1994, 'Commentary—the qualitative/quantitative debate: Moving beyond acrimony to meaningful dialogue', in *Qualitative Research in Social Work*, E. Sherman & W. J. Reid (eds), Columbia University Press, New York.

Travers, P. & Richardson, S. 1993, *Living Decently: Material Well-being in Australia*, Oxford University Press, Melbourne.

Trinder, L. 2000, 'Reading the texts: Postmodern feminism and the 'doing' of research' in *Practice and Research in Social Work: Postmodern Feminist Perspectives*, B. Fawcett, B. Featherstone, J. Fook & A. Rossiter (eds), Rontledge, New York, pp. 39–61.

Tutty, Leslie M., Rothery, Michael A. & Grinnell, Richard M. Jr 1996, *Qualitative Research for Social Workers*, Allyn & Bacon, Boston.

University of New South Wales 1991, *Suicide Prevention: Sutherland Shire: Needs Analysis Report*, Southern Sydney Area Health Service Health Promotion Unit/Sutherland Hospital and Health Service, Sydney, State Health Publication Number (SSAHS) 91–108.

Wadsworth, Y. 1997, *Do It Yourself Social Research* 2nd edn, Allen & Unwin, Sydney.

——1997, *Everyday Evaluation on the Run*, 2nd edn, Allen & Unwin, Sydney.

Wadsworth, Y. 2001, 'The Mirror and the Magnifying Glass, the Compass and the Map: Facilitating partipatory action research' in *Handbook of Action Research: Participative Training and Practice*, P. Reason & H. Bradbury, Sage, London, pp. 420–32.

Walpole, Ronald E. & Myers, Raymond H. 1978, *Probability and Statistics for Engineers and Scientists*, 2nd edn, Macmillan, New York.

Wechsler, Henry, Reinherz, Helen Z. & Dobbin, Donald D. 1976, *Social Work Research in the Human Services*, Human Sciences Press, New York.

Weeks, Wendy 1988, 'De-Professionalisation or a new approach to professionalism?' in *Australian Social Work*, March, vol. 41, no. 1.

Weinbach, Robert W. & Grinnel, Richard M., Jr 2001, *Statistics for Social Workers*, 5th edn, Allyn & Bacon, Boston.

Whyte, William F. 1955, *Street Corner Society*, University of Chicago Press, Chicago.

Williams, Margaret, Tutty, Leslie M. & Grinnell, Richard M. Jr 1995, *Research in Social Work: An Introduction*, Peacock Publishers, Itasca, Ill.

Winter, Richard 1987, *Action Research and the Nature of Social Enquiry: Professional Innovation and Educational Work*, Avebury, Aldershot.

Wodarski, J. S. 1997, *Research Methods for Clinical Social Workers: Empirical Practice*, Springer Publishing Co., New York.

Wood, C. 1997, 'To know or not to know: A critique of postmodernism in social work practice' in *Australian Social Work*, vol. 50(3), pp. 21–27.

Yegidis, B. L., Weinbach, W. W., Morrison-Rodriguez, B. 1999, *Research Methods for Social Workers*, 3rd edn, Allyn & Bacon, Boston.

Zapf, W. 1986, 'Development, Structure and Prospects for the German Social State' in *The Welfare State, East and West*, R. Rose and R. Shiartori (eds), Oxford University Press, Oxford.

Zapf, W., Glatzer, W., Noll, H. H., Habich, R., Berger-Schmitt, R., Brever, S., Diewald, M., Kerber, U., Mohr, H. M. & Wiegand, E. 1987, 'German Social Report: Living conditions and subjective well-being, 1978–1984' in *Social Indicators Research*, vol. 19 (1).

Author index

SUBJECT INDEX